LOCAL POLITICS AND PARTICIPATION
IN BRITAIN AND FRANCE

Local participation can and does influence the political process. *Local politics and participation in Britain and France* provides a unique comparative study of the involvement of average citizens in local politics and government between national elections. The work of Professor Mabileau and his colleagues will illuminate the nature of contemporary processes of participation at a time when the local level of government, administration and participation democracy are topics of renewed interest in all Western democracies.

French and British teams explore the salient differences between the two local government systems – both of which have recently been reformed. Through a series of local case studies, they examine levels of individual and group participation, mobilisation into single issue protest groups, links between councillors and the local electorate, and the importance of local context in participation patterns.

Local politics and participation in Britain and France is a product of collaborative research carried out at the Universities of Manchester and Bordeaux. The results are based on surveys of ordinary people as well as on interviews with local leaders. They will be equally of interest to academics – students and specialists of British and French politics, local government, participation and democratic theory – and to local party workers and activists.

T0371326

LOCAL POLITICS AND PARTICIPATION IN BRITAIN AND FRANCE

ALBERT MABILEAU
INSTITUT D'ETUDES POLITIQUES DE BORDEAUX

GEORGE MOYSER
UNIVERSITY OF VERMONT

GERAINT PARRY
UNIVERSITY OF MANCHESTER

PATRICK QUANTIN
INSTITUT D'ETUDES POLITIQUES DE BORDEAUX

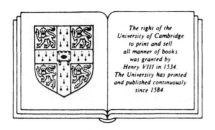

The right of the
University of Cambridge
to print and sell
all manner of books
was granted by
Henry VIII in 1534.
The University has printed
and published continuously
since 1584.

CAMBRIDGE UNIVERSITY PRESS

CAMBRIDGE
NEW YORK   PORT CHESTER
MELBOURNE   SYDNEY

CAMBRIDGE UNIVERSITY PRESS
Cambridge, New York, Melbourne, Madrid, Cape Town, Singapore,
São Paulo, Delhi, Dubai, Tokyo

Cambridge University Press
The Edinburgh Building, Cambridge CB2 8RU, UK

Published in the United States of America by Cambridge University Press, New York

www.cambridge.org
Information on this title: www.cambridge.org/9780521122870

First published 1989
This digitally printed version 2009

A catalogue record for this publication is available from the British Library

Library of Congress Cataloguing in Publication data
Local politics and participation in Britain and France / Albert
Mabileau ... [et al.].
p.   cm.
Bibliography.
ISBN 0–521–34576–6
1. Local government – Great Britain – Citizen participation.
2. Local government – France – Citizen participation.
3. Political participation – Great Britain.   4. Political
participation – France.
I. Mabileau, Albert.
JS3209.L63 1989
320.8′0941 – dc20   89–7193CIP

ISBN 978-0-521-34576-7 Hardback
ISBN 978-0-521-12287-0 Paperback

Contents

Figures and tables

Notes on contributors

GERAINT PARRY is W. J. M. Mackenzie Professor of Government at the University of Manchester. His previous publications include *Political Elites* (London, Allen and Unwin, 1969), *John Locke* (London, Allen and Unwin, 1978). He is editor of *Participation in Politics* (Manchester University Press, 1972) and co-editor of *Democracy, Consensus and Social Contract* (London, Sage, 1978). With George Moyser he is co-director of the British Political Participation Study which will appear in book form from Cambridge University Press as *Participation and Democracy* (forthcoming).

DR RICHARD BALME is Chargé de Recherche at the Fondation Nationale des Sciences Politiques, and works at the Centre d'Etude et de Recherche sur la Vie Locale in the Institut d'Etudes Politiques de Bordeaux. His research focuses on organised groups and policy building, leisure policies and fiscal policies. He published 'La participation aux associations et le pouvoir municipal', *Revue Française de Sociologie*, XXVIII, 1987, p. 601–637 and 'Determinants of Fiscal Policies in French Cities', in *The Political Implications of Policy Change*, ed. S. Clark.

DR PHILIPPE GARRAUD, Chargé de Recherche at the CNRS, works at the CERVL in the Institut d'Etudes Politiques de Bordeaux. His research focuses on different topics related to local politics: voluntary organisations, parties and elites, public policies. He is the author of '*Profession: homme politique. La carrière des maires urbains*' (Paris, L'Harmattan, 1989).

ALBERT MABILEAU is Professor of Political Science at the University of Bordeaux I, Director of the Centre d'Etude et de Recherche sur la Vie Locale (Institut d'Etudes Politiques de Bordeaux – CNRS). He has studied French political systems and institutions (*La personnalisation du pouvoir*) and comparative politics (*Les partis politiques en Grande-*

Bretagne). His work focuses on local politics. He has contributed to several recent books on this topic ('Les institutions locales et les relations centre-periphérie', in M. Grawitz and J. Leca eds., *Traité de Science Politique*, Paris, PUF, 1985; *Gouverner les villes moyennes*, Paris, Pedone, 1989).

DR PATRICK QUANTIN is a Chargé de recherche at the French National Foundation for Political Science. He is the author of *Les origines de l'idéologie* (Paris, Economica, 1987) and has published articles on voting and on local politics in French reviews.

DAVID CLEAVER has undertaken research on Welsh history and politics at the Universities of Wales and Manchester. He has published articles on Welsh local history in the *Welsh History Review, Morgannwg* (The Journal of Glamorgan History) and *Llafur* (The Journal of Welsh Labour History).

GEORGE MOYSER has taught politics at the University of Manchester and, currently, at the University of Vermont. He is editor or co-author of several books, including *Church and Politics Today* (1985), *Research Methods for Elite Studies* (1987) and *Church and Politics in a Secular Age* (1988). With Geraint Parry he is co-director of the British Political Participation Study.

Preface

This volume is the culmination of a comparative enquiry undertaken on the theme of political participation and mobilisation in local communities in France and Britain. It was conducted within the framework of the Franco–British programme launched jointly in 1984 by the Centre National de la Recherche Scientifique and the Economic and Social Research Council. Our thanks are due to these bodies not only for their financial assistance, without which this study would not have been published, but also for their encouragement of cooperation between the British and French research teams.

The present study is the result of a collaboration between the British Political Participation Study (Department of Government, University of Manchester) and the Centre d'Etude et de Recherche sur la Vie Locale (Equipe de Recherche Associée au CNRS, Institut d'Etudes politiques de Bordeaux). The two teams pooled their respective specialised skills, the former dealing with the theory and quantitative analysis of political participation, the latter with the politico-administrative features of society in local areas. Between 1984 and 1987 a series of regular meetings took place: the two groups met for the first time in July 1984, and the final stage of synthesis and revision began with the meeting which took place in Bordeaux in April 1987. Coordination was further maintained by exchanging and discussing working papers.

During these three years, we encountered difficulties inherent in comparative investigations carried out by two teams whose scientific backgrounds sometimes differ markedly, with each of them being accustomed to particular theoretical approaches, or familiar with specific methodological tools. We have probably not avoided all these stumbling blocks, and it is perhaps an advantage that each team retained its distinct identity and interests. But the efforts to understand, and the concessions made by both sides, enabled us to advance the comparative study.

Much of the volume was written by, in alphabetical order, Albert

Mabileau, George Moyser, Geraint Parry and Patrick Quantin. They were also jointly responsible for chapter 1 of the first part, as well as for the concluding chapter. Richard Balme, David Cleaver, and Philippe Garraud were involved in writing individual chapters. The British experience was examined by the BPPS, the French by CERVL, but the comparisons between the specific topics are discussed in an introduction and conclusion written jointly by the authors of the relevant chapters.

Our thanks are due to all those who have helped us in carrying out these studies. The British team is particularly grateful to Neil Day and Kurshida Mirza who were research associates in the BPPS team, to David Adams and Peter Humphreys for assistance with translation, and to Kate Baker, Tricia Pygott, Catherine Smith, Michelle Dicken, Stephanie Hamer and Jean Ashton for their patient typing of successive versions of the volume. They would like to thank the anonymous reader for Cambridge University Press for many helpful comments and Michael Holdsworth of the Press for his patience, encouragement and advice. The French team is grateful to Lise Mounier, who assisted with data-processing, to Véronique Hoffman-Martinot, who translated into French the chapters written in English, to its research administrator Christiane Pucheu, and to Maryse Ducournau who transcribed the text onto a word-processor.

BPPS–CERVL

PART I SCOPE AND CONTEXT

1

People and local politics: themes and concepts

ALBERT MABILEAU, GEORGE MOYSER, GERAINT PARRY
and PATRICK QUANTIN

The daily lives of most people are circumscribed by the locality in which
they live. In some respects this may appear a strange observation. It is usual
nowadays to think of people as members of a 'global village'. The news
media bring pictures of political happenings in other continents into our
homes. Movements in the international economy render people unemployed in industries across the world. The structure of society is shaped
by forces which have their origins outside the local arena and which
regulate all countries within the same mode of economic organisation.
International organisations, such as the European Economic Community,
legislate across national boundaries. Meanwhile, within particular countries the State is increasingly able to surmount the resistance of local
administration and customs. What are ostensibly local political events,
such as elections for councils, are often heavily influenced by the conditions of national politics. Finally, populations are far more mobile than
at any previous time and able, with greater affluence, to encounter a much
wider range of experiences.

Yet, despite these often dramatic developments, the locality remains the
arena within which most lives are conducted. The problems people face in
their daily lives arise for the most part within the area in which they reside.
They may be concerned with the quality of schooling for their children, the
provision of hospital facilities within easy reach, the state of the roads, the
need for a place of worship for a religious minority. These are the ordinary
problems which face the average person and they constitute much of the
stuff of local politics. Whilst the problems may seem unique to those
affected they are in fact common to many localities and they engender
relatively standard patterns of actions and responses. Moreover, these
problems are recognisably similar, though never precisely the same, in
different countries. However, the processes by which the citizen brings

issues to the attention of authorities and the ways in which the problems are handled by them can display as many differences as similarities – which it is the object of the series of case studies in this book to illuminate. The organising theme is local political participation, a complex phenomenon involving a myriad of forms of political behaviour which are, taken together, of central importance to the life of democracy. Amongst the many aspects of such local political behaviour that might be examined the study has selected four themes: political participation, political mobilisation, the relations between leaders and citizens, and the effect of locality and community on participation. They provide a picture, though not a complete one given the complexity of the subject matter, of the distinctively local aspects of citizen participation.

Political participation is, of course, not an entirely novel topic in either Britain or France. Much of the British and French literature has, however, concentrated on participation in elections, as in the research conducted by the Fondation Nationale des Sciences Politiques in France and the series of British election studies sponsored by the Economic and Social Research Council or associated with David Butler in the Nuffield series. Our approach differs, however, in that it consciously pays less attention to electoral participation in order to concentrate on the participation of the average citizen in day-to-day politics and government, outside the electoral period when political involvement is artificially heightened and distorted by partisan polarisation and the activities of a 'political class'. In that respect its general orientation shares something in common with the approach developed by Verba and Nie (1972). Whilst their study had a local component it nevertheless was principally focused on national patterns. By contrast, our aim is to give greater weight to the particular character of the local milieu and its effect on participation. Thus, we pay special attention to the way in which local activity is concerned with issues that affect people in an immediate manner and which may often be at least partly resolved within the locality. The immediacy of the problems gives local participation an added meaning. At a time when the local level of government and administration and participatory democracy are topics of renewed interest in all western democracies, the study of local communities or collectivities can shed a distinct light on the nature of contemporary processes of participation.

I PARTICIPATION

That the locality should be a major focus for public participation in Britain is, perhaps, not surprising given the localist tradition in British politics. In Britain, as also in the United States, there is a long-standing belief, which may be more myth than reality, that in matters of government and public services there is an autonomous sphere open to influence and determi-

nation by local citizens and their representatives. As Lagroye and Wright
suggest, 'the powers of the local authorities in Britain belong to a *residual
domain* preserved by the local authorities as their legitimate and traditional terrain against encroachments from the centre' (Lagroye and
Wright 1979: 5). The importance of this notion of the prior legitimacy of
the local over the centre is not necessarily reduced by the fact that (as
chapter 2 relates) the centre has been increasingly forceful in imposing its
will over local authorities. There is a presumption of local responsibility
for problems and solutions and this has been seen, in theory at least, as an
inducement to local political participation. It was the potentiality for civic
participation within an autonomous local structure, as opposed to a
centralised bureaucratic system, which inspired the classic participatory
theories of John Stuart Mill and Tocqueville.

This presumption in favour of local autonomy is in striking contrast to
the situation in France. The Jacobin tradition of France has ensured a
centralisation of administrative powers which has no institutional parallel
in Britain, whatever the pressures the British centre can impose on its
periphery. Much of what in Britain is run by local politicians and local
government officers is managed in France by a centrally appointed and
controlled bureaucracy. Whilst it remains appropriate to speak of local
government in Britain, in France it is a matter of local administration. As
Lagroye and Wright again put it, 'the powers of French local authorities
belong to a *conceded domain* – to areas traditionally belonging to Paris
but resentfully transferred to the localities' (Lagroye and Wright 1979: 5).
At the same time there are political linkages between centre and periphery
quite unlike anything in Britain as a consequence of the *cumul des mandats*
whereby politicians hold office at both national and local levels – as
deputies (or even ministers) and as mayors or local councillors. Whilst the
French national and local elites are integrated, however unevenly (Becquart-Leclercq 1983), in Britain the two elites are at some distance from
one another, observing a kind of division of labour, and creating what has
been called a 'dual polity' (Bulpitt 1983; see also Page 1983). There has,
indeed, been an attempt to bridge the gap in Britain by national level local
government pressure groups but these intermediary bodies have proved
relatively ineffective, especially during the post-1979 period of Conservative government (Rhodes 1986).

The consequence of these differences is that while in Britain it has been
standard practice to think in terms of a distinctive local politics, somewhat
apart from (but far from uninfluenced by) national politics, in France the
notion of 'political' activity was for long commonly applied solely to
electoral activities and even then only where these involved competition
between parties. Behaviour which might therefore be construed as 'political' participation in Britain would possibly not possess a 'political' quality
in a French locality, though even there the idea of 'total politics' appears to

be on the increase. This 'apolitical' tradition means that 'political' participation at the local level is less readily regarded as legitimate and proper in
France.

Political participation may be defined as taking part directly or indirectly in the processes of formulation, passage and implementation of
policy. However, at the local level much involvement in decision-making
arises out of a person's social position and lacks a political character. In
both countries there remains, though to a decreasing extent, an arena of
politics which is not very distinct from civil society in which socially
prominent people are involved in making decisions and may be elected to
office even though they do not identify themselves with any ideological
position or display any party political affiliation. This 'apolitical politics' is
particularly to be found in rural areas and has survived longer in France
than in Britain where party involvement in local politics has been much
more widespread. Activity directed at influencing decisions in such areas
may be regarded as belonging as much to the social as to the political
realm. Distinctively political local systems emerge with the appearance of
competition between party entrepreneurs at the local level. Hence, action
targeted at such decision-makers might be interpreted as distinctively
political participation. But even in this case the participants themselves
may, as is shown in chapter 3, perceive their behaviour in trying to
influence decisions as non-political, perhaps regarding it as akin to a
consumer complaining about services.

The modes of participation are various (Verba and Nie 1972). We have
chosen to look in particular at the extent to which people contact the local
council, take part in groups and protest about local issues. Local voting
behaviour is not our prime concern except to the extent that the political
leanings of citizens shed light on other aspects of their behaviour. Important as electoral activity is, it is a mode of behaviour quite distinct from
other kinds of participation (Verba and Nie 1972; Moyser, Parry and Day
1986).

The greater part of the participation we look at follows the conventional
channels whereby people engage in group activity or contact authorities
whether individually or through their groups. Such activity is mainly
instrumental in character, concerned to achieve or defend the interests of
the individual or group. This has been very much the dominant model in
studies of participation, such as those by Verba and Nie (1972) and
Barnes, Kaase *et al.* 1979. According to this conception the bulk of
political behaviour is characterised by a rational assessment of the costs
and benefits of action – a view borne out by much of the evidence reported
from both countries in subsequent chapters. Some individuals, on the
other hand, may be motivated more by communitarian than by narrowly
conceived benefits. Their involvement may take on an altruistic dimension

concerned more with the good of the whole local community than with the advantage of particular groups or sectors within it. Indeed the concern for others may be such that individual benefits become irrelevant and participation ceases to be instrumental but is, instead, expressive in character, establishing a person's solidarity or sympathy with those whom they believe deserving of their support. Finally, another motivation may be the developmental or educative effect of action, enhancing one's understanding of the political world although this may well be regarded more as a by-product of action than an impetus to it (Parry 1972, 1974). The extent to which these non-instrumental attitudes are at best minor themes in understanding the quality of local participation is explored, particularly in chapters 9 and 10.

Not all participatory actions are spontaneously generated by citizens who seek to bring problems to the attention of local government and administration. In very many cases participation is reactive as individuals and groups respond to measures initiated by the authorities themselves. It is when people are faced with a threat to build a road near their property or to close the local school that they are most likely to voice their feelings and take action. Even then the extent of participation is partly determined by the opportunities provided within the local institutional structure for citizens and groups to make themselves heard. A very powerful campaign may force its views upon authorities but to a large extent participation is dependent on the access provided, which varies not only between countries but within the various institutional structures of any one country.

Participation is a minority activity. Apart from voting, most people do not involve themselves in public life. Non-participation is, therefore, as important a phenomenon to examine as participation. The social composition of the participants and the non-participants is potentially important to the operation of liberal democracies such as France and Britain and is the prime focus of the case studies reported in chapters 3 and 4. To the extent that public action is effective in carrying messages about needs and problems to the authorities, it can be of some significance that these messages are being transmitted only by that sector of the population which is most active. It is possibly that participation, far from helping to rectify the inequalities arising in civil society, may end by reinforcing bias.

2 MOBILISATION

Among the various forms of political action may be distinguished a type of collective behaviour which has important specific characteristics and is worth treating separately as a phenomenon of possibly growing importance. The notion of mobilisation has not been widely employed by British political scientists outside the study of developing countries where it refers to the attempts by elites to direct the local population and its resources towards programmes of modernisation. To a lesser extent it has made its appearance in the discussions of mass society and the dangers of its exploitation by anti-democratic elites (Kornhauser 1959). In France, however, the concept of mobilisation has wider currency within the social sciences (Chazel 1975). But even in France the term has taken on a multiplicity of meanings. In this study it is used to describe a process whereby individuals are led either to take on new political commitments or to rediscover old ones and as a result to act collectively and particularly intensively to achieve common ends (Oberschall 1973: 102). This may occur in two very different ways. People may be mobilised to act against the established authorities culminating even in acts of violence – ascending mobilisation. Alternatively, elites may themselves mobilise their forces to coordinate resistance to threats to their policies or their existence – descending mobilisation. There is both mobilisation and counter-mobilisation.

Mobilisation, in this sense, involves three major characteristics. The action is, in the first place, collective. It is a matter of assembling individuals into groups to pursue common objectives which they bring to the attention of the authorities. Secondly, and following from the first, it is organised action. Although action may initially be more or less spontaneous, once mobilised it becomes organised and structured by agents of mobilisation which may be parties or voluntary associations. Hence, mobilisation involves the work of political entrepreneurs. This mobilisation is a process which is induced and in which the action of political entrepreneurs (leaders, elites or institutions) forms an essential component (Nettl 1967: 32–3). Finally, mobilisation is, on this view, typically conflictual. In the case of ascending mobilisation it seeks to activate the population to oppose a public decision or to challenge established values and norms. For this to occur the relevant population must be 'mobiliseable'. There must be grievances, values or goals, explicit or merely latent, which can be activated and, very often, symbols by which these can be recognised and even internalised by those being mobilised (Nettl 1967: 33). The possibility that a population is mobiliseable in certain circumstances places the inactivity of large sectors of society in a different perspective. To discover, as studies regularly do, that most people are not actively involved does not mean that they could not be activated quite readily by skilled agencies of mobilisation. The dangers and the opportunities provided by this possibility were much debated in the discussions of the nature of mass society (Kornhauser 1959; for a critique see Oberschall 1973: 102–13). Sometimes both those mobilising and those mobilised may individually be active participants in other directions. In distinguishing the processes of mobilisation for special attention, therefore, we do not assume that in practice mobilisation and conventional channels of participation can be sharply distinguished. Descending mobilisation is very frequently directed at countering challenges. This may be achieved by mobilising the various sectors of the elite to defend the policy. Alternatively it can involve an attempt by the authorities to drum up support amongst the wider population to support the status quo.

Thus part III of the book will be looking at the ways in which, in reaction to decisions with potentially very severe repercussions on the locality, individuals were activated to form groups. Typically, leaders took on the task of organising often diffuse concerns into collective action with an agreed strategy. Examples of such issues include the building of a nuclear power station and the introduction of policies undermining a major source of employment and wealth. In several cases the threat originated from sources outside the locality, but the mobilisation was directed in the first instance at those more local authorities which appeared to bear responsibility for allowing the danger to develop. Often the action is extremely intense but short-lived, with the group dispersing once the objective is achieved or the leaders find themselves unable to sustain the new commitment or to reinvigorate old loyalties long enough to see a major campaign through to a conclusion. This is especially the case where the authorities have been able to mobilise their own response in which, as chapter 5 reveals, the integrated French elite system has considerable resources.

3 LEADERS AND CITIZENS

The orthodox democratic image of local politics is one where citizens bring their problems to the attention of their elected representatives who, in turn, respond to the demands which are placed upon them. This process is sometimes described as one of the articulation and aggregation of interests in which demands expressed by individuals and groups are packaged into sets of policies by political entrepreneurs, usually parties, and converted into policies and policy outputs. However, as part IV seeks to show, this account is far too simplistic. Leaders exercise a considerable degree of autonomy in modern democracies. Indeed, it has been argued that a more comprehensive explanation of policy-making in modern democracies would ensue from concentrating on the preferences and actions of leaders than of the social forces which strive for influence (Nordlinger 1981). Certainly no picture of politics, local or national, could be complete which does not bear in mind this dual perspective – from the centre of policy-making downward and from society upward (Alford and Friedland 1985). Hence, although our focus is on the response of councillors in France and Britain to the issues and problems raised by the local population, the reaction of councillors has in part to be understood in relation to their position at the intersection of a number of political and social forces.

Councillors as well as needing to take into account the problems of the particular area of the town they are responsible for representing, are also faced with demands from a variety of groups and associations speaking for the interests of different social sectors. Whilst having to respond to these expressions of often sectional interests, councillors generally conceive themselves as acting for the collective interest of the locality by reconciling conflicting aspirations and, to a degree, integrating local society. They can thus justify a belief in priorities which deviate from those of the local populations. This notion of a collective interest may itself be a myth but, as a political formula, it is often part of the language of political leadership. In formulating local policies and decisions the councillors are influenced by forces other than pressures from the electorate – forces which may be overlooked in studies of participation. The impact of the strategy of the council as a whole, especially where parties are strong, and the influence of the local bureaucracy, particularly in Britain, have to be borne in mind.

Nevertheless, when all this is admitted, local democracy, if it is to have some meaning, must imply a significant degree of agreement between leaders and citizens as to the local agenda. The conditions favourable to such agreement include the integration of the leadership into the locality. Such integration is not merely socially and economically based, in the sense that councillors can be rooted in the locality by length of residence or by their sharing the social and economic experiences of the population at large. Councillors can also be integrated into the social, economic and political structure of the locality through membership of the most import-ant effective groups. The case studies suggest that this integration is apt to go rather further in France than in Britain. In this way, messages about the needs and problems of the area can be communicated to the decision-makers on the council. The linkages can also be utilised in a downward direction by the councillors to influence the composition of the issue agenda. Indeed, they may go so far as to activate the groups themselves, thus helping to shape the agenda and channelling the direction of the very demands which the council is to handle.

Comparisons between the priorities of citizens and councillors, such as those made in chapters 7 and 8 are therefore only one measure of the success of a local political system in democratically establishing a common understanding of its priorities. There are sound reasons why the council-lors' concerns might diverge from those of their constituents. There are even reasons to think that the agenda of citizens is not entirely spon-taneous and beyond manipulation. It also has to be acknowledged that there may be, in addition, a suppressed agenda which our study of effective political demands has been unable to tap. The ample theoretical literature on the possible existence of non-decisions and of covert agenda construction (Bachrach and Baratz 1962; Lukes 1974; Parry and Morris 1974; Cobb and Elder 1983) coupled with a certain number of empirical investigations (Crenson 1971; Gaventa 1980) show that there are dangers in accepting overt issue agendas at their face value. For this reason the several questionnaires employed in the course of the study made use of very open, non-directed questions in order to elicit as unconfined a set of agendas as possible. Arguably, the processes by which elite and, especially, citizen attitudes on issues may subtly be structured by social and economic as well as political forces can mean that there is no guarantee that even unpressured answers to questionnaires will bring to the surface those needs and problems which have not yet achieved public expression. Whilst acknowledging this limit to our methodologies we do nevertheless claim that the overtly expressed agenda represents a highly significant part of the basic material of local politics. Indeed the extent to which the very different French and British systems are capable of permitting local concerns to be articulated and communicated is some evidence of their democratic quality.

4 COMMUNITY AND LOCALITY

It was pointed out above that most public participation occurs within a given locality. Very few people cross the local political boundaries in order to conduct political activity. The few who do so are in general the professional politicians seeking to promote or defend the interests of the locality at regional or national level. If most action goes on within a locality how far is it possible also to say that perceptions of the nature of the locality have an effect in encouraging or discouraging political involvement?

One view of the relation between participation and the locality which has received much attention in British and American thinking is that political involvement might be expected to increase, the more that residents identify the area in which they live as a 'community' (Putnam 1966). The characteristics of a community are notoriously contestable and involve a mixture of descriptive and evaluative considerations (Plant 1978). They are generally applied to an area which is thought to have a reasonably clear spatial identity, a strong degree of social integration and a degree of political autonomy (MacIver 1924; Rossi 1972).

The appeal of this approach almost certainly reflects some British and American beliefs about the nature of local government – beliefs which, as critics have noted, may have more to do with aspirations than reality (Bulpitt 1972; Saunders *et al.* 1978). Thus it has been one view guiding

discussions of British local government that the boundaries of governmental areas should ideally bear some relation to 'communities'
(Hampton 1970: 1–23). The assumption appears to have been that a sense
of identity with a distinct, long-standing autonomous village, town or
county stimulates political interest and involvement. This communitarian
principle, however, pointed towards units of local government of a relatively small scale which were not necessarily compatible with the needs for
regional coordination and planning in a complex mobile industrial society. Moreover, the financial and administrative reality of increased
central government control and supervision reduced local autonomy in
fact and often in law. The Local Government Act which came into force in
England and Wales in 1974 generally favoured the principle of efficiency
through scale rather than that of respect for communities. The abolition or
merger of smaller authorities resulted, in the view of traditionalists, in the
disruption of old loyalties and a loss of local democracy (Byrne 1985:
48–59). It is not clear, in fact, either that the old authorities were closely
related to genuine communities or that the new authorities gained efficiency through scale. As Hampton has argued, local government may
need to be both smaller *and* larger to combine the virtues of both ideals
(1970: 302). The extent to which a sense of community exists and to which
it contributes to political involvement thus remains relevant to any future
discussion of local government organisation and is also a very open
question, as chapter 9 will indicate.

This concern for community has no counterpart in French political
science. The reason lies partly in criticisms of the relevance of community
sentiment in the modern world and partly in the very different assumptions about the system of local administration. An interest in community is
largely confined to rural sociologists for whom it is a residual element in a
generally more urbanised society. French political writing prefers the
notion of local 'collectivity' to that of community. The collectivity takes
institutional form in the *commune* which is an administrative and political
unit rather than a social phenomenon marked by feelings of solidarity.
Moreover, within the French political and administrative system no local
area could make the claims for autonomy traditionally advanced in Britain
(see chapter 2).

Given these factors, the approach of French political science is to view
the local commune as a social unit (*Gesellschaft*) marked by social contradictions, conflicts and compromise rather than as a community (*Gemein-
schaft*). This is not to say that community is not a value towards which
leaders and citizens might in theory aspire, but studies start more from the
view that participation is likely to be associated with the pursuit of
sectional interests within the collectivity. The hypothesis is, therefore, that
it is those who are aware of and involved in the active social forces in the

locality rather than those with consensual attitudes who will be in the forefront of participation.

This approach has more in common with the 'social interactionist' perspective on participation which has been advanced as an alternative to the community identification theory (Putnam 1966). According to this view it is the frequency with which people interact with other members of their locality which determines the level of participation. The more that people know others in the area and the more that they join local groups the more likely they are to engage in public activity. Their attitudes may not necessarily be consensual nor may they direct their activities towards collective goals. Their relations with others in the area may involve only sectional interests and their consequent action be directed towards achieving the objectives of particular groups.

If this hypothesis about participation is upheld, the lessons for local government are more ambiguous than in the case of the communitarian theory. An active, involved citizenry will be more likely to occur where there is a multiplicity of interests and, perhaps, a council which plays a major role in distributing resources, thereby stimulating the attention, whether positive or negative, of the interest groups. Participation may be higher in larger, more urbanised areas where a multiplicity of groups form to press their demands upon the local authorities. More decentralised local governmental systems may not then make any obvious difference to levels of participation, which could depend more on the propensity of people to interact with one another and to form groups. This propensity is itself associated strongly with education and social status. The argument for greater decentralisation would then turn more on the possibility that 'small' makes for better communication of needs and problems than on the possibility that it makes for a greater level of citizen involvement.

5 PROBLEMS OF COMPARATIVE STUDY OF LOCAL PARTICIPATION

Needless to say, the investigation of this set of themes, surrounding the notion of local participation in the two countries, was not an entirely straightforward matter. As we shall indicate later in this section, we found ourselves addressing many of the problems typical of cross-national or cross-cultural research. But first we briefly consider the benefits or potentialities, as we see them, of the exercise. In general terms, what did we hope to gain in setting our separate research efforts side by side?

At a very basic level we were each, no doubt, responding to the nature of the times in the study of politics which now stresses much more strongly than once was the case the comparative aspect (Czudnowski 1976: 9). The reason for this, of course, is that ultimately it is the only way in which empirical theory can be developed beyond the contingent circumstances of single-country observation, and the culture-bounded vision of political scientists, or so it is argued. More specifically there is the legacy of Gabriel Almond and Sidney Verba's *Civic Culture* (1963) within the field of political participation itself. Whilst, perhaps naturally, only imperfectly surmounting a particular vision of political action rooted in their American experiences, nevertheless it firmly established the comparative principle within this sphere of enquiry, and provided a classic benchmark against which subsequent research has been implicitly judged.

The fruits of such an approach are potentially numerous. Perhaps most central, as we have indicated, is the critical capacity to establish common patterns of a broader geo-cultural basis and to identify those which appear to be contingent upon particular circumstances. Thus, we might want to examine whether social inequalities are manifested to the same extent in the patterns of local political participation of the two countries. Similarly, we might wish to compare the processes of local political mobilisation, integration or other aspects of our substantive agenda. The results of such enquiries will then add to our knowledge about the scope of generalisations in this area and hint at the nature of the systemic contingencies which may be involved (see also Lijphart 1971, 1975).

However, insofar as we are dealing with local materials in both countries, such considerations represent more of an extension of a logic already present within each national study than a totally new departure. In other words, the comparison of local 'micro-polities' in the search for generalities and the specification of contingencies is an entirely analogous procedure to that when cross-national materials are used. What this points to, perhaps more clearly than in avowedly 'national' comparisons, is that system properties which in part provide the basis for explicating similarities and differences may be defined both sub-nationally as well as cross-nationally. This serves to underscore just how difficult comparative analysis can be. On the other hand, multi-national or bi-national research may entail other, perhaps more modest and immediately attainable goals than the development of cross-culturally valid empirical theories. One that seems particularly salient in the present instance is the fresh light that the comparative perspective throws on analyses of one's own country.

Part of this process also involves a reexamination of the intellectual luggage that each political scientist subconsciously acquires within a particular cultural and academic ethos (Dogan and Pelassy 1982: 8–16). Linguistic and cultural boundaries still play a significant role in the way social scientific concepts are defined and operationalised (Hymes, 1970). On the positive side, such exercises help to sharpen the sense of the relativity of political enquiry and of alternative ways of dissecting the world. More negatively, perhaps, it also emphasises how far political science has yet to travel in the search for theories and concepts which transcend the particularities of language and culture through which they are expressed and given meaning.

Clearly what is needed in the long term is a set of 'transcultural' concepts (Frey 1970: 187; see also Dogan and Pelassy 1982: 24–45) through which patterns of local participation, indeed politics more generally, can be consistently comprehended across a wide variety of milieus. Certainly, our initial experiences were, like Frey, that many of the key analytic terms deployed in French and Anglo-American political science are 'false friends': they look the same, but their definitions and meanings are significantly different. This was true, for example, of 'community' (see chapters 9 and 10), 'integration', 'mobilisation' and even, to some extent, of 'participation' itself. Part of our endeavours, therefore, was to seek to understand these nuances and then to establish enough of a common framework within which we could jointly operate.

Some measure of the potential difficulties we faced can be gleaned from a consideration of two concepts with which we were concerned, party membership and social class. Neither of these would, on the surface, appear to cause great difficulties, referring as they do to fairly concrete phenomena – certainly more concrete than pinning down 'community' for example. Nevertheless, if they are scrutinised closely, they both reflect that 'element of cultural arbitrariness', that 'plain parochialism' to which Frey (1970: 188–9) refers as undermining comparative analysis.

In the case of party membership, indeed, parochialism, at least at the measurement level, can be found within each political party one examines. As Duverger (1964: 61) put it in a now classical analysis:

How do we define a party member? The reply varies according to the party: each holds to a concept of membership which is peculiar to it. The expression 'party member' does not mean the same thing to ... the French Socialist party and the British Labour party ... For American parties, it even has no meaning at all.

Equally, the notion of a 'supporter', an 'activist' or a 'militant' would no doubt also carry not insignificant variations of meaning not only across parties but also across national party systems (see also Thomassen 1976; Kaase 1976; Converse and Dupeux 1966).

Turning to social class, one also finds that the respective operational procedures for measuring it in Britain and France differ significantly from one another. The experience of a team of sociologists working specifically on this issue in trying to compare national mobility rates between the two is salutary:

For our own part, we have become well aware in the course of our work that occupational groupings that would appear functionally similar – and that are perhaps described in similar terms – from one society to another may nonetheless still differ in various non-negligible ways: for example, in the precise nature of the work-tasks and roles that their members perform, in their requisite qualifications for entry, in the nature or relative level of their economic and other rewards etc. In other words, it is dangerous to take apparent similarities among countries in the form of their occupational groupings of labour at face value (Erikson *et al.* 1979: 419).

In particular, they point to the difficulties of distinguishing between the upper and lower echelons of the 'service class' of professionals and managers. Not only do definitions of the relevant occupational groupings differ, but there are significant variations imparted by the way management and the professions are institutionalised in the respective countries. Equally, what counts for 'skill' in separating 'skilled' from 'semi-skilled' and 'unskilled' workers is also a matter of divergence in the different schemas.

As these examples are much more the norm than the exception in comparative research, the reader may perhaps be forgiven for wondering whether there is a future in this sort of undertaking. Can there be 'any certain and stable spot from which ... to erect a reasonable investigation' (Frey 1970: 190)? Some practitioners would give a resounding 'no'; all must be relative, all meaning must inevitably be particular (MacIntyre 1971: 260–79; Winch 1958). Such relativism appears excessive. France and Britain are polities which share a common European cultural history, a similar level of economic development and democratic practices. They encounter many of the same political problems. There is therefore enough in common for it to be worthwhile to consider how far variations in political institutions and practice between the two countries occur within what is still recognisably a shared democratic experience. It is within that general context that our particular approach – a series of comparative case studies – should be viewed. Case studies can have a number of different purposes (Brundal 1982; Molnar 1967). We have used them here, however, principally to provide in-depth analyses of political participation and other related themes in carefully chosen comparative milieus. In this way we intend to contribute to more general theories and debates, as well as highlighting some of the difficulties and problems that often remain hidden from view in larger and more thoroughly statistical treatment. Not that we eschew quantitative evidence in either country. Although some tend to equate the case study method with a qualitative style, in fact this need not be so (Walker 1973: 262). We have indeed used both quantitative and qualitative techniques as the occasion demanded – but, of course, remained consistent in this respect as between the two countries. All in all, therefore, although case studies are not, ultimately, a substitute for broader and more all-embracing research, the latter strategy often depends upon the detailed preliminary work of the former. Possibly in recognition of this, our impression of the present state of knowledge about political participation in western democracies is that detailed case studies in particular localities are a much needed and even innovative counter-weight to work previously done on a national basis. As we will argue, the roots and context of participation is substantially at the local level. It is in that spirit, therefore, that this volume has taken its present shape.

6 PLAN OF THE BOOK

As the preface indicated, the research on which this book is based emanates from two research teams who were working independently on aspects of local political participation in their respective countries and who were brought into a collaborative arrangement by a joint programme of the Economic and Social Research Council in Britain and the Centre National de la Recherche Scientifique in France. Consequently we are not reporting the results of an identical research programme carried out in both countries so much as a series of studies which have a number of elements in common and which are intended to illuminate various aspects of the relations between citizens and their local political systems in the two countries.

At the same time the collaboration permitted the researchers to make use of some shared approaches and to develop some explicit comparisons. Thus, the survey approach developed by the British Political Participation Study was employed in adapted form in one of the French localities and forms the basis of the first and the last of the pairs of chapters. Moreover, in chapters 7 and 8, although the method of interview was rather different in the French study to that employed in the British counterpart, there were, again, many questions developed in common. However, there are also differences in emphasis. The British design was developed as a component of a large-scale survey-based study of participation in Britain conducted at both national and local levels. Accordingly it tends to be more quantitative whilst the French research is based on a more qualitative set of interviews.

The national basis of the British research allowed localities to be chosen from around England, Wales and Scotland which are, in many ways representative of types of residential patterns. The localities were selected on the basis of a statistical analysis of local government districts in England, Wales and Scotland which took account of 40 variables including indicators of family structure, occupation, ethnicity, housing type and average length of residence. This examination permitted the identification of clusters of locality types in Britain such as market towns, inner London areas, northern industrial towns, from each of which one representative example was chosen after local research. Hence, in the present volume, chapter 3 will be based on the politics of one of Britain's most typical commuter towns, chapter 8 on the archetypal English market town and on an industrial town, and chapter 9 on an inner London area and a Welsh mining village. Chapter 6 is concerned with a more rural Welsh town and rests on a different, qualitatively-based style of research. By contrast, the French study is based on a mixture of localities of different sizes and types in the region of Bordeaux where the research team is based and where it has conducted previous studies on an intensive basis over a period of years. No claim is made that the two sets of localities can be precisely comparable, although in some cases we have attempted to indicate certain features in common between the areas under study. For these reasons one must be cautious, as ever, about generalising from case studies to the pattern of a nation as a whole. However, the emphasis is intended to be less on the detail of the specific towns and villages than on the ways in which the processes of citizen participation and political response are conducted in the two countries.

The book is constructed around the main themes we have singled out for treatment – participation, mobilisation, leaders and citizens and the 'spirit of the place'. Corresponding to each theme is a pair of chapters preceded by a common introduction setting out the orientation of the section and followed by a common conclusion drawing out some of the comparisons and contrasts which emerge. Preceding these sections is a review of the two systems of local government and administration and their general implications for participation. The concluding chapter looks forward to other areas of research interest and seeks briefly to draw some lessons from the experiences of the two countries for the future of citizen participation.

2

Local government in Britain and local politics and administration in France

ALBERT MABILEAU

There is a gap of ten years between the Local Government Act of 1972 and the Act of 1982 dealing with 'the rights and liberties of communes, departments and regions', which is more usually called the 'decentralisation act'. The style and scope of the two reforms look very different: local government in Britain was to be tidied up and simplified, whereas local government in France was to undergo radical overall reorganisation. London's concern with the efficiency and technical capability of local authorities contrasts with the declared political and ideological determination to decentralise expressed in Paris. Conversely, a profound change took place at the territorial level in England, Wales and Scotland, whereas in France the picture presented by local and regional levels of action remains practically unchanged. These contrasts are striking, but they are deceptive, since they do not really disguise the resemblances between the two systems, even if the arena of local politics is marked out in different ways, and power at the local level is unevenly distributed.

I EVOLUTION: FROM CONTRASTS TO ANALOGIES

It has probably not been sufficiently recognised that the disparities, and even the contradictions, between the two local traditions have been greatly reduced by changes in social conditions, such as to produce in recent years an unusual degree of convergence between the British and French systems of local government.

Differences in the two politico-administrative traditions

History has produced in the two countries local political cultures which are firmly established and practically polar opposites. The British tradition

17

of local autonomy has created 'local government', a notion the French reject, having a tradition of centralisation dominated by the State which entrusts local authorities only with lesser administrative functions.

The main reason for this is the search for national unity which has been a permanent preoccupation of France whether under the monarchy, or during the Revolution, or as a republic – 'France one and indivisible' – and was intended to offset the geographical and cultural differences of the country. There is nothing of this kind on the other side of the Channel, where central authority has never been particularly bothered about the sense of overall national identity shown by local communities, or even by Wales and Scotland. In Britain, national integration has been achieved by having a government which represents local areas, whereas in France its character has been determined by the fact that the State has penetrated local society with the system of Prefects. Hence, it is not surprising that Britain bears witness to the individuality and diversity of local administrations which have been criticised by every Royal Commission on reform since the nineteenth century. In France, however, every commune and every department is uniformly governed by the same administrative rules and subject to identical control by the State.

Indeed, the role of the State and of central government is the crucial element distinguishing the two systems of local government. The French State long ago organised a network of institutions to control, through the presence there of its agents (the Prefects) and its supervision of local authorities, even the most remote area of its territory. 'Local government' in Britain, by contrast, is completely the opposite: each local community has its own government, whose task is to administer services for the citizens independently. Furthermore, until recently, Whitehall did not dispatch any of its representatives, apart from the Inspectorates, to the local level which was regarded as the 'private domain' of the local authorities.

Relations between the periphery and the centre are, therefore, inevitably set in very different contexts. They are particularly close in France, not only at the administrative level, but also in the political arena, where local elites are a breeding-ground for recruitment into national politics (through the accumulation of offices – *cumul des mandats*). By contrast, the links are less close in Britain, and the autonomy which prevails both at the centre and at the periphery is built into the conventions of the Constitution. Thus, in Paris, a centralising power grants concessions to the periphery, whereas in London it must justify its incursions into local government. Equally, the French government has no hesitation in imposing its decisions on local authorities, whereas the British government in the past, at least, has cooperated with its local government partners. Yet another result is that the separation of the levels of power is not perceived in the same way: political personalities in France point with pride to the opposition between the State and the local authorities, and blame the State for their difficulties. Local opinion in Britain has not traditionally been in the habit of viewing the State as oppressive. Indeed, until recently, its interventions were seen rather as a way of defending the rights of the citizens against the abuses of local power. But it has not, perhaps, been sufficiently appreciated that these contrasts, which were supported and perpetuated by the political culture, have greatly diminished as traditional local society disappeared.

Comparable constraints arising from a new socio-economic environment

The gap in time between the modernisation of local society in the two countries is considerable. Whereas, in the years following the last war, France still lived 'according to the village clock', the British had already had long experience of the movement towards industrialisation and urbanisation. This indeed began in the nineteenth century with an Industrial Revolution that was much earlier than in the other countries of Europe. Hence, when the same process was getting under way in France in the 1950s, local authorities in Britain were concerning themselves more with the process of 'suburbanisation', which is typical of the gradual disappearance of the distinction between urban and rural society. It was not until the early 1980s that attention was focused in France on the problem of the 'periurban areas', and even then in a local setting in which rural life is still a reality, albeit one that is different from what it was.

Nevertheless, in both countries, the authorities are attempting to maintain some control over urban planning, though in very different circumstances. Britain is already confronting the problem of industrial decline and decision-makers are cooperating at the national and local level in joint action to achieve more efficient management of local affairs. In France, on the other hand, a period of strong economic growth has allowed the central government to launch a huge town and country planning exercise aimed at building up the plant and equipment of local authorities which have in this way benefited from the financial largesse of the State.

However, the onset and development of the crisis in the 1970s was once again to place both countries in a similar socio-economic situation. The Welfare State, having provided a greatly increased number of services to its citizens in both countries, especially at the local level in the form of individual or collective benefits (housing, transport, social services, etc.), is from now on in charge of handling the crisis. Its task is to maintain the level of services while limiting their cost in relation to the State's resources.

These new objectives of government policies have had two immediate consequences. The pressure of government action on local affairs is increasing, at the same time as the State's control over local authorities has been legitimised through the need to 'implement' national policies in a satisfactory way over the country as a whole. It was in the mid-1970s that local councils in Britain began to feel the first effects of State pressure, first through the multiplication of central regulations and the setting of expenditure levels, and then, with a Conservative government, through a change of attitude towards the periphery (Wright 1986). In France, the process has been marked by an ever more visible interlocking of the policies of the State and those of the local authorities. Another consequence of the crisis has been the reduction of the distributive capability of central government. While there is an ever-increasing demand for services and benefits, especially in the face of unemployment, the urgent need to limit costs weighs heavily on local budgets. The importance which government subsidies have taken on in local authority finances, and the State's determination to limit or even to reduce them, play a large part in the crisis in local finance which has become apparent in both countries.

The disquiet aroused by this situation was to count for a great deal in the emergence of a positive obsession with reform intended to increase the ability of local authorities to solve the problems confronting them. The sole difference was that the reorganisation of structures and functions occurred in Britain in 1972, whereas it is still awaited in France, even though several government commissions have been set up. Yet it is not inappropriate to draw a parallel between the series of measures taken by the Thatcher Government (the Local Government Planning and Land Act of 1980, the Housing Act of 1980, the Local Government Finance Act of 1982 and the Rates Act of 1984) and the Defferre law on decentralisation and the copious legislation intended to implement it (the laws of 1983 on the allocation and transfer of responsibilities and the laws of 1984 and 1987 on the regulations of the territorial civil service). Indeed, all these measures are the result of unilateral government action, which, if not a matter for surprise in France, is the outcome of a major change in the rules of the game in Britain. Even so, the measures taken in Britain form part of a policy of centralisation just at a time when the policy of the French seems to be to abandon its centralising Jacobinism. This is, in appearance at least, a reversal of traditional tendencies, and it is helping to produce a degree of similarity in the overall political organisation of the two countries.

A comparison of the two systems of local government

In fact, recent developments enable us to see a number of analogies in the structuring and regulation of the two forms of local government. For a long time it was thought that relations between local and central government took diametrically opposed forms in the two countries partly, no doubt, because they were viewed from a legal–institutional perspective which remained the dominant mode of interpretation until the 1970s. Since then a good many scholars in France have demonstrated that centre–periphery relations are more a matter of less formal transactions – described even as a 'complicity between the prefect and the notables' (Worms 1966: 249) – than of the domination by the centre which has been emphasised by the earlier, institutional approach.[1] Nevertheless, it is difficult to accept in its entirety the analysis of Ashford according to which the British system can, in fact, function in a much more centralised manner than the French (Ashford 1976: 62). The claim may, however, begin to appear more valid at a time when the Thatcher Government is steadily tightening its control over the local authorities whilst, at the same time, the Defferre law of 1982 is providing some genuine autonomy to the French equivalents by granting local representatives responsibility for certain local-level decisions arising out of the allocation of new responsibilities to the localities. It would probably be an exaggeration to see in these developments a total break with the past rather than the outcome of an evolutionary process begun earlier (Thoenig 1985), but it remains true that the French local system has undergone a considerable change as much in its internal structure as in the relations between centre and periphery: the marginalisation of the prefect through the devolution of executive functions at departmental and regional levels to the elected representatives; the replacement of the system of administrative supervision by one of *a posteriori* control of local decisions; and direct elections to regional councils (Mabileau 1983; Belorgey 1984; Rondin 1985).

In the light of all these changes it has to be acknowledged that a good many of the processes which shape the relations between the centre and the periphery operate on both sides of the Channel. The interdependence of the two levels of government – the national and the local – is now a reality in Britain, and has not been abandoned by the French, even though one of the aims of decentralisation has been to clarify the respective areas of responsibility of the State and the local authorities.

The legal principle of *ultra vires*, according to which local authorities can exercise only those functions which are given to them by law, is common to both systems of local councils. The control exercised by the State over local authority taxes and finances is a further restriction common to both, even if the mechanisms differ in their complexity. Even the legal establishment of relations with central government, which is traditional in France (though it was further developed in 1982 with the creation of *Chambres Régionales Des Comptes*), is being introduced into Britain at the present time. It remains true, none the less, that relations in Britain are essentially functional or departmental in character, whereas in France the centre deals with each locality as a territorial entity.

However, the politicisation and nationalisation of the local system cannot be ascribed to legal reforms or to new regulations. Politicisation is long-established in Britain, and is linked to the party system, at least in elections – even though a relatively small number of 'independent' councils still exist. In France, a new situation has grown up gradually under the Fifth Republic, with parties being established at the local level, and also with the bi-polarisation of political life. But it is difficult to assert that this has any specific effect on the way in which the citizen takes part in elections. In spite of the hopes nurtured in this respect for the 1972 reform, the British citizenry continues to ignore local elections (only 42% voted in 1983). By contrast, the French elector remains unfailingly interested in them (as many as 78% voted in the municipal elections of 1983). Voting may be only one basic and conventional form of participation, but it is far from insignificant. Moreover the importance of politicisation goes beyond electoral processes. British observers have noted a new political element in the actions undertaken by local councils, just as the policies of municipal councils in France, and even the successive reforms which are more or less closely linked to the prevailing political climate, are nowadays often determined by political choices. The fate of the Metropolitan Counties and the Greater London Council in Britain, which tended to support the Labour Party and were abolished by the Conservatives in 1985, was dictated by party political considerations. The same was no less true of the advantage which the French Socialists hoped to derive from the 1982 reform of local councils on which they had a majority.

Politicisation goes hand in hand with the nationalisation of local life. Thus, the nationalisation of political cleavages is apparent in both countries, except, no doubt, for the regional interests represented on Scottish or Welsh councils which find little parallel in France outside the communes and departments of Corsica. There are 'ruling party' towns and 'opposition' towns in both countries, whose elected representatives regard themselves as such. What is more, the fate of local elites is closely linked to the national political situation – French mayors, who are noted for their longevity, suffered the same fate in the municipal elections of 1977 and 1983 as local councillors in Britain, whose period in office has always been shorter. In short, a number of factors have contributed in both countries to the 'delocalisation' of the local system, whose impact on the organisation and working of local institutions cannot be ignored.

2 THE POLITICO-ADMINISTRATIVE ARENA: THE STRUCTURES AND
FUNCTIONS OF THE LOCAL SYSTEM

Even if the interpenetration of the centre and the periphery is far more
marked than it once was, especially in Britain, there exists in both countries a distinct local politico-administrative arena, which is structured by
local institutions providing services for the citizens insofar as local authorities have the ability to do so.

The institutionalisation of local communities and authorities

In both countries several layers of local institutions exist which form, in
concentric circles set one on top of the other, a 'Chinese box' structure.
There are three levels (communes, departments, regions) in France and
two levels (districts and counties) in Britain.[2] The population of both
countries is of almost equal size, but their areas are very different,[3] as is the
socio-geographic distribution of local authorities: the 520 British local
authorities contrast with more than 36,500 communes, 96 departments
and 26 regions in France. This is the source of the very great disparity
frequently emphasised by British and French observers. And yet it is not
certain that this apparent disparity is entirely accurate, since no account is
taken of the 'local councils' in Britain (parish or town councils in England,
community councils in Wales and Scotland), even though their responsibilities are minimal and marginal. It may be argued, after all, that the
mayors and town councils of the 22,500 French communes with less than
500 inhabitants have, whatever their legal rights, no more powers in
practice than the 11,000 British 'local' councils. And yet the gap between
them remains significant, especially in relation to the optimum size of the
geographical area they control.

The reason for this is simple. In France, the division of the country has its
roots in history, and is an integral part of the political culture which no
reformer has dared to attack.[4] As a result, the local political arena is
over-institutionalised, and the only outcome of the reforms has been to
add still further to the number of local units (urban communities in 1966,
regions in 1972). In contrast, the British reform of 1972 aimed at simplifying the local system by leaving in place only two levels of local authorities
whose size was related to the urbanisation of the country.

Any attempt to compare local authorities on the basis of their population size, however, has only limited relevance. Since 1972 Britain has
been divided into comparatively equal areas (of roughly 125,000 inhabitants) reflecting both the relative homogeneity of the country in socio-
economic terms, and the desire to include, apart from the big cities,

both urban and rural zones in the same administrative units. In France, on the other hand, there is a considerable disparity between local authorities at all levels and, with the obvious exception of the regions, they have not been much altered since the Revolution.

In such circumstances, it is very difficult to draw analogies between the two systems of local authorities. The parishes of Britain have something in common with the rural communes of France, so far as their limited role in the system of local government as a whole is concerned. This arises in Britain because their powers are marginal. Equally, in France, they also have limited powers to act on their own and therefore depend largely on other local authorities or on State representatives. Yet a disparity remains in that the small commune in France is a rural phenomenon, whereas in Britain town councils are responsible above all for ensuring that citizens are represented locally, and they are also found in some urban areas.

Moving up a tier, the 423 British districts can be sub-divided, for purposes of comparison, into metropolitan and non-metropolitan districts, the former equivalent in France to large cities or urban communes and the latter to French departments. In both instances their powers are broadly the same – responsibility for housing and urban planning in towns, or local roads in departments. But the 62 British counties – including the nine regions of Scotland – are also similar to the departments of France both in the size of their populations and in some of their responsibilities (welfare services, main roads and public transport). The creation in 1965 of the Greater London Council with its 32 boroughs did, until 1985, offer some parallel with the new status (since 1982) of the City of Paris, in which councils were elected for each arrondissement.

The picture would not, however, be complete if we omitted two further points. First, the distinction between metropolitan and non-metropolitan areas in Britain involved giving a broader range of powers to the metropolitan districts, and reflected a policy of providing a specific organisational framework for the large urban conurbations (London, Birmingham, Liverpool, Manchester, Leeds, Sheffield and Newcastle). Similar concerns have also guided French reformers both in creating urban communities and in remodelling the administrative organisation of Paris, Lyons and Marseilles. Secondly and conversely, there is no British equivalent of the French regionalisation programme – except, perhaps, for the formation of Scottish regions which are far larger than the English counties but have the same powers. The question of a regional structure has not so far passed beyond the economic sphere, although even this has some bearing on the provision of local public services.

The distribution of local services

Nowadays, citizens generally regard local governmental institutions as agencies for providing services for the population. Local authorities both in France and in Britain, cannot escape this shared responsibility and obligation, even though such functional responsibilities are more apparent in Britain than in France, where the intervention of the State in local affairs means that it takes prime responsibility for solving the most critical problems.

At first sight, the distinction which exists in France between State services and local services seems not to exist in Britain. British local authorities are the executive agencies of the central administration whereas in France they share this responsibility with the local offices of the State. This has considerable implications since services as important as education, police and public health – which in France are the responsibility of the State – are under the control of British local authorities. Except for social welfare and employment, and the public inspectorate, there are no central agencies playing a part in the affairs of local authorities.

Nowadays, however, the contrasts between the situations in France and Britain are perhaps not quite so stark. In France, decentralisation in 1982 brought about a significant transfer of responsibilities from the State to the local authorities. For example, the running of secondary schools and colleges devolves respectively upon the regions and the departments. Similarly, sanitation and welfare have become in part the responsibility of the departments. For the British, on the other hand, the tendency has been the reverse since responsibilities have recently become more centralised. The result is that central government now exercises ever-tighter control over those services for which local authorities once had discretionary responsibilities. The Housing Act of 1980 and the Transport Act of 1985 are both cases in point.

Underlying this trend in Britain lies the principle of obligatory responsibility which forces local authorities to carry out all the tasks or obligations assigned to them under central regulations. These regulations are, in turn, becoming ever more precise and detailed. The French system, however, is rather different, being based on the view that local authorities should be responsible for 'local affairs', and for 'protecting the economic and social interests of the population'. As a result, the disparity in French local services, especially those provided by the communes themselves, is far greater than in Britain where national regulations impose relatively uniform standards.

Nevertheless, contrasts between the two countries in the functioning of local services have not prevented identical problems from arising in recent years. The division of responsibility for services between local authorities is not always clear, even though British and French reformers attempted to clarify the matter. In consequence, spheres exist in both States in which the various echelons of local government are more competitive with one another than complementary. Thus, we see in Britain a degree of 'vertical disintegration' as a result of the district authorities having been given powers in the areas of planning, roads and traffic. The overlap of responsibilities is particularly apparent in planning, where the county is able to lay down general lines which the district must then follow. In France, despite the determination to give each echelon of local government a set of special responsibilities, some services are still shared between several levels of local government. Action on economic questions, for example, often produces rivalry between the regions and the departments.

The privatisation of local services is yet another recent phenomenon which can be found in both countries. In France, after a long period of 'municipal socialism' between the wars, the great increase in the number of local services was never an obstacle to using the private sector to solve the problems of local development. The Offices d'Habitation à Loyers Modérés (HLMs), for example, were set up as mixed economy companies. But, with a few exceptions, and then in only special circumstances (such as undertakers in some towns), France has, unlike Britain, not experienced a deliberate policy of privatising local services imposed by central government (such as the selling of local authority houses or the management of urban transport). It has to be said, however, that this policy, as implemented by the Thatcher Government, has met with a good deal of local resistance – especially from Labour councils – which makes one speculate as to how effective it will turn out to be. Moreover, the transfer of some services to the private sector does not appear to have changed significantly the overall image of local authorities. Even less in evidence is any recognition of their capacity for independent action.

The ability of local authorities to take action

The powers of local authorities can be gauged not only from the functions assigned to them, and from the areas in which State regulations allow them to intervene, but also – and above all – from their ability to take action, i.e. the latitude which they are allowed in taking decisions about the services for which they are legally responsible. The problems here are all the more acute in that local government agencies are facing ever-increasing demands from the population to provide more comprehensive and varied services.

It should first be noticed that there has been a great increase in the number of standards laid down by government, which reduce the freedom of action of local decision-makers. There have been many complaints in

France, for example, that technical standards have become more numerous, especially in town planning, a situation which the decentralisation legislation was intended to simplify – obviously so far without success. Similarly, local authorities in Britain are undeniably responsible for much of education, but are tightly controlled by the rules laid down by Whitehall as regards the school-leaving age, school services, the qualifications of teachers, etc. Adherence to these rules is, in turn, monitored by an inspectorate. Furthermore, both parliament in London and ministers in Paris have powers to set these standards, powers that have been regularly asserted with the development of, and the crisis in, the Welfare State. The result is that national and local policies interlock more and more, a process emphasised by State intervention at the local level to correct inequalities between the regions (town and country planning in France), or nowadays (in Britain) to favour, through subsidies, those local authorities most affected by the crisis. This, in turn, has the effect of removing from local authority agencies their functions as self-governing providers of resources and services.

We therefore come back again to the essential problem of the organisational and financial capacities of local authorities. So far as their structure and organisation are concerned, local authorities in Britain have, as we shall see, greater resources at their disposal than their French counterparts. They have long had the advantage of a professional local bureaucracy, in France a privilege until recently confined to the large towns. However, since the modernisation of the local government system, medium-sized French towns have also set up services (especially technical services) which enable them to rival, or at least to negotiate with, the local administrative representatives of the State.

The financial resources of local authorities need to be examined with caution. Although they have traditionally complained of being impecunious – and have been more willing in France than in Britain to blame the State for this – their financial situation has indeed gradually worsened in real terms in the last ten years. The limitation or reduction of State subsidies and indebtedness as a result of spending on plant and equipment have both lessened considerably the financial capacities of local authorities in the two countries. However, a major difference in the organisation of local finances lies in the control exercised by the State. In France, local authorities have been given increasing scope for action by handing them overall responsibility for management, for public works, and for setting the level of rates (albeit within a range specified by law). Despite such moves, the State continues to exercise a decisive role through the mechanism for providing subsidies and making financial adjustments. In Britain, on the other hand, the State's financial control has greatly increased in recent years, until it now seems, in the view of most observers, to be the principal instrument or agent of centralisation. Thus, Whitehall has arrogated to itself the power to fix a ceiling on the level of local rates (rate-capping) and to reduce local expenditure by imposing penalties on certain spendthrift local councils who ignore the targets set by the government. It also now keeps a detailed check on public works expenditures and on the operational costs of local authorities through the Local Government Finance Act of 1982. Although these measures have not turned out to be fully effective, they have none the less considerably reduced the financial capabilities of local councils, without producing any noticeable corresponding gain in the standard of services. This is a factor which obviously changes the position of local decision-makers.

3 LOCAL ACTORS AND REPRESENTATIVES: THE POWER OF DECISIONS

The internal process of decision-making is undoubtedly the area in which the face of local power in the two countries is most different. If we leave out of account peripheral figures, the range of strategic decision-makers appears to be identical in the case of the local elected representatives and the bureaucracies which go with them, whereas it differs profoundly in respect of the local political parties.[5]

The elected local authorities

If the election of local councils became accepted once and for all in both countries at the end of the nineteenth century (the Local Government Act of 1888 and the *Loi Municipale* of 1884), the position and role of the local authorities are none the less very different. Thus, one finds no real equivalent to the 'notables' of French local politics within the British system: nothing comparable to the personality cult, the authority or the prestige of a French mayor, or of the chairman of a general or regional council; nothing comparable with the domination he exerts over his constituency, and sometimes beyond it. In other words, a French mayor is a 'notable', who often owes his appointment to the fact that he is well-known in local society, holds the reins of power in his commune and has a privileged place among the electorate as an intermediary for distributing rewards and offices to groups or to individuals. The British mayor, by contrast, is, in the last analysis, merely the honorary representative of his council which is responsible for administering the locality. In France, the mayor is a figure-head of local society, often retaining his seat for many years. This advantage of incumbency in successive elections is unknown in British local government, which is better characterised by a rapid turnover of councillors. If both are generally recruited from the middle classes, the quality and the level of competence of the local elected representatives bear witness to another seeming difference. The Redcliffe-Maud Report complained that candidates at local elections in Britain were not sufficiently qualified, and it is by no means certain that the 1972 reforms have necessarily improved matters. In France, by contrast, it is widely believed that the fact that the 'new middle classes' have increasingly taken up council posts has noticeably raised the quality of local elected representatives over the last ten years.

This discrepancy between the two systems goes hand in hand with differences in the ways that decisions are taken by local councils. In France, most such decisions are taken by individuals, and not only just by the mayor (who generally keeps personal control of local finances) but also by his deputies (*adjoints*). The latter are given delegated authority in specialised areas of local management such as town planning, welfare and culture. In Britain, decisions are more often taken collectively by numerous committees, although belonging to the Policy and Resources Committee gives its members the right to oversee the general administration of the locality. One might compare the former system to presidential government, the latter to parliamentary government.

However, we ought not perhaps to push the parallel too far, since, in the final analysis, the difference between the two sets of local representatives is to be explained in large part by the specifically French practice of accumulating offices (*cumul des mandats*). No regulation forbids a British local councillor to challenge an MP for his seat, but it would be unthinkable for him to hold both offices once he had gone to Westminster. The French arrangement has a number of important implications. The *député*/mayor, or the senator/general council chairman, find that prestige with local voters increases upon gaining national office. They also take advantage of their direct access to ministers in Paris. Indeed, the accumulation of offices is an incomparable method for ensuring good relations, via the elected representatives, between the centre and the periphery. Britain, in contrast, has to fall back on local government officials and their opposite numbers in Whitehall, thereby diminishing the role played by parliamentary representatives in the local government system. In fact, in France, most *députés* and senators are local elected representatives, and therefore act both as intermediaries for their constituencies and as the privileged defenders of local interests. British MPs, on the other hand, tend to be less involved with the local authorities in their constituencies, and even if they interest themselves in local problems, their fortunes are not directly linked to them, unlike their French colleagues. One cannot, therefore, be surprised that the difference in the position of the local elected representative finds its counterpart in a similar contrast in the role of the local officials.

Local bureaucracies

If the French local government system is most outstandingly characterised by the presence of notables, in Britain the dominant feature is its professionalism. Local administration has indeed developed differently in the two countries. In France the central government agencies have put in place, over the country as a whole, a network of services which go right down to the lowest level of local administration. What is more, until the last war, only the large towns had their own separate administrative apparatus, and rural communes merely had a town clerk who was, in any event, rarely a full-time official. Only in the last 30 years have local bureaucracies come into being in small towns, or technical services developed in medium-sized cities, while regional and departmental administrations grew out of the 1982 decentralisation.[6]

In Britain, by contrast, provision of local services has traditionally been fundamental to the autonomy of local governmental institutions. Indeed, each local authority has had a responsibility to provide administrative and technical support for the full range of local services. This has produced a compartmentalised administrative arrangement in which the running of each service is also to a large extent autonomous. Such a specialised and horizontal administrative structure is the opposite of the pyramidal organisation of a unified local administration under a chief executive (*secrétaire général*) which is to be found in French towns.

The difference between these two types of administration has a significant effect on the position and role of local authority staff. Whereas in France, local bureaucracies are in the hands of generalists, in Britain they are run by technicians and specialists (accountants, lawyers, engineers, etc.), the only major exception possibly being the chief executives who might well be considered generalists. The distinction between local authority staff and the central civil service is watertight, and is indeed wholly a part of the administrative traditions of the country. In France, on the other hand, a series of laws dealing with local administration has been passed (1952, 1972, 1984 and 1987) with the specific aim of assimilating it more closely into the State civil service.

The relative autonomy of local authority officials in Britain strengthens their role in regulating the system of local government. They operate face to face with the elected local representatives, and decisions are reached by negotiation based on a more or less equal relationship. In France, however, the rule has traditionally been that the elected representatives exercise authority over their services, according to hierarchical principles which decentralisation left intact – and has even strengthened. What is more, relations with ministers in London are established through specialised administrative channels, whereas in France the elected representatives, and especially those who have accumulated several offices, reserve this role for themselves. This does not mean, however, that professional corporatism amongst administrators is more developed in Britain than in France. Indeed, British local officers are usually noted for their loyalty to their own authority.

In these circumstances, the responsibility of local authority employees in the decision-making process is certainly greater in the British than in the French system. Furthermore, the existence of the committee system through which the different departments are controlled makes it easier for them to be involved alongside the councillors in decisions. None the less, it has recently been noted in both countries that small specialised management teams have been set up by the leading elected representatives (committee chairmen in Britain, mayors and deputy mayors in France) and administrative heads (chief officers, directors of services). These teams are comparable to politico-administrative technostructures, and this in turn could give rise to fears that local authorities and local administrations are being diverted down a technocratic road. It seems, however, that this risk can be largely ignored, since in France elected representatives retain full responsibility for local decisions, whilst in Britain the presence of local parties continues to be a significant factor in maintaining political direction.

The influence of the local political parties

The two national party systems reflect contrasting traditions. In Britain the national organisations of the two major political parties in the nineteenth century were built upwards from the local constituency associations and, hence, the influence of the parties in the political system was due in part to their local presence.[7] In France, by contrast, the process was the reverse and the central party apparatuses were established before the local party committees. As a consequence party implantation at local level was, for a long period, weak. Furthermore, until recently, the parties showed only a moderate interest in local politics, leaving local notables in charge of elective offices. This situation encouraged the development of an apolitical stance at local level, with à language and ideology which served as a vehicle for local elected representatives who regarded the management of a local council as something beyond party divisions. It was not until the 1960s that party struggles became gradually more widespread in municipal and cantonal elections, and not until the 1970s did the major national party organisations judge that the conquest of local power might provide a spring-board for gaining national power. At the same time, the new parties of the Fifth Republic, particularly the Socialist Party and the Gaullist

Party, were making considerable efforts to establish roots in local authorities.

This does not mean that in either country the totality of local councils is dominated by the political parties. However, the number of non-partisan councils run by 'Independents' (in Britain) or by representatives elected without a party label (in France) has decreased considerably in recent years – earlier in Britain than France, probably because of the greater pressures imposed by the two-party system. Nowadays, in both countries, most local councils are in the hands of one or other of the major parties, and local elections are to a great extent politicised. Thus, in 1980, only 16% of local councils in Britain were predominantly (60% or more of the seats) composed of Independents (Byrne 1985: 112). Equally in France, 'Divers Droite' and 'Divers Gauche' (Independents who have some partisan leanings) – many of which, indeed, have been indirectly supported by the main parties – represented a mere 22% of the general councillors elected in 1982. It has generally become the case that local elected representatives in towns and cities belong to a party, the only exceptions now being in rural areas. The penetration of the parties into local life has been still further strengthened by the fact that minority parties are also represented on councils. In Britain, this is helped by a system which permits electors to vote for only one candidate, an arrangement reintroduced into town council elections in France by the law of 1982.

However, the politicisation of local elections does not mean that the parties can be sure of controlling local decision-making. This is certainly not the case in France where, on the contrary, mayors make every effort to distance themselves from their local party organisation in order to obtain a wider consensus from the population as a whole in favour of the council's actions. In Britain, the parties' control over local decisions is far more direct which makes it easier for collective decisions to be taken. Every important problem is discussed at a preliminary meeting of the party groups on the council at which their position is laid down. The leader of the majority party is therefore politically a much more important figure than the 'chairman of the council', and his influence in the decision-making process is equivalent to that of committee chairmen in France. In this way, it seems that party policy plays a far greater part in shaping local council affairs in Britain than it does in France.

All these findings and observations show beyond doubt that there are still considerable differences between the systems of local government in Britain and France. This is, perhaps, despite the common context of changes which have come about in all western democracies following the crisis and birth of 'post-industrial' society. It is far from pointless, however, to draw attention to their similarities as well as their differences, since these features constitute the immediate environment of the studies which follow in the remainder of the book. In short, they provide the structural parameters for assessing, comparing and interpreting political participation and mobilisation at the local level in the two countries.

At this stage, it is difficult to say whether one system rather than the other is more conducive to local democracy in the sense of the access afforded to citizens and groups, and of the political interest it evokes. It is true that the proximity of local administration and the personalisation of elections constitute factors which should facilitate citizen involvement in France. But it is also the case that the wide responsibilities accorded to British local authorities might be expected to stimulate interest in the operations and output of local government. In any event, it is clear that the hopes for a higher level of participation by ordinary people in their local affairs expressed by the British reformers of 1972 and their French counterparts in 1982 have been largely disappointed.

NOTES

1 It is not possible to refer here to the large body of critical literature directed at the institutional approach to the study of local administration notably by students of the sociology of organisations, but see in particular Crozier and Thoenig (1975) and Gremion (1976). British authors who have adopted the same approach include Machin and Wright (1980) and Hayward (1983).
2 No account is taken here of Northern Ireland, where the administrative system is quite distinct.
3 230,000 km² in Great Britain, 550,000 km² in France.
4 The 1971 law on the fusion of communes has been a total failure.
5 We shall not deal here with the external services of the State in relation to the system of local government in France.
6 In 1981 it was estimated that local authority employees numbered 725,000. British local authorities in 1979 employed 2,350,000 people. The figures for the State civil service are almost the reverse: 600,000 in Britain, 2,600,000 in France.
7 The Labour Party broke with this pattern.

PART II PARTICIPATION

Introduction

One of the advantages of studying public participation at the local level is that it is somewhat easier to establish the specific context which gives rise to action, particularly by individuals. The national political stage tends to be one in which great issues are debated, about which individual citizens may have views but the outcome of which they cannot affect in any very direct way. For this reason, the 'great issues' do not necessarily produce the largest amount of participation (Moyser, Parry and Day 1986). However, as was argued when discussing the existence of a distinctively 'local' form of participation in the introductory chapter, it is not possible to exclude entirely the national dimension from many aspects of the local context. Moreover, many of the problems which arise in a locality, concerning housing or education, will have their close parallels elsewhere. Indeed, one of the objectives of the study of participation is to examine the almost routine patterns of political life between the highlights of election periods.

Nevertheless, problems do take on more specific forms in different localities and the prevailing social and demographic structure, the party political alliances and the social norms will give their own bias to the outcome. This in turn leads us to a consideration of the methodological choices which lie behind the two chapters.

We can distinguish two broad approaches to the study of political participation. The first focuses on the long-term personal predispositions which affect behaviour. The second is based on the responses of individuals to the immediate circumstances in which they find themselves. Both, of course, are essential ingredients for any fuller account of why people participate (or fail to) in political life. Nevertheless, they do represent differing emphases in research on the subject.

Thus, when participation is viewed principally in terms of the socio-psychological predispositions of individuals, citizens are regarded as having a variable potential for activism which can be evaluated largely independently of the particular context. The question of whether or not specific issues or problems within that context prompted intervention is, in a sense, superseded by a concern for a more generalised propensity to participate that can be linked to the various sociological and psychological characteristics of individuals. Thus, participation is not examined in relation to local issues and problems or to the nature of political demands. The approach, in short, only considers participation as instrumental – as an act intended to solve a problem (Orbell and Uno 1972: 475) – in a very loose sense.

This contrasts with the second approach. In this perspective, the individual intervenes, or participates, only when he or she is adversely affected by a concrete situation. In other words, this model tends to view participation as a sign of dissatisfaction, a response towards a system which, from that individual's point of view at least, is working badly. This is, therefore, somewhat different from the view of Almond and Verba (1963) and others, who see participation, or rather a judicious blend of activism and quiescence, as the hallmark of the civic-minded citizen and as an indicator of integration into a properly functioning socio-political system.

These approaches tend also to influence the methods used for data collection. The 'predispositional' approach, being so closely associated with the individual *per se*, is especially identified with the deployment of sample surveys, particularly on a national basis. As a result, one might say that the dominant paradigm of such studies, as exemplified by Verba and Nie (1972) and Barnes, Kaase *et al.* (1979), and being based on national samples, has tended to de-contextualise participation and 'atomise' individuals (Segal and Wildstrom 1970; Boyd 1971). In fact, however, the individuals included in such samples presumably find themselves in a series of localised situations which vary to a greater or lesser extent in respect of the problems involved and the issues at stake. Thus, although we can relatively easily quantify the patterns of participation with respect to such factors as age, gender and class, this tends to be at the expense of discounting the particular character of the issues and circumstances which might have been their immediate trigger.

Such considerations suggest that this responsive or reactive element must form an essential feature of the study of participation. It also implies that it can be most effectively incorporated in local studies. However, this can give rise to difficulties over making valid comparisons. One instance would be a community faced by a major issue affecting most, if not all, of the local population. This creates specific conditions which structure participation in ways not found in other areas where issues may be less pressing, or only affect limited segments of the population. The siting of a nuclear power-station in a rural community may generate levels and types of reaction atypical of normal patterns of participation. However, most local political life is far more mundane. Whilst issues are in one sense specific, such as the building of a new shopping development, the actions surrounding them assume patterns which are recognisable in other localities and, perhaps, also in other countries. Issues prompt action, yet at the same time some types of people are more readily prompted than others. For this reason, we aim in both the following chapters not only to consider participation in relation to individual predispositions but also as a direct response to local issues and problems.

In consequence, we have, in the two chapters that follow, limited the localities which we have investigated to two – one in Britain and one in France. Their choice was governed, to the extent possible given the range of materials we had available, by the relative similarity of their socio-economic contexts. Both areas, Mérignac and Sevenoaks, are small towns on the outskirts of larger urban centres. Both are mainly middle class but in the English case, professional and managerial occupations predominate whereas in Mérignac it is much more a case of technicians and 'white collar' forms of employment. Neither town faced a major single problem that created special circumstances, although, as we shall see in chapter 3, Sevenoaks does bear the imprint of two special issues, at least one of which stimulated a local referendum which is highly unusual in the British context. However, the populations of Mérignac and Sevenoaks have never witnessed any major collective protest activities such as those experienced by the Welsh mining community discussed in chapter 9. Nor has either locality been the subject of any concerted attempt to raise the level of citizen involvement. In short, they are relatively ordinary towns particularly as regards levels and types of participation.

At a more technical level, it should perhaps be noted that this common substantive focus was supported by the deployment of a very similar questionnaire. This allows some cautious comparisons of levels of participation, although, as Verba, Nie and Kim (1978: 40–2) point out, great care should be exercised in such endeavours. But at least the categories of political activities, the range of behaviours included and, not least, the response alternatives provided, assist this type of comparison. Furthermore, they provide a firm basis for assessments of those social and political traits of individuals which seem particularly to predispose some to be active participants and others inert non-participants.

Although the two chapters range fairly widely across the theme of local participation, they do not, of course, exhaust all the questions that might be raised in this connection. Indeed, the remainder of the volume represents an unfolding of many other related aspects – mobilisation, linkages with local leaderships, the impact of 'community' and 'locality', to mention some major instances. Nevertheless, within the limitations imposed by the comparison of two single case studies, this opening pair of chapters does represent a 'clearing of the ground'. They provide, in short, an initial 'fix' on the patterns and processes that are involved in Britain and France. As such, they represent a step towards putting local participation into some comparative perspective.

3

Participation and non-participation in an English town

GEORGE MOYSER and GERAINT PARRY

The theme of this chapter concerns the character of local political participation. This is an important subject, raising, as it does, questions about the
democratic nature of political life at the base of the whole system. Equally,
it throws light on how citizens contribute to decision-making about those
matters that most directly affect the quality of their daily lives. So what are
the local issues that are raised by citizens? How do these personal concerns
get translated into interventions by them in the public affairs of a given
locality? And what types and levels of interventions are involved here –
demonstrations, or pluralist-style group activities, or is it more a matter of
individualistic, one-to-one contacts between 'citizens' and local 'leaders'?

In assessing the cumulative impact of citizen participation, we also have
to consider how those concerned view the local political domain. Which
issues and actions do they see as falling within this ambit and which do
not? This set of cultural assumptions, seemingly neglected in other studies,
must shape in subtle but important ways the whole character of local
political life. More concretely, however, we also need to examine what
type of person is most active. Is it the case, as has been found on the
national scale in other countries, that participation tends to advantage
those already advantaged in other ways? Or is the immediacy of the local
system sufficient to equalise matters? Whatever the case we must, finally,
give close attention to the non-participants for it is their voice which is not
heard and it is they, therefore, who potentially provide the sharpest
critique of how the system as a whole operates.

I THE RESEARCH LOCALITY

In this chapter, the context is provided principally by the town of Sevenoaks in Kent – whilst drawing comparisons from other localities as appropriate. Sevenoaks itself is an old-established town. Growing up in the
vicinity of the great seventeenth century stately home of Knole, it

39

contains many buildings dating from the seventeenth and eighteenth centuries. The population of the town is around 24,000 but the local government district, which contains one other moderate-sized town and several
smaller villages, has a population of nearly 110,000. With a frequent train
service to London, Sevenoaks is an extremely attractive residential location for commuters. It is one of the most typical of a distinct group of
affluent towns around London in the 'Home Counties', a group which also
includes Guildford, Windsor and Maidenhead, and St Albans.

Its affluence may be measured in a number of ways. One major indicator
is the fact that Sevenoaks, according to the 1981 Census, contains three
times more households whose head has a professional occupation than in
Britain as a whole. Compared with the rest of the country, it also has twice
the proportion of men with higher educational qualifications and a substantially higher than average proportion of qualified women. Two-thirds
of the houses are owner-occupied compared with 56% for the rest of the
country. The houses are also generally larger – 30% having seven or more
rooms, compared with under 12% nationally. Car-ownership is higher,
with over a quarter of households owning two or more, whereas this is true
of only 15.5% in Britain at large. As an official report put it, 'Figures of
over 1 car per household are rare in urban areas with populations of
20,000 or more, and nearly always indicate higher status areas with a
life-style in which cars are heavily involved' (OPCS 1984: 14). In this
connection one must always remember that a large proportion (20%) of
the Sevenoaks working population use the train to commute to work,
mainly in London.

Sevenoaks is not, however, entirely commuter country. It contains a few
substantial firms including a nationally-known supplier of building materials, a leading publishing company, and an international insurance firm,
among others. For these reasons the proportions employed in construction
(nearly 8%), and in distribution and catering (just over 20%), are very
close to the national average. The highest proportion is in 'other services'
which at 48% is much higher than the national average of 34% but is quite
typical of urban areas in the South-east of England. Compared with the
rest of the country, the numbers in manufacturing are low, 14% compared
with 27%. Concomitantly, the proportion unemployed at 5% was less than
half the national average of 11.6% – again at the time of the 1981 census.

2 ISSUES, ACTION AND THE LOCAL POLITICAL DOMAIN: AN
OVERVIEW

Our 1985 survey focused attention on issues, needs and problems facing
the local area, or facing the individual and his or her family. Those
interviewed were not presented with a 'menu' of local problems on which

to comment but were asked to suggest any matter which had arisen in the 'last five years or so'. The objective behind such an open and wide-ranging question was to avoid, so far as possible, any restriction on the range of issues, which might bias it according to any preconceptions of the investigators. However, people were asked to consider only those types of issue about which action might be taken, such as contacting a local councillor or official, signing a petition or working in a local group. In this way, the study sought to emphasise those issues which could, at least in principle, give rise to some form of more public action whilst avoiding matters which were entirely personal.

As well as obtaining an overview of all the issues, needs and problems mentioned in the interviews, the study also probed in much greater detail one issue (and associated action) selected because it was of highest priority to the individual, judged either by the fact that it was the matter on which he or she took most action or, if no action had been taken, which was described as being most important. Just under a fifth (18.2%) of the total sample in Sevenoaks offered no issue, need or problem whatsoever.[1] A further 24.6% took no action although naming an issue. Their significance as 'non-participants' will be discussed later in the chapter.

Local action

In table 3.1 the actions taken on these 'selected' issues by the remaining 57.2% in Sevenoaks are reported.

They are sub-divided into broad and largely self-evident types: those of a 'personal and private' nature, 'contacting', 'protesting' and 'group activity'. The first of these comprises essentially any initiative kept entirely within the private domain and arises, albeit very infrequently (2.6%), in spite of our attempts indirectly to screen out issues that would be associated with this form of outcome. At least, it shows that issues having a 'public' potential need not necessarily be associated with action exclusively conducted in the public arena. The relevant linkages and boundaries are just not that watertight in British local politics.

Contacting, by contrast, clearly is 'public' and refers to any attempt to get in touch in person, by letter or by telephone, with an elected representative, a government official or even a group in order to affect an issue. This was done by 40.9% of the sample, the vast majority being at the local level. Another small group contacted a variety of other persons and bodies, such as Members of Parliament and private businesses.

The selected priority issue prompted 44% of those taking action to undertake some form of protest. In the context of Sevenoaks, protest takes on a fairly mild form. Over half of the relevant group (or 24.9% of the total) had signed a petition and a quarter had attended a public meeting

Table 3.1. *The distribution of action on local issues and their perception as being 'political'*

Action	%	% 'Political' ?*			Number
		Yes	Depends	No	
Personal and private	2.6	(0.0)**	(0.0)	(100.0)	5
Contacting	40.9	6.3	6.3	87.5	80
Local	33.7	3.1	7.7	87.7	65
National	4.1	(33.3)**	(0.0)	(66.6)	9
Other/NA	3.1	(0.0)**	(0.0)	(100.0)	6
Protesting	44.0	15.5	8.3	75.0	84
Signing a petition	24.9	17.0	6.4	74.4	47
Attended public protest meeting	11.9	8.7	8.7	82.6	23
Other protest action	7.3	(21.4)**	(14.3)	(64.3)	14
Group activity	5.7	(18.2)**	(5.6)	(72.3)	11
Other	6.7	(18.2)**	(5.6)	(72.3)	11
Total	100.0	11.5	7.3	79.6	191

* 'Don't know' and 'Not ascertained' responses not included.
** All bracketed percentages should be treated with caution because of the low base N (under 20).

called to remonstrate about the issue in question. The remainder had taken a variety of other protest actions such as circulating a petition, taking legal action or registering a protest vote in a local referendum. None of these would be regarded by most people as very extreme although the use of a referendum is a relatively unusual step in British local politics.

Petitioning and attending public meetings have been shown elsewhere in the British study to be often associated with activity in groups (Moyser, Parry and Day 1986). However, supporting organised groups and working informally with others was the response of only 5.7% to dealing with their major issue. There remain, finally, 6.7% who took a variety of other actions. Overall, therefore, no one mode or style of action is dominant. Rather there is a diversity of ways in which people express themselves, encompassing collectivistic as well as individualistic, and unconventional alongside more established forms of engagement.

Table 3.1 also reports the extent to which people regarded their actions as 'political' in any way. Every single type of activity was seen as 'not political' by the vast majority – nearly 80% overall. Nevertheless, some variation can be detected, although in several instances it is advisable to exercise caution in interpreting the figures in view of the small numbers involved. There are grounds for arguing that the more conflictual kinds of activity, represented by protesting, are viewed in a more political light, with 15.5% describing them in this way and a further 8.3% recognizing some political element to their action by opting for the response, 'Yes, in some ways; no, in others'. It could also be hypothesised that the more collective types of action were viewed somewhat more politically in that a little under a fifth (18.2%) would use the term to designate group activity, with an additional 5.6% feeling ambivalently about the matter. Whilst it is tempting to argue that protesting also has a collective aspect, and that it is for this reason, as well as because of its conflictual dimension, that it is seen as relatively more political, this appears not to apply to attending a protest meeting. Finally, though on very tenuous grounds in view of the numbers involved, it might be claimed that when a national element is drawn into a local problem, action takes on a more political aspect. Thus, contacts with national figures or agencies are described as political by one third of the very few who made them.

Local issues

Action can also be analysed by reference to the type of issue which gave rise to it. Action, it has been pointed out above, is not necessarily spon-taneously generated by the individual participant but may be a response to a situation created by others in the local environment, or may form part of a collective action aimed at mobilising opposition to, or support for, a policy.

Table 3.2 reports the broad categories of issue mentioned by the popu-lation in Sevenoaks. (In this instance, *all* the issues mentioned are reported and not just the sub-set of 'most important' issues which were the subject of table 3.1.) The issue responses were sorted into a large number of substantive areas and were then re-grouped into a smaller number of categories for purposes of easier exposition. However, issues are not, in the real world, always classifiable into such neat compartments. Some problems which are raised have more than one aspect to them. Thus, a problem concerning youth unemployment might be regarded either as concerning youth or unemployment. The solution adopted has been to regard any issue as having a maximum of two such aspects and to count each aspect as a separate issue for the purpose of analysis. This makes but a small difference to the overall picture since, of the full set of 556, only 106 (or 19% of the total) were classified as having a second aspect.

It will be readily seen from table 3.2 that the dominant category of issues in Sevenoaks is 'environment and planning', comprising 44.2% of all the issues mentioned. Within this broad category, the largest specific topic concerned the provision of leisure facilities, raised 106 times, comprising 16.0% of the total number. Two-thirds of the references in this instance were about the location in the town of a new swimming pool, which had

Table 3.2. *The distribution of issues within the locality and their perception as being 'political' (662 issues, 216 respondents)*

Issue category	% all issues	% 'Political'
Environment and planning		
(leisure and sports facilities; conservation; planning permission; refuse collection; litter)	44.2	29.3
Transport and traffic		
(road traffic; car parking; public transport)	17.7	27.7
Health		
(national health service; hospital provision)	16.0	63.8
Youth		
(provision of facilities)	5.3	14.3
Housing		
(repairs; availability of housing)	3.2	40.0
Education		
(provision; primary and secondary schools)	2.9	68.4
Economic (excluding unemployment)		
(taxes; wages; inflation; pensions)	2.7	50.0
Elderly		
(care and facilities)	2.0	–
Law and order		
(crime; vandalism; drunken driving)	0.7	–
Unemployment		
(unemployment; redundancies; closures)	0.6	–
Race		
(race relations; problems of minorities)	0.4	–
Other	4.2	53.5
Total	100.0	38.1

occasioned a great deal of local controversy. Indeed, this was the subject of the local referendum previously mentioned. There was also a substantial number of problems concerning planning and about the collection of refuse.

Some way behind 'environment and planning' came issues about 'transport and traffic' – a mixture of problems concerning local road conditions. There was also a relatively substantial number of references to health issues, a category which covers the National Health Service and such matters as hospital provision. In fact, virtually all the references here concerned one single issue – the threatened closure of a local hospital.

The remaining issue categories, as can be seen, represent very small proportions of the total. Nevertheless, one deserves some comment. A very striking feature is that so few references were made to unemployment, one of the major issues facing the country at the time. This can, perhaps, be explained in two ways. Unemployment tends to be regarded as more of a national than a local issue (Moyser, Parry and Day 1986) and is, for this reason, less likely to be raised in a local context.[2] Secondly, Sevenoaks is an area far less troubled by such matters, as was shown earlier. Its relative affluence would perhaps lead one to expect the pattern in fact found, in which economic issues come low on the scale and matters to do with the quality of life receive relatively greater priority. However, this is not necessarily to endorse the post-materialist thesis of Inglehart (1977) according to which relative affluence might be expected to result in a shift away from concerns with material economic matters toward a less materialist involvement with the environment. To be concerned with planning decisions and with the environment in a pleasant suburban town may well reflect as much an interest in conserving the value of individual property as in protecting the quality of life *per se*, although few might be found publicly to acknowledge this possibility (Barker and Keating 1977).

The local 'political' domain

The readiness to use the word 'political' to describe issues (rather than actions) varies markedly in table 3.2 and the explanation for the variation is not self-evident. Amongst the larger categories of issue it is only those concerning health which are described as political by a majority of those mentioning them. Part of the explanation may be that the ultimate provision of health facilities is a matter for national rather than local government. At the local level, Regional and Area Health Authorities and Community Health Councils are only in part subject to local authority influence. The ambiguous role of health matters, neither within nor totally outside the governmental structure and with a national and regional dimension (Boaden *et al.* 1982: 112–29) may affect the way in which participation in this sphere is conceived. Somewhat similar considerations may be behind the large number of educational issues viewed as political, given that this is a responsibility not of the Local District Council in Sevenoaks but of the higher tier Kent County Council. It is also the case that resources for education are very much dependent on national policies, including national salary negotiations, and have also been the subject of considerable controversy between the political parties in Westminster.

Where issues come more firmly within local responsibilities the proportion regarded as political declines to less than 30%. Most environmental and planning matters are the responsibility of the District Council, including some of the more frequently mentioned 'issue areas' in Sevenoaks – leisure and sports facilities, planning permission and refuse collection. These are less likely to be matters of partisan controversy. Smaller problems of planning permission would in the main be routinely handled by officials and not be a matter concerning elected representatives. Major

issues of conservation and planning development could generate controversy, but not necessarily along party lines. It is perhaps the combination
of local responsibility and non-partisan bases to problems which helps to
explain the infrequency with which such issues are seen as 'political'.[3]

It might be anticipated that those who had taken action on issues they
believed to be political would also describe their actions in political terms.
However, even in this case no more than a quarter of the relevant respondents were clear that their action was political, with a further 13.2%
recognising the possibility of some political element. The majority, in
other words, still thought what they did was *not* political.

It seems to follow, therefore, that, by whatever set of measures one
takes, actions of the sort which are commonly considered as political
participation by political scientists – contacting representatives and officials, working in groups, protesting – are not generally regarded as
coming within the realm of politics by the majority of the population in
this particular locality. It would appear that to warrant the description,
actions and issues have on the whole to be within the sphere of party
controversy. If the latter point is true (and we have only hints that it is)
something of a paradox emerges. Local politics in Britain is increasingly
being fought on a partisan basis in elections and the outcomes of those
elections are profoundly influenced by national political party fortunes.
Furthermore, recent issues such as the local control of education or the
changes in the system of local rating and taxation have been couched in
'political' terms. And yet it would seem from the evidence of both our
national and local surveys that the actions taken by people in connection
with the local issues they focus on are not, by and large, seen as 'political'.

This raises, of course, the question of the framework being used, if it is
not a party-political one. In the French case, it would seem, the idea of a
field of 'administrative action' is well developed. But in Britain this would
appear not to be the case, at least to the same extent. Quite in what terms
such issues and actions are viewed by the populace is a matter for conjec-
ture. They may derive from the era before mass politics and mass parties,
or they may be entirely personal and idiosyncratic. Certainly, it would be
an interesting topic for further investigation.

3 PARTICIPATION

Issues and participation

Regardless of whether the action taken by the people of Sevenoaks is to be
viewed as political or not, it involved issues which most people accepted
could in principle be raised in a public manner. When asked whether the

issues they mentioned might conceivably be acted upon by taking them up with a councillor or working in conjunction with a group, people generally replied in the affirmative. The fact that the majority of people have not taken action does not therefore reflect any sense of the impracticability of such steps. Indirectly, this could be interpreted as some measure of the political awareness and efficacy of those living in this area.

Just under half (45.3%) of the issues raised by our respondents led to some action being taken by them. In the broader context of other localities[4] this is not exceptional as in two other instances (part of the northern industrial town of Rochdale and part of the inner London Borough of Lambeth) the proportion was the same. However, in both relatively rural locations, the market town of Oswestry and the isolated villages comprising the Machars, the activity rate is significantly lower – 26.1% and 36.9% respectively. All of this suggests, therefore, that the relationship between issues and action is analogous to an iceberg floating in the sea: more local issues remain unacted upon and, therefore, hidden from view than become the subject of visible, public intervention. Even in Sevenoaks which, along with Lambeth, had the most issue-oriented or articulate set of respondents, only a minority of issues (albeit a large one) surfaced in some tangible way.

This was not, however, true of every category of issues. Indeed, the most action was taken over health issues and by a clear majority of those concerned – 60% in this instance. Conversely, least action arose in connection with youth concerns where only 11.8% of the relevant group had tried publicly to raise such matters. But, despite such significant differences, they did not greatly change the overall range or pattern of the issue agenda (as recorded in table 3.2). In short, the varying proportions taking action over issues does not alter the fact that public participation in this locality has been dominated by three types of matter – environment, transport and health.

In general, what led people to act was the feeling that they themselves, or their families, were affected. Where individuals reported that the matter affected themselves or their families they were twice as likely to take action than when its effect was confined to other people (62% to 31%). In most instances, however, they took up problems in which their individual interests and those of others were intertwined and in these situations nearly half (48%) prompted action. From the evidence a good example is the problem of health, the only major issue category where a majority were sufficiently concerned to take action. As previously mentioned, the references here in the main related to the threatened closure of a local hospital which clearly affects the community and, potentially, any individual in it. An instrumentalist view of participation (Parry 1972) receives a good deal of support from these findings. In this interpretation the prime justification

Table 3.3. *Levels of local participation (N all items = 264)*

A Non-voting	% 'At Least Once'	% 'Often'*
Contacting		
Local councillor	23.5	3.9
Town Hall official	22.0	3.0
Member of Parliament	12.9	1.0
Central government official	12.5	1.4
Group activity		
In an organised group	17.4	3.5
In an informal group	20.5	4.6
Protesting		
Attended protest meeting	23.1	1.0
Organised a petition	6.8	0.4
Signed a petition	73.8	4.9
Blocked traffic	2.3	0.0
Joined in protest march	2.7	0.4
Joined in political strike	1.9	0.0
Joined in political boycott	5.3	0.8
Used physical force against opponents	0.4	0.0
Campaigning		
Fund raising for political party	6.5	2.4
Canvassed/door knocked for party	5.7	1.6
Party clerical work	4.6	2.0
Attended party rally	10.4	2.3

B Voting	% 'Yes'
1983 general election	87.1
Local elections	
'Every' election	46.5
'Most' elections	26.7
'Some' elections	17.8
'Never'	8.9

* This % is also included in the first column along with those having done the activity 'only once … in the last 5 years or so' and those having done it 'now and then'.

for action is to defend or promote one's interests, as distinct from participation oriented to the well-being of the community as a whole, or justified by its contributions to the development of the individual.

Despite appearances, however, these patterns of behaviour are susceptible of a more generous interpretation. It is possible that although most people accept that action can be taken on wider issues, nevertheless there is a feeling that the chance of success for an individual is less likely (Moyser,

Parry and Day 1986). Concentration on action in the more personal and more localised spheres may, therefore, reflect a rational assessment of the costs and benefits of participation rather than a purely self-interested view of life.

Levels of local participation

So far, public participation has been examined as a response to local issues. An alternative approach is to analyse levels and forms of action without specific reference to the issues which may be involved. In this way we can obtain a more systematic and accurate 'map' of local participation. The relevant figures for Sevenoaks are shown in table 3.3. (The equivalent table for the French case study is table 4.1.)

The table brings out vividly the fact that, in strict numerical terms, participation, and especially frequent political action, is a minority taste. Outside voting, the only partial exception, but a very marked one, is the proportion who have signed a petition 'at least once' which is little short of three-quarters of the sample. But even this figure requires some qualification. First, there is no indication of the subject of the petitions signed. Secondly, once one asks whether a person actually, in much more positive manner, has taken around a petition for others to sign the proportion drops to a mere 6.8%. No other type of non-electoral action has been taken by as many as a quarter of the population although contacting a local councillor and attending a protest meeting approach that figure.

However, if we compare Sevenoaks with other localities in the BPPS study, we find that the rates recorded in table 3.3 are in general somewhat higher than the norm. Contacting a civil servant or the mass media, for example, is the highest in this particular area. Equally, Sevenoaks manifests a relatively high level of voting in local elections and of informal and formal group participation. Indeed, this confirms the impression of 80% of our respondents who thought that the town was an area with a thriving group life. Overall, therefore, the levels recorded in the table suggest a more participatory populace than is found in the generality of other areas. Only amongst our inner London and mining village interviews were activity rates typically so high, a finding which echoes our results for the issue-linked analysis of participation previously discussed. Similarly, it is unsurprising that we again found the lowest involvement in the two rural areas of Oswestry and the Machars. Clearly there are systematic differences between localities in the propensity for the individual overtly to intervene in the affairs of his or her locality.

The question remains, however, as to the extent to which such participation is indeed distinctively 'local'. One way of throwing light on this is to examine the 'targets' of such actions. When this is done, it turns out that contacting involving such local figures as a councillor or town hall official

Table 3.4. *The effect of various demographic, socio-economic and political characteristics on participation in the locality*

	Unadjusted score*	(eta)	Adjusted score*	(beta)	N
A Demographic					
Age (years)					
18–25	−0.24		−0.15		26
26–40	−0.14		−0.01		53
41–64	+0.22		+0.07		79
65+	−0.07		−0.01		50
		(.20)		(.07)	
Gender					
Male	+0.02		−0.13		90
Female	−0.01		+0.10		117
		(.01)		(.09)	
B Socio-economic					
Education					
No Qualific's	−0.17		−0.04		69
'O' Level & less	−0.09		−0.12		62
'A' Level	+0.02		+0.00		16
College	−0.01		−0.00		26
Degree +	+0.48		+0.29		34
		(.25)		(.15)	
Class					
Working class	−0.09		+0.17		32
Petty bourgeois	[−0.08]		[−0.21]		8
Routine non-manual	−0.09		−0.04		42
Prof. & managerial	+0.15		−0.01		87
		(.23)		(.14)	
Wealth					
Poor	−0.54		−0.36		21
Intermediate	−0.11		+0.04		67
Rich	+0.12		−0.02		82
Very rich	+0.25		+0.19		38
		(.26)		(.17)	
C Political					
Interest					
Not at all	−0.46		−0.32		20
Slightly	−0.20		+0.01		49
Fairly	−0.16		−0.16		93
Very	+0.74		+0.45		46
		(.44)		(.28)	
Party identification					
Labour	−0.07		+0.04		44
Lib/SDP	+0.14		+0.12		59
Conservative	−0.04		−0.09		105
		(.09)		(.10)	
Strength of party identification					
Not very	−0.15		−0.10		93
Fairly	−0.09		−0.11		88
Very	+0.82		+0.70		27
		(.35)		(.30)	

Multiple R = 0.63
R^2 = 0.40
N = 207
Overall mean of participation scale = +0.27
* Scores represent average deviations in level of participation for each category from overall mean for the locality, standardised by the standard deviation for that locality (SD = 1.365)
[ ] = very low N, to be treated with caution.

is twice as frequently undertaken as the equivalent activities oriented towards the national arena. In so far as this finding is not dependent upon any prior 'bias' in the sort of issue on which the action was predicated, it therefore serves to emphasise the importance of the local arena for individual political action, and the infrequency with which most people move politically outside its boundaries.

This is not, however, true in the case of voting. As we have mentioned previously, local elections are very much conditioned by national imperatives. This is reflected in turnout differentials as between the two levels of representation. The imprint of national factors is also reflected in responses to a question we posed as to whether they voted in local elections on the basis of national or local concerns. As many as 41% said their decisions were principally conditioned by the former. Given also that 'local issues' may well reflect national policies and agendas, the intrusion of such elements is obviously very pronounced indeed.

The structure of local participation

One important question which arises from this analysis is whether or not the individuals who became active in these different ways are drawn from distinct social strata and political groupings, or have particular personal characteristics.

To investigate this we developed a single measure of political participation encompassing all those various specific activities itemised in table 3.3.[5] This overall scale showed, as previously mentioned, that our Sevenoaks respondents were indeed more participatory, on average, than those in our other five localities (their average score being +0.27 as against 0.00 overall). Nevertheless, and in common with the other areas, those with very high scores were still relatively few in number, and hence highly atypical. Conversely, those who were inactive were much more numerous and thus much closer to the general norm. Indeed, our evidence indicates that in the locality the most politically active citizen (with a scale score of +9.17) was more than eleven times more 'remote' from the average Sevenoaks resident than was the most 'inert' individual (with a score of −0.50).

We then examined the relationship between this general participation scale and a number of important demographic, socio-economic and political characteristics.[6] The results of this analysis are set out in table 3.4 and indicate the effect, in terms of a deviation from the overall average for Sevenoaks, of having each of the characteristics in question. The first column of effects are those where only the particular (bivariate) relationship between each characteristic and the participation scale is considered. The second column, however, is the (multivariate) relationship obtained when the effect of all the other variables in the table is taken into account. As can be seen when the two sets of figures are compared, there are several instances where these relationships diverge.

If we look first at the two basic demographic factors that have been included we can see that age does indeed have a modest impact on one's propensity to participate. The detailed pattern, being curvilinear, is very typical of other studies: young people participate least (-0.24) and the middle-aged participate most ($+0.22$) (see Verba and Nie 1972: 138–45). Furthermore, we also find, as in the other studies, that if we take into account in the table relative disadvantages, in terms of socio-economic and political resources, experienced by the youngest and oldest age groups, then the patterns change somewhat. The young still under-participate more than any others and the middle-aged remain the most active. But all the divergences are much reduced. In other words, the apparent effect of age is to a considerable degree the result of related advantages or disadvantages deriving from other factors. A rather different pattern, however, is found associated with gender. Here, the initial differences are tiny, although women in Sevenoaks do seem to participate to a very slightly lesser extent than men do – again reflecting a finding that has been repeatedly established elsewhere (Milbrath and Goel 1977: 116–17). But in this instance, it is interesting to note that once the socio-economic and political differences between the two genders are taken into account, this pattern not only reverses itself, it also becomes somewhat more pronounced. Nevertheless, the gap is still rather small, possibly reflecting the fact that Sevenoaks is, generally, a middle-class locality. And it is amongst the middle class that gender differences in participation are typically found to have largely evaporated.

A measure of that middle-class ethos can be found in the distributions of our respondents across the three measures of socio-economic characteristics. In the educational sphere, as many as 16% of our Sevenoaks interviewees have a degree (34 out of 207), which is some three times the national average. On the other hand, the largest fraction, one third, is still that group without any formal qualifications at all. The effect on participation represented by these two extremes is initially quite considerable. Unsurprisingly, it is the most educated who participate most, and those without formal qualifications who participate least. However, we again find that the relationship remains true only to a more modest extent when class, age and other factors are taken into account. Here, the only significant effect is the positive impulse imparted by the holding of a degree.

Class, too, generates a pattern in Sevenoaks that is found in most other contexts. Those with professional and managerial backgrounds who, consistent with the general character of the area, comprise as many as 42% of the total are also the most participatory. Conversely, all those not of that high social status, be they routine non-manuals, members of the petty bourgeoisie or even the working class, under-participate to the same extent. However, it is interesting to note that when their base of relative disadvantage is taken into account, it is the workers who seem the most active. This, therefore, indicates that the source of their non-intervention in politics lies more in their lack of other advantages rather than anything intrinsic to being 'working class' *per se.*

It is clear that wealth is another resource which had some bearing upon participation. Indeed, in this general area it has the most powerful effect. As elsewhere, it is the poor who are the least active in Sevenoaks, and the very rich (those possessing a car, their own home, company shares and a very high annual income) who are the most active. In part, as can be seen in the table, the differences reflect other factors but important effects remain. Thus, even with those other characteristics taken into account, being very rich confers an additional advantage which is converted by those concerned into a higher rate of political participation. Equally, being poor in Sevenoaks is an even greater handicap.

Across these two broad domains, therefore, we can identify a multi-faceted syndrome that tends to distinguish the active from the passive in Sevenoaks. The key to the former seems, thus far in the analysis at least, to be the holding of degree level educational qualifications. But being very rich and middle-aged (in that order) also helps. Conversely, the inert citizen is most centrally defined by being poor. But, equally, having no educational qualifications and being young also intensify the propensity not to intervene in pursuit of one's issue concerns.

We turn, thirdly, to the contribution the different political traits make to the picture. In fact, our results show that it is this area where the strongest and most significant linkages with the overall participation scale are to be found. In particular, levels of political interest and the strength of one's psychological identification with a given political party both have an impact that is far stronger than that of wealth or education. Thus, those that claim to be 'very interested ... in politics and national affairs' have a relatively pronounced tendency to convert that interest into personal involvement. Equally, those who have a 'very strong' attachment to a political party (of whatever hue) are even more likely to become active. Conversely, those who are 'not at all interested' and who have only a fairly weak partisan attachment are the least likely to become participants. Finally, we might note that the particular party that is the subject of such attachments in itself contributes relatively little either way. It is the case that in Sevenoaks the Conservative Party attracts the strongest levels of adherence and the Alliance parties the weakest (see also Himmelweit *et al.* 1981: ch. 10). But when we separate out the effect of having an attachment to a particular party from the strength of that commitment, it is what was

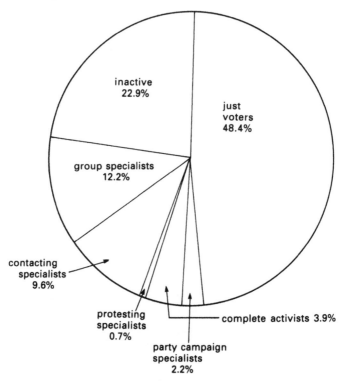

Figure 3.1 An empirical typology of local political participation (N = 264)

then the Liberal–SPD Alliance connection that seems to provide the main, albeit mild, impulse to participate. This is, of course, of a piece with those parties' ideological stress on bringing about a more participatory society and their stress at that time on an active style of 'community politics'. Equally, although the association between the Labour Party and participation is on the positive side, this is hardly sufficient to counteract the usual effects of market position.

Overall, therefore, we can add much clearer political markers to those of a socio-economic and demographic variety in distinguishing the active from the passive. The active are not only typically well educated and well endowed with material resources, but political ties of interest and party attachment also provide major, indeed dominant, additional impulses to become involved. Conversely, the lack of such impulses tends to add to the apparent unwillingness of the poor, the young, and the uneducated, to stand up and be counted.

What all this means, at least for the activists, can perhaps best be illustrated by looking at participation not so much in terms of the power of given traits to predict levels of participation, but rather the socio-political profile of those who, by their responses, clearly identify themselves as the most active of citizens. To look at the matter in this way we placed each of our Sevenoaks respondents into one of seven empirically occurring types of participant, according to how their particular activity profile best allocated them.[7] The results are set out in figure 3.1. In the latter part of this chapter we will examine those who fell into a category we identified as containing the least active (some 23% of the total). Here, however, we wish principally to look at the two groups at the other end of the spectrum, the 'campaigners' (who focused their energies mainly on working for a party but were also quite active in other ways) and the 'complete activists' who were the closest approximation of the 'amateur politician' – the citizen who is active right across the board, in contacting, campaigning, groups, voting and even political protest.

In so far as, together, these two categories only comprise some 6.1% of the total sample, this serves powerfully to reinforce our earlier observation not only that participation in Sevenoaks is a minority taste, but that the effective bedrock of citizen involvement (outside elections) amounts at best to no more than a quarter of the local adult populace and arguably extends merely to a relative handful of perhaps well under 10%. Once more, however, we might stress that this is not atypical. Indeed, as we have mentioned previously, if anything Sevenoaks throws up more than its proportionate share of activists. In the rural areas of Oswestry and the Machars, for example, that inner core who make the most sustained contribution to the total sum of citizen political inputs amount to an almost indetectible 0.6% and 2.7% respectively. In most types of localities, therefore, it would seem, that 'amateur politicians' are very thin on the ground. This may well create that climate generally conducive to autonomy in decision-making perceived by our elite respondents which is further discussed in chapter 8.

The 'biases' induced by the differential effects of socio-economic, demographic and political characteristics discussed previously are very visible within the inner core of Sevenoaks activists. Thus, not one of them was drawn from the youngest age grouping of 18 to 25 year olds. On the other hand, the middle-aged were massively over-represented in that the activists were almost twice as likely to be aged between 41 and 64 compared with the sample as a whole. A similar pattern also was found in respect of educational differentials. None of the activists was from the least educated segment of the population. Rather, they were far more likely to be very well-educated than the population at large. Furthermore, this discrepancy was also reflected in class and wealth differences, which in Britain tend to form a mutually reinforcing system of individual advantage and disadvantage affecting both the economic and the political market-place.

Finally, we might note that, above all, those advantages of a directly political nature seem to provide the most vivid hall-mark distinguishing the 'amateur politician' or citizen activist. We have already seen the powerful effect of having a strong psychological commitment to political affairs. However, when we look at more tangible linkages, institutional ties between citizen and politically relevant groups, we find the greatest differences of all. Thus, those without such ties are, like young and uneducated people, largely absent from the inner participatory core. Conversely, those with a substantial number of ties to local social and political institutions are well over four times more likely to be found amongst their ranks than in the populace as a whole. It is this, of course, that puts the hyper-activists in a position not dissimilar to that of local political elites who are themselves also well integrated into the public life of the locality (see also chapters 8 and 9). In this way, the character of the relationship between these two groups is no doubt a crucial determinant of the democratic qualities of public life in any given area.

4 NON-PARTICIPATION

The findings discussed in the previous section already give some substantial clues as to the character of the non-participants in Sevenoaks. Here, however, we take the matter further in two ways. First, we will look briefly at the 'inert' citizenry – the 22.9% who fell into the almost totally 'inactive' category. Secondly, we will then examine in some detail the linkages between issues and inaction – those who mention no issues, and those who take no action. In doing so we seek to emphasise the importance of examining non-participation in the understanding of democracy at the local level. Even in a town with an affluent and relatively well-educated population such as Sevenoaks, the majority of adults are either non-participants or restrict their contribution solely to periodic elections. Hence, the concerns of the inactive, the social strata from which they are drawn and the reasons for their passivity, are of considerable import in both numerical and evaluative senses. They provide a 'second face' to Sevenoaks' political process (Bachrach and Baratz 1962).

The demographic profile of the 'inactive' stratum is more or less the reverse image of the hyper-activists'. Gender makes very little difference, but age does. As expected, it is the more youthful who are over-represented in this category. In similar vein, the educational and class patterns show that it is the manual working class, and those least educated, who are also very prominent. Finally, group ties also make a further contribution to the picture that is again the opposite pattern to that observed amongst the very active. All in all, therefore, the non-participants do have an identifiable image, although one that is not perhaps so sharply drawn as for their polar opposites. This may, of course, simply reflect the fact that they are nearly

Table 3.5. *Characteristics of issues that led to no individual action*

Issue category	% Issues	% Political	N (Issues)
Environment and planning	43.8	31.4	158
Transport and traffic	18.0	24.6	65
Health	11.6	57.1	42
Youth	8.3	20.0	30
Housing	2.5	(77.8)	9
Education	3.3	(83.3)	12
Economic and unemployment	4.2	64.3	15
Law and order	0.8	–	3
Other	7.5	51.9	27
All issues	100.0	37.5	361

four times more numerous. But this merely serves to emphasise their importance. They represent nearly one fifth of the town's population whose voice is little or very infrequently heard. This heightens one's sense of the possible social implications that the inequalities of local political participation entail.

One measure of those implications can be gleaned from looking at the set of issues where no subsequent action was taken. (This does not mean, of course, that the individual did not take action about another issue on his private agenda.) The distribution is set out in the first column of table 3.5. In fact, if we compare it with the total set of issues recorded in table 3.2 we can see that there is very little difference between the two, once any sampling fluctuations are taken into account. There are no significant differences either in total, or in the rank ordering, between those issues which led to no action and the complete set of issues.

Part of the reason for this can perhaps be found in responses to the question as to whether, in principle, the given issue was amenable to action on their part. Clearly, the vast majority (86.9%) were. Furthermore, in no particular issue category did the proportion fall significantly below this norm. Thus, it is apparent that there is no major impediment or barrier that the respondents see which might systematically prevent certain types of issue from being articulated in the political arena at the expense of others. The two 'faces' are, in this respect at least, virtually the same.

The same conclusions can also be drawn about whether issues not acted upon were seen as more (or less) political. One might have expected, possibly, that 'political' issues would have been more likely to lead to action than those of a non-political variety. But this is not the case to any discernible degree. Overall, the 'inactive' issues were viewed as less 'political', but the difference was entirely too slight to support the proposition.

Nor was there any equivalent, noteworthy deviation within each particular issue area. On the basis of this analysis, therefore, significant differences, if they exist, must lie not amongst the issues themselves but elsewhere.

We therefore turned, by way of concluding our investigation of this area, to the reasons those individuals (and others in a similar position) gave for not expressing themselves at all in the public arena. Perhaps here might be found some important clues as to why they held back from taking action whilst others did not.

Though the group who remained totally silent about all their issue concerns was a relatively small one (just under a quarter), it should be remembered that, on any given issue, taking action was in fact the minority response. Thus, in one sense, it may seem curious to ask those in the majority the reasons why they took no steps to deal with a matter which they thought important enough to the locality or to themselves to mention. If inaction is the norm, perhaps it is the participants who must explain themselves – which of course they do when recounting issues and action. Nevertheless, the reasons for inaction can themselves be important. At its most simplistic, it is relevant to know whether people did not act because they felt fairly satisfied with how things were being dealt with, and hence saw no need to intervene, or because they felt powerless to do anything.

It is a standard view in much of the literature on participation that high levels of action are associated with a sense of political efficacy and that this, in turn, is a feature of those with high economic status (Verba and Nie 1972). Alternatively, it can be argued that such persons tend to have relatively better access to those in positions of political power. The greater certainty of successful outcomes to action is what prompts them to participate compared with persons from poorer sectors of society who may rationally calculate that there is less advantage in doing so (Goodin and Dryzek 1980). On either argument the high status town of Sevenoaks would, as has indeed been seen, produce relatively fewer non-participants and also not many with an acute sense of powerlessness. Comparisons do indeed support this expectation in that fewer people in Sevenoaks than elsewhere were prepared to agree that, as individuals or as members of groups acting together, they could have no influence on local councillors.

In fact, the inactive produced a variety of reasons for their failure to participate. Just under a quarter (23.6%) cited powerlessness as a reason. In some cases this was born out of experience:

I went to a lot of trouble over an education issue several years ago ... wrote letters ... formed groups ... all came to nothing and people are still arguing and still nothing happened.

Others displayed a general dissatisfaction about the possibility of influencing outcomes and spoke of the 'futility of trying to do anything' and of 'beating your head against a brick wall'. For some it was a mixture of powerlessness and a sense of the complexity of government – 'not knowing who to go to and there being so many channels and probably not getting anywhere anyway'. One person possessed a very clear calculation of relative power when wishing to complain about the building of council offices near his home: 'As it is the council office, and they are the ones that give approval, there would not have been any point in protesting whatsoever.'

For around 15% the idea of acting did not occur to them and a few felt that they could not act alone and were not aware of other active groups with whom they could associate: 'I haven't heard of anyone in particular doing anything about it and I can't do it alone.'

The other substantial group serve to remind one of the ways in which the nature of the community impinges on participation. They were too busy, but many were busy in London, rather than in Sevenoaks. 'I don't concern myself sufficiently with Sevenoaks perhaps because the town is a commuter town, and I commute daily.' This person put forward the argument that, having been voted in at the election, it was up to the Council to deal with things, rather than, it was implied, the busy individual citizen – a rational division of labour, as Schumpeter (1954) would have viewed it.

The proportion who took no action is lower in Sevenoaks than in our other communities and, on the basis of the answer to a further question, could be lower in the future. Respondents were asked whether, if a similar problem were to arise again in the future, they would then take any action. A quarter still would not and 14% were uncertain. However, 60% believed that they would act, of whom half would take some form of protest action and a third would contact a representative or an official. Only a small proportion (under 8%) would think of joining in some form of collective group activity. Compared with actual participation in the town, this is a low figure for group activity but a slightly high one for contacting and protesting. One would not deduce a potential for radical protest, however, given that attending a meeting and signing petitions are the only significant forms of protest activities in the area.

Sevenoaks cannot stand for all local communities in England. If it is representative it is so of a number of more affluent towns most, though not all, of which are located in the South on the periphery of London. Localities do differ in their patterns of participation as has been briefly indicated above and has been elaborated elsewhere (Moyser, Parry and Day 1984). Nevertheless, Sevenoaks, or towns like them, provide valuable case studies in that their populations are very much composed of the types of people who have been supposed to possess many of the attributes which make for higher rates of participation (Milbrath and Goel 1977). In particular they are, on average, better-educated and better-off. On this basis ordinary participation levels could be expected to be high. This turns out to be so, but only in the most relative of senses. Even in such apparently favourable circumstances participation is the indulgence of a minority, not a norm for the majority. Other factors are sometimes supposed to stimulate participation – the sense of community, or the awareness of threats to fundamental local interests which other chapters will discuss. But the present study suggests that it remains the case that in the current state of British local politics, without some extra stimulus, public participation falls a long way short of what idealistic democrats would desire.

NOTES

1 It is interesting to note here that this was the lowest proportion across any of the six localities in the overall BPPS study. In our very rural and isolated locality, for example, 44.2% had no issues to offer. This underscores the potential importance of the 'inert' fraction of a given community, both numerically and politically.
2 This pattern whereby the national level actions are more likely to be viewed as political is supported by evidence from the national survey of participation in Britain (see Moyser, Parry and Day 1986).
3 For a more extended discussion of this general topic see Parry and Moyser (1988).
4 For details see note 1, chapter 8.
5 In effect, this scale was computed through a factor analysis of all the items listed in table 3.3. See Moyser, Parry and Day (1986) for details as applied to our national sample.
6 For table 3.4 we have used a statistical technique known as Multiple Classification Analysis (MCA) (see Andrews *et al.* 1969). This produces, first of all, a set of figures labelled in the table as, respectively, 'unadjusted' and 'adjusted' scores. The former represent the average levels of participation for the particular group in question. They are expressed as deviations from the average for the Sevenoaks sample as a whole. For example, those aged between 18 and 25 years had a level of participation that was 0.24 points below that for all individuals on the scale. This scale runs from a minimum of -0.70 (for the least participatory person) to $+7.22$ at the top (for the most active individual). Two thirds of respondents, however, were located approximately in the range $\pm.50$. A measure of the extent to which the given set of categories (in this case, age) collectively discriminate between different levels of political activity is provided by 'eta'. In the example of age, the value of eta is .20 which suggests that this characteristic is, taken by itself, a moderately powerful explanation of why some individuals participate more than others. In general, an eta of less than .10 indicates a very weak relationship, while anything above .30 would suggest an increasingly strong association. (The statistic itself can theoretically range from 0, where no relationship exists, to 1.0 where perfect predictability would be afforded.) We

need to know, however, whether such relationships are 'true' effects or merely the spurious result of some third factor. Here we might ask, for example, whether young people participate less than those of middle age (−0.24 to +0.22) because of their *age* difference, or because young people are less interested in politics than their elders. Is it this factor and not age *per se* which is at work? The results of the tests we apply for this possibility are set out in the second main column of the table. Here we present the deviations associated with each category having made allowance for all the possibly confounding effects associated with the other explanatory factors included in the analysis. Thus, in our specific example, we find that those aged 18 to 25 still participate less than average (with an adjusted score of −0.15). However, compared with the original unadjusted figure, we can see that part of the reason at least why young people participate somewhat less is, indeed, because of the social and political factors we brought into consideration in the rest of the table. At the same time, it remains true that even when we make allowance for all these other effects, young people still seem to participate less than those of middle age. In other words, within the terms of our analysis, age still retains some explanatory power and this is summarised in the 'beta' statistic. We can see that for age this is .07 which would make it a rather weak residual relationship – having only about a third of the explanatory power that age had when considered by itself. The third column, headed 'N' indicates the numbers of individuals from the Sevenoaks sample that fell into each of the categories under review. Where a given category comprised less than 15 (one instance in table 3.4) we have put square brackets around the associated score to indicate that these results, given the small numbers, should be treated with particular caution. Finally, we should note that we specifically exclude from our discussion at this point the effects of 'community' and 'locality' which are fully considered in chapter 9. Their effects, however, have been taken into account statistically.

7 The procedure used to define the different categories of participant, and to allocate individuals appropriately, was a form of cluster analysis. See Moyser, Parry and Day (1986) for details as applied to our national sample.

4

Participation and non-participation in a French town

PATRICK QUANTIN

I THE NATURE OF THE TOWN

This chapter is based on the analysis of data collected using a question-naire very similar to that employed by the British Political Participation Study in its investigation of a number of British communities. The questionnaire was administered to a representative sample (N = 237) of residents in Mérignac, an urban commune forming part of the metropolitan area of Bordeaux.

This is a commune which today has more than 50,000 inhabitants. Its expansion is relatively recent as, in 1954, its population was only 23,000. This rose to 32,000 in 1962 and to 46,000 in 1968, increases that are mainly due to a movement in the population from the centre of Bordeaux to suburban residential areas. The commune has also taken in a number of new residents who have come from other parts in the *département* and from elsewhere in France. This explains why the proportion of adult inhabitants who have resided in the commune itself for more than 20 years is now less than half the total.

The breakdown by age of the population of Mérignac is quite close to the average for the nation as a whole. Natural growth is slight, because half the households have no children. Population density is also low, the area covered by the commune being very large; indeed, one of the largest in France. As a result there are only 1,100 inhabitants per square km, compared to the 5,100 we find in Bordeaux itself. A large section of it still consists of pine forests. The inhabited area is chiefly to be found in the eastern part of the commune, whereas the two thirds to the west are occupied principally by civil and military airports, by two industrial zones and by areas which are still rural.

The industrial enterprises which have been set up locally employ a large part of the salaried population. Alongside the many small enterprises, the presence of 'high tech' industries such as aeronautics (Dassault) means that economic activity takes a very specific direction. However, many people have jobs in other parts of the Bordeaux area. Hence, Mérignac's local economy does not exist in isolation. It is partly a 'dormitory town' for the inhabitants who work in Bordeaux or in other neighbouring communes.

The economically active population is noticeably greater than the national average, and is characterised by a large proportion who work in the 'intermediate professions' or who are employees. Thus, statistically, Mérignac is no longer the working-class town that it was until the end of the fifties. At that time, workers represented nearly 50% of the employed population. The figure has fallen today to below 30%, while at the same time the numbers of middle-rank managerial and office staff have risen from 23% to over 40%. Conversely, the agricultural population is now only a residual one: less than 1%. Overall, therefore, in the last thirty years the number of employees has risen from 85% in 1954 to 95% today. And the numbers of small traders and craftsmen have also fallen proportionately.

The type of housing has also changed from the private detached house, which predominated before the war, to modern apartment blocks. More than 75% of present-day residences in Mérignac were completed after 1949, the most intense period of construction occurring between 1962 and 1967. Today housing is divided more or less equally between blocks of apartments and detached houses. More than half the residents own their own homes, the figure being particularly high in the case of detached houses.

The commune of Mérignac could be regarded as an excellent example of what in the 1970s was called 'the rise of the middle classes'. This type of 'laboratory' of social change in fact took some time to develop fully, but specific forms of political participation derive from the process. In particular, a large network of associations has developed which has taken the place of the old forms of political militancy and patronage. Mérignac, a town with a classic socialist tradition, has thereby undergone a political transformation – the result of the thorough restructuring of its population. However, the traditional political apparatus is still effective amongst the people who occupy leading positions. But the rules which govern how that apparatus works have been greatly changed. This can be seen from a study of political participation in the locality.

In presenting the results of the investigation, carried out in 1985, we have not made direct use of this historical dimension. Our investigation necessarily deals mainly with phenomena as they were at a given time. It does, however, provide information with a diachronic element in as much as it helps us to understand the social and political changes which are taking place in the commune, a commune in many respects, very typical of the present-day French urban milieu.

2 LEVELS OF POLITICAL PARTICIPATION

Measurements of levels of participation aim principally to indicate the order of magnitude of the phenomena being observed. These measurements must, of course, also be adjusted to take account of the intensity of the various participatory actions. Equally, their significance can only be fully assessed in relation to the issues which triggered off these actions.

The frequency of the activities recorded in the Mérignac survey ranges from very common types of behaviour, such as voting, to types which are quite rare, such as belonging to a political party. The resulting rank order of such actions then gives us an initial idea of what the hierarchy of participation looks like and gives us clues about the various levels of involvement amongst the citizenry. Some political actions are clearly very easy to carry out, while others are harder to perform, requiring more personal competence or commitment and calling upon resources not equally distributed throughout the population.

When we come to assess the degree of political participation, we have to make an initial choice about measurement. Should we regard an action performed only once as a sufficient indicator, for example signing a petition on one occasion? Or is only a repetition of the action significant? In other words, should we only take into account the regular performance of, say, petition signing? If the first point of view is adopted, then we can say that there is a high degree of participation in Mérignac. For, if we leave aside the special case of voting, we still find, as set out in table 4.1, that as many as 77% of respondents have signed a petition at least once, that 58% have attended a meeting to protest against a decision or to support a cause and 41% have taken part in a demonstration. Equally, nearly half (45%) have contacted a town councillor and 17% a deputy. (Comparisons may be made with table 3.3 giving the corresponding data for the British case study.)

These figures certainly give an impression of intense activity. But in fact it is somewhat intermittent – not to say exceptional – since, when we consider only those who frequently resort to each type of activity, the rates all fall considerably. Thus, as we can see in the second column of table 4.1, only 13% have 'often' had occasion to sign a petition, 14% have 'often' attended a protest meeting, and 5% have 'often' taken part in demonstrations. Similarly, those who have 'often' contacted a town councillor number only 14% of the sample, with 3% for contacting a deputy. These results can, in turn be compared with other regularly performed social and political activities. Thus, for example, over a quarter were active in the

Table 4.1. *Levels of local participation*

A Non-electoral	% 'At least once	% 'Often'*
Contacting		
Municipal councillor	45.1	14.3
Mayor	34.2	7.6
Conseiller général	13.9	3.4
Deputy	17.3	3.0
Senator	5.9	4.2
Administrators in charge of town services	47.3	13.9
Section of ministry responsible for a department	26.6	7.2
Local press	27.0	5.5
Group activities		
Formal, social or political association within the commune	48.9	25.3
Informal group within the commune	36.7	10.1
Protesting		
Taken part in a demonstration	41.4	5.5
Signed a petition	77.2	13.5
Attended a protest meeting (or to support a cause)	58.2	14.3

B Electoral		
Election campaigning	% 'Yes'	
Candidate in an election	0.8	
Put up posters, distributed leaflets	1.3	
Voting		
Presidential elections 1981 (2nd round)	81.9	
European elections 1984	63.7	
Local elections:		
'always'	73.8	
'sometimes'	16.0	
'never'	7.2	
no response	3.0	
Member of a party	3.0	

* This % is also included in the first column along with those having done the activity 'only once … in the last 5 years or so' and those having done it 'now and then'.

social clubs and associations of Mérignac, and 10% of respondents were active in informal groups dealing with local problems. Only 3%, however, claimed to be members of a political party.

From all this one initial conclusion has to be drawn. Insofar as involvement in participatory action is largely 'occasional', only a small proportion of the population is 'habitually' engaged in local political life. However, this result is in no way surprising in view of the research findings of other investigations. And yet what is remarkable is the high level of occasional participation, which leads one to ask questions about the validity of the responses. Are they indeed inflated in order to please the investigator?

It is certainly the case that those who answered the questions were not at all reticent in doing so, very few refusing to answer. But even if one has slight reservations about the true level of actual behaviour, none the less we have to admit that the phenomenon of participation is quantitatively an important one. In these terms, the practicalities of political participation, and the fact that a limited group of 'specialists' are involved, are not due to the incompetence or ignorance of the majority. This in turn suggests that interpretations of low rates of participation as being due to the hegemony of a dominant class or group are invalid. On the contrary, our own observations tend to support a more 'culturalist' reading of the situation. From this perspective, we can see political participation as being in conformity with prevailing norms, but as engaged in by only a limited number of the members of a given community. In this respect, therefore, the present case-study seems to constitute an example of a less than completely participatory culture.[1]

3 ASSOCIATIONS

The structure of political participation can also be compared with that of experiences acquired in local associations. Membership (present or past) of such associations shows the relative weight of the different sectors in which collective activities take place. To deal only with the main features, we find that in Mérignac the groups most likely to mobilise people into action are in the fields of sport and leisure. In comparison, activity in political organisations, in the strict sense of the term (such as within a party or a political club), is very limited. Indeed, our evidence suggests that whilst 59% of those questioned belong (or have belonged) to a sports club and 45% to a leisure group, only 5% say that they belong (or have belonged) to a political organisation of some sort. From such figures we can then gain some indication of the more important policy areas in which local demands and problems will arise. They also enable one to see what position the people who run these associations will be in as regards to negotiations with local decision-makers.

In this way, political participation draws much of its strength from local associational life. Indeed, belonging to a political party often goes with belonging to a non-political association, although unfortunately our sub-group of party activists[2] is too limited to build up an adequate statistical interpretation of this general linkage. Nevertheless, we found that all of them have had personal experience of such associations. On the other hand, as many as 41% of the population belong to no association at all. This category of citizens can therefore make no demands of a collective nature, but that does not, of course, rule out more individualised methods of getting their views across.

4 PROBLEMS AND ISSUES

Types of issues

The fact that most local demands are formed by associations probably explains the kind of responses given by residents when asked about the issues which concern them. The problems which they mentioned relate to areas in which local interest groups have no direct voice: employment, the cost of living and, to a lesser extent, law and order. The question asked was open-ended: 'What are the specific problems which have seemed most important to you in the last few years, and about which you would like to do something?' This way of asking the question was intended to bring out the genuine and spontaneous concerns of the population.

The relative absence of strictly local issues in the responses set out in table 4.2 is perhaps disappointing given our general focus. It nonetheless remains a result of considerable importance which has to be taken into account in the analysis. Thus, closed-ended questions offering a list of local problems and issues would no doubt have produced material closer to the presuppositions implicit in our investigation. The results, however, would have given a biased impression of the views of the citizenry as a result of the intrusion of the researchers' hypotheses.

Theoretically, it is possible to object that nothing *a priori* prevents there being actions demanding local solutions for such problems. However, the population does not seem to think in this way. Rather, they appear to take the view that responsibility for such problems lies beyond the framework of local institutions. The State is indeed regarded as being principally responsible for the major problems on their agenda. Sometimes employers, and sometimes individuals, are also seen as having such re-sponsibilities, but never the commune itself. All in all, the ways in which

Table 4.2. *The agenda of issues*

Issue category	% Mentions	N*
Social	*17.1*	*93*
racism	4.0	22
law and order	5.1	28
other	8.0	43
Economic	*47.2*	*257*
unemployment	28.6	156
cost of living	8.5	46
poverty	5.5	30
small businesses	1.3	7
other	3.3	18
Political	*19.8*	*108*
French politics	4.4	24
inequality	3.8	21
international politics	7.2	39
other	4.4	24
Family	*9.9*	*54*
teaching	3.6	20
housing	0.4	2
other	5.9	32
Local	*6.0*	*33*
roads	1.6	9
pollution	1.3	7
other	3.1	17
Total	100.0	545

* Up to three responses were recorded: 98.3% made 1 response, 76.8% made 2 and 54.9% made 3.

these links (between problems, those responsible for dealing with them, and solutions) are viewed therefore leads to the conclusion that the local arena is *not* where the most important issues in the lives of the citizens can be dealt with.

On the other hand, the local context retains the advantage of being a familiar and reassuring world in which only issues of 'lesser' importance, such as culture or sport, arise. It is striking to note that the struggle for employment is not seen as a *local* issue by the population, whereas the maintenance and development of business enterprises, which have been set up within the commune is an obvious (and probably the major) concern of the council. The latter see it not only as the main lever for satisfying the demands of the local inhabitants, but also as an important financial resource which allows domestic rates to be reduced and collective amenities to be provided.

Similarly, law and order produces no explicit demands for the council itself to act. This at least is what the survey responses indicate. On the other hand, it is not the view taken by the police in the commune, who feel that they are being hard-pressed by local demands for urgent action to which they are trying to respond by making the presence of their officers more visible on the ground. But through which channel do such demands flow? In this instance, the issue probably arises principally from complaints made on the spur of the moment as a result of minor offences, which are generally agreed to have increased. There is no sign, however, of a properly organised movement which would result in demands being advanced by local groups calling for a clear public policy response on the issue.

These two very key examples suggest that the issues which are seen as the most important in Mérignac do not necessarily lead people to participate. Indeed, between the problems experienced by individuals on the one hand and those raised and given importance by the national media on the other, there seems to be little place for distinctively local political action. Thus, the general assumption amongst the citizenry of Mérignac seems to be that those responsible are the State and its administrative apparatus; only they can provide solutions. It therefore presents a good example of a 'subject political culture' (Almond and Verba 1963) which does not encourage people to participate fully and persistently. The council, therefore, runs the risk of having to interpret demands which are not directly addressed to it and for which – and this is more to its advantage – it is not thought to have any particular or prime responsibility.

It is highly significant in this respect that when our respondents were asked who was responsible for solving the main problem each mentioned, only one referred to the commune. As can be seen in table 4.3, most of the answers naming just one responsible agency referred to the 'State' (38.8%) or 'the citizen himself' (8.4%). However, many of those questioned refused to name any one person or institution as responsible, stating that all those in positions of responsibility who were mentioned were responsible 'to some extent' (27.0%). This latter type of response is a clear indication both of indecision in selecting a particular target, and of the difficulty in triggering off the processes of participation. For many people there are, indeed, issues at stake, but there is no specific responsible individual with whom the issues could be discussed. Furthermore, the absence of any groups set up around a given issue also means that no clear objectives are designated, and nobody is asked to undertake discussion of them. Identifying the adversary is perhaps the first dynamic and creative action per-

Table 4.3. *Responsibility for issues and problems**

	% Mentions	N
The state	38.8	92
All those named	27.0	64
The citizen himself	8.4	20
Trade unions	5.9	14
Employers	3.8	9
The region	3.8	9
The commune	0.4	1
Other/don't know	11.9	28
Total	100.0	237

* Responses to the question 'Who is in a position to solve the most important problem which you have just mentioned?'

formed by a group when it emerges onto the political stage to make a demand.

Reactions to the issues and problems

In this context, it is not surprising that the identification of issues should so often be accompanied by statements of non-involvement, not to say impotence. Indeed, nearly half of all those questioned (48%) either did not know what they could do personally to solve the main problem[3] which they had mentioned, or else they said that 'nothing could be done'. Either way, it is hard to see what purpose would be served by participation. Another group of respondents (11.4%) who also took no action on their problem offered much more strongly opinionated reasons. These consisted largely of denouncing the behaviour of others, or of the French government. Some, alternatively, did clearly articulate demands, but ones which implied no personal action on their part – such as asking for more police or for greater equality.

In the event, therefore, only 39% of those surveyed believed that they could take action to deal with their main problem. Some (17.8%) espoused individual action, actions such as persuading others, or communicating with them in some other way. A further 21% thought of more collective forms of actions, ranging from signing a petition to joining a political party. The most widespread responses under this heading were those which advocate joining an organisation (4.6% of the whole sample) or else making a financial contribution, either in the form of money given to an association or of taxes (5.5%). Of course, whether these would have led to actual behaviour is a moot point. But at least they are indicative of the general direction of thinking amongst those concerned.

5 ATTITUDES TOWARDS NON-PARTICIPATION

We now turn briefly to explore further the attitudes of respondents underlying the decision whether to take action about issues which they said were important, or to remain silent. How would people react to such issues? In particular, why might they *not* participate in order to get the issue addressed?

To provide some understanding of the principal lines of thinking behind this question, all respondents were asked to give their opinions about a number of alternative reasons as to why they might or might not be willing to take action. The resulting distributions are set out in table 4.4. This shows that the single most favoured explanation for why people might not participate was their lack of specialised knowledge. Indeed, three out of four (75.1%) took this view. To this extent, political action is assumed to be essentially the prerogative of specialists – or rather best undertaken within an organisation, where the relevant skills are available, rather than as an individual. Another major source of potential inaction can be identified from the fact that two out of three respondents believed that the authorities should be responsible for solving the major problem. But, to the extent that citizens might distance themselves from action, this was not because they were afraid of being criticised by their fellow residents. Only 19%, indeed, viewed fear of being regarded as a trouble-maker to be a reason for inertia. Nor was it because they had a fatalistic outlook on things for, again, fewer than 30% thought that the problem could not be solved.

As for the remaining possible reasons for inaction, they showed a more or less equal division between those who have a seemingly deprecatory view of themselves as citizens and those who exhibited a degree of self-confidence. For example, those who would stand aside from the world of politics by accepting the view that 'the authorities never take any notice of what people like me think' represent just over half (54.4%) of the total. Equally, 57.0% agreed that they 'wouldn't know what should be done', and 56.1% thought that 'other people can deal with these matters better than I can'. Finally, and perhaps in a more neutral vein, 46% cited lack of time as a reason why people do not participate.

6 PROFILES OF PARTICIPATION

The data collected concerning the various types of participation enable us to develop a typology based on the distributions of the responses that were made on five criteria. These were as follows:

Table 4.4. *Attitudes towards non-participation**

	% Agree	% Disagree	% Don't know	% Total
'I don't have the knowledge to engage in this sort of action'	75.1	23.6	1.3	100.0
'This is the sort of problem which the government or local authorities ought to deal with'	65.8	31.2	3.0	100.0
'I don't know what should be done about this sort of problem'	57.0	39.2	3.8	100.0
'Other people can deal with these matters better than I'	56.1	34.6	9.3	100.0
'The authorities never pay attention to what people like me think'	54.4	40.1	5.5	100.0
'I live with this sort of problem'	52.7	44.7	2.5	100.0
'I have no time'	46.4	52.4	1.2	100.0
'Other people acted before I could do anything'	34.8	54.6	10.6	100.0
'This sort of problem can't be solved'	28.7	68.4	3.0	100.0
'I'd get a reputation as being a trouble-maker'	19.4	75.6	5.0	100.0

* Figures are distributions of responses to each alternative in the table as an answer to the following: 'There are many reasons why people might not participate, or not take action in order to get things changed...'

A   Has often contacted at least 2 levels mentioned in the list   (9.0%)
B   Active in an association   (29.0%)
C   Demonstrations + petitions + meetings   (3.8%)
D   Been a candidate or worked for a candidate + member
of a party   (1.2%)
E   Always votes at local elections   (73.8%)

On this basis, we can define a pattern of reported activity that would identify, at one extreme, the 'complete activists'. These individuals would have undertaken every type of activity included in the scheme. At the other end of the spectrum are the 'inactives' who take part in no form of action, and do not even express themselves by using the ballot. The intermediate types are made up of different sorts of 'specialists' who largely focus their involvement on one mode of activity, to the exclusion of the others. The precise make-up of each type, and the resulting size of each is set out in table 4.5.

We can distinguish three principal groups of behavioural patterns in the table. The 'participants', whether complete or specialised (excluding those who 'specialise' in voting), represent about one quarter of the total sample. The inactive form another quarter. The rest, nearly one half, is made up of individuals whose participation is limited to putting a voting paper in the ballot box at local elections. From this we can conclude that as many as three electors out of four do not participate in any substantial way in the life of the commune. This finding in turn throws some light on the way in which the practical problems of mobilising votes are presented to the candidates.

Thus, those citizens who simply vote may well also be those who believe that the running of the commune should be entrusted to specialists in local political affairs. Their participation then consists solely of supporting or lending their voice to the actions of the council. The inactive, on the other hand, in effect exclude themselves from the democratic process. They live within the commune, but not in any political sense. They behave, in fact, as though they had deprived themselves of civic rights. The different kinds of active participants (other than those who 'specialise' in voting) form that minority from which those who run Mérignac are drawn. However, the precise type of participation within this group clearly varies considerably.

The largest group, amounting to 17.7%, is represented by people who involve themselves mainly, but not exclusively, in associations. As indicated in the chart of response patterns, they are also all active voters (if not always, at least from time to time) and have occasion to contact the local authorities at one level or another – if only in connection with the association in which they are personally active. However, no people in the survey specialised solely in group activity to the entire exclusion of even voting and contacting.

What is the significance of the large numbers of this type of participant? This kind of associative activity is just within the bounds of political participation. A more restrictive definition would certainly exclude it from consideration and, what is more, those concerned would themselves be the first to say that when they are dealing with their association, they are not involved in 'politics'. Indeed, the associations are principally active in sport, culture or education. They work with the local authorities only

Table 4.5. *A typology of local political participation*

Participant type	Response pattern					Distribution	
	A	B	C	D	E	%	N
Complete activists	+	+	+	±	+	2.6	(6)
Specialise in election campaigns	−	−	−	+	+	0.0	(0)
Specialise in protesting	−	−	+	±	±	1.2	(3)
Specialise in contacting	+	−	−	−	±	4.0	(9)
Specialise in associational activity	±	+	−	−	±	17.7	(42)
Specialise in voting	−	−	−	−	+	48.1	(114)
Inactive	−	−	−	−	−	26.4	(63)
Total						100.0	(237)

indirectly, in so far as they voice demands for goods and services. However, we know from elsewhere that they are breeding-grounds from which the members of the council are recruited, and that the demands which they voice are of the highest importance when the mayor comes to draw up his agenda. The active members of the associations in Mérignac are in this sense, therefore, the most typical examples of purely local political participation.

In comparison, other types of participant involve only small minorities. The 'complete activists', for example, constitute a mere 2.6% of the sample. But among their numbers are the citizen-elite of local politics. They are, however, too few for us to be able to analyse them with any accuracy.

Those who specialise in contacting, on the other hand, are slightly more numerous (4%). It is an activity which they practice seemingly to the exclusion of any other (again except for voting). Since they are also clearly not active in any association, there is every reason to think (although the investigation does not allow us to be certain) that they act on their own behalf as individuals. Or, at least, if they do not always work for themselves, they deal with particularised problems. To that extent, it would be interesting to know more about the kind of demands which they make. Unfortunately, a survey of the sort used here does not permit us to inquire into the details of subjects which most of those who might answer would regard as wholly private and personal.

Specialists in protesting are even rarer than complete activists – a mere 1.2%, or just three people, if we count solely those who have repeatedly engaged in demonstrations, petitions and 'protest meetings'. However, it is only with these restrictive criteria that we can identify those who are the true protest specialists. In this respect, we saw earlier that these activities are indeed carried out by a relatively large proportion of the sample, but for most of them it was only on occasion. In most cases, therefore, such activities are not part of a regular political repertoire, nor one which excludes other more conventional actions.

Finally, we find that the sample includes no individual who fits the model of an election campaign specialist. Unless such people refused to identify themselves as such in their response pattern – and this is unlikely – it seems rather that the presence of associations in Mérignac leads the party activists to belong to one or more of such organisations. And, if they did not belong, they would certainly be active in contacting. The probability, therefore, of finding any individual whose participatory activity is exclusively concerned with the election campaigns of political parties is thus very slight.

Examination of these findings confirms just how varied are the participatory styles encountered. There is no average – or normal – pattern of behaviour tied to one unique set of cultural assumptions or a specific plan of political participation. Instead, what we have brought to light, through a simple analysis of the various indicators taken in conjunction, is the very unequal distribution of positions which individuals take up on political action. On the other hand, it is a rather static picture which does not take into account the attitudes which lead each person to take a more or a less active role. But an examination of certain social and demographic factors may bring the picture to life by making it apparent that people do not play simply any role in politics. This is what the last part of the analysis, in the next section, tries to demonstrate. In doing so, however, we must avoid falling into the trap of making partial interpretations which would either emphasise the degree of non-participation, or else pay no attention to it and concentrate only on the various groups of political activists.

7 WHO PARTICIPATES?

Is the propensity to participate distributed randomly through the population as a whole, or is it the effect of certain predisposing factors? The study of the correlations between participatory activities and a set of social, economic and political variables enables us to give some relatively precise answers.

Participation is, first, determined to a far greater extent by the degree to which the individual is integrated into the social life of the community than by social or demographic characteristics such as age, sex or occupation. These latter variables do indeed contribute to an explanation of the overall pattern, but do not determine behaviour in any strict sense. Indeed, classic sociological variables tend to fade into the background beside the power of more explicitly organisational and political factors. For example, mem-

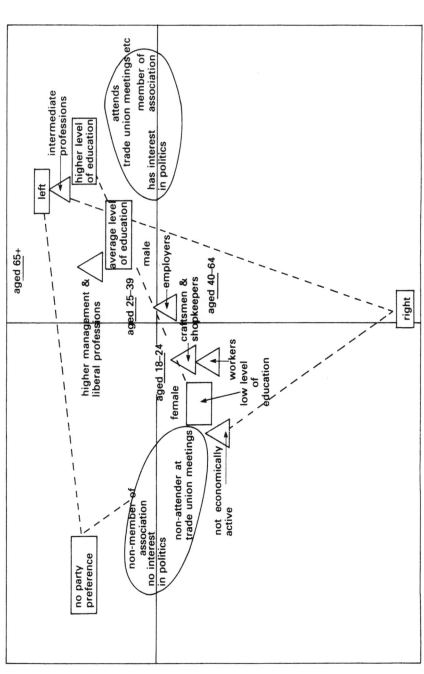

Figure 4.1 First analysis of correspondence: political participation, party preferences and background characteristics

bership of an association is a much stronger factor favouring political participation than being male or a senior executive. Equally, partisan political preferences have an important role in shaping the way in which the population participates. However, the analysis also shows that party loyalties and participatory activities are distinct and, in that sense, independent phenomena.

Two analyses of correspondence were undertaken for which results are presented.[4] The variables included overlap to the extent that the same explanatory or background factors have been deployed in each. The two diverge in the measures of participation included. However, this was done merely to avoid excessive clutter in the figures which the analysis generates. In any event, as we will see, the two sets of results corroborate each other.

First analysis of correspondence

The results of an analysis of correspondence are set out in the form of a graph or figure in which are located the categories of the participation and background variables included. The interpretation arises mainly from the spatial relationships between the categories. In addition, axes have been inserted to help the exposition of these graphical 'correspondences'. The first axis, in figure 4.1, is defined principally, and in participatory terms, in two ways. First by the 'opposition' between those who have experience of associations and those who have none, and secondly by whether or not they had taken part in political or trade union meetings. It is around these two poles that the picture of participants and non-participants is largely built.

The relative proximity of the participant categories (so defined) both to those claiming an interest in politics and to the way in which affairs in the commune are run suggests a strong connection between involvement and overt behaviour. Indeed, other evidence shows that the participants know several councillors by name. They also hold (or have held) office in the associations of which they are members and prefer collective action as a means to solving problems. In partisan terms the figure suggests that they tend to categorise themselves as being on the left. This is confirmed by their voting in disproportionate numbers for Mitterrand in the second round of the 1981 presidential election.

The non-participants, by contrast, are clearly associated with a lack of interest in politics. Equally, they show little concern for the way in which the affairs of the commune are run. They also do not know the name of any councillor, and have never been in contact with one. As for the problem which was most important to them, their responses about the possibilities of taking action was that they could do nothing about it themselves, or that nothing can be done anyway. Finally, in terms of party preferences, their position in the figure associates them closely with an outright refusal to locate themselves on the left–right axis, or even to say for whom they voted in the 1981 election.

The series of categories which make up these two juxtaposed profiles reveals a remarkable symmetry, except possibly for party preferences, which are apparent in the case of participants, yet either hidden or non-existent in the case of the non-participant. The second axis of figure 4.1, however, clarifies this relationship by providing evidence of a further set of associations involving party preferences. Further scrutiny of the relevant responses suggests that a preference for the right is accompanied by two closely linked attitudes. First, they regard voting in a local election as an opportunity for giving a verdict on the national government. Secondly, they are marked by a tendency to offer dogmatic and simplistic solutions to important problems, prefaced by such phrases as, 'the only thing to be done is ...' Conversely, a preference for the left is correlated with a different set of answers: that local elections are *not* the opportunity for expressing an opinion about the government, and that solutions to the main problem are to be found through positive and collective forms of action.

Turning to the associations between activism and the various background factors, we can see that age has only a slight influence on participation. No one age category is very close to the participatory categories but, clearly, the projection of the four age cohorts onto the first axis suggests that participation does increase slightly with years. The occupational category most closely correlated with participation, and above all with voting for the left, is that of the 'intermediate professions'. Conversely, the non-participatory categories are linked to those who are not economically active. Craftsmen, like the workers and employees, are in an intermediate position between the two roles, close to the centre of the axis. Finally, the spread of the educational categories along the participant axis strongly suggests that this is the most important variable in explaining the degree of participation. Those possessing the highest qualifications indeed do report the highest numbers of participatory activities, whilst those who have no qualifications are at the opposite end and include those with only the slightest propensity to participate.

The close relationship between active participation and political preferences for the left needs, however, to be assessed in the particular local context of this study. Thus, it is important to note that the Socialist Party has been in control of the council in Mérignac for 40 years. As a result, the activities of local associations are to a large extent channelled through activist members of that party. What is more (though this is merely conjectural as the study was undertaken in a pre-election period before the cantonal elections in March 1985), a considerable number of those questioned may have thought that the research was being 'remotely controlled' by the Town Hall (despite all the precautions taken), and therefore, tended to opt for a legitimist position by refraining from expressing views hostile to the local political forces in power.

But, even with these reservations, a strong relationship seems to exist between participation and the holding of left-wing views. On the other hand, as we have seen, this connection is not complemented by an equivalent relationship between non-participation and right-wing stances. What seems to be happening in figure 4.1 reflects to a large extent the fact that activists close to the Socialist Party control all local official institutions and the activities of associations. However, this situation probably does not affect the way in which the citizens react to the parties in a broader, national context.

Second analysis of correspondence

By choosing, for figure 4.2, another set of participatory indicators, we can further explore, and possibly corroborate the configuration of positions and attitudes that emerged in the previous analysis. As we can see, the sample again divides into two polarised clusters. On the one hand, there are those response categories which delineate a set of non-participants. This includes individuals who have never participated in a political demonstration, express no party preference, never discuss politics, think that their vote serves no purpose and do not know the name of the *conseiller-général*. These features coexist in turn with two other significant traits: holding the view that the State is responsible for dealing with problems, and a lack of knowledge about the political preferences of their parents.

There is also, again, a juxtaposed group which emerges from the analysis that manifest opposing tendencies. These are, clearly, the participants – those who have taken part in demonstrations, know, by name at the very least, the *conseiller général*, are members of an association, and express satisfaction with the way in which decisions are taken in the associations with which they have been involved. They also have contacted the mayor of Mérignac at least once.

Defining the active in these terms again produces an association with strongly-marked left-leaning party preferences – as indicated in this figure by their voting support for the socialist candidates at the European elections in 1984. Their cast of mind is confirmed in a more generalised way by the fact that they felt close to the Socialist Party. Amongst the participants, those active in demonstrations can also be associated in this way with the Socialist Party. Interestingly enough, their second most powerful linkage is the possession of an average or higher level of education. And, so far as the

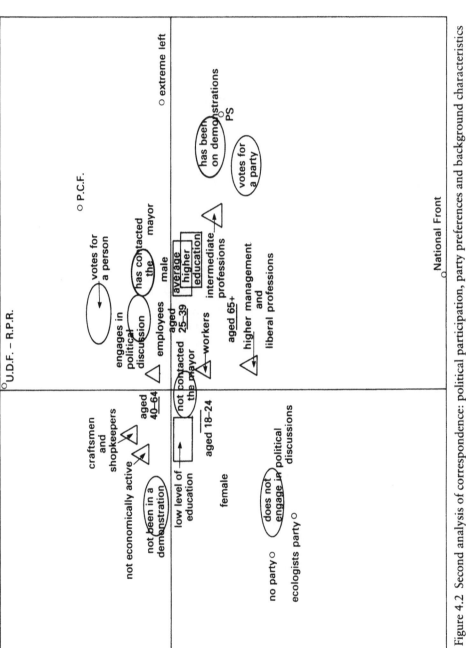

Figure 4.2 Second analysis of correspondence: political participation, party preferences and background characteristics

main problem or issue of the protesters was concerned, they seemed to have a greater idea of the complexities involved in so far as they answered neither 'the State' nor 'the individual', but 'everyone to some extent' when questioned about responsibility for finding solutions. They also, perhaps surprisingly, had a relatively positive view of elections, thinking that one's vote does serve some purpose. Finally, and like activists in general, they were certainly clearly in the habit of discussing politics with friends and colleagues.

Who, then, participates? The results obtained by the analysis of correspondence give us a rather dichotomised view along the main participation – non-participation axis (and, incidentally also along the left/right spectrum). However, there is nothing surprising in the dichotomisation itself as this is merely a product of the way the categories of the participation variables were combined in preparation for the analysis. This does mean, unfortunately, that some of the fine detail in the responses has been lost. Nevertheless, it was certainly not obvious *a priori* that all these dichotomised participation measures would appear so closely clustered in both analyses. What we may conclude, therefore, is that the analyses have not only brought to light the network of relationships which underpin participation and non-participation, they have demonstrated how the partisan history of the local political system exerts its influence over the way citizens become politically involved.

NOTES

1 For a discussion of this concept see Almond and Verba (1963).
2 A mere seven individuals in the sample.
3 1.7% see no problems.
4 As the interpretation of political participation calls on a large number of variables, it seemed preferable to replace a lengthy series of contingency tables by a multivariate analysis. The technique used is analysis of correspondence. In order to interpret the figures presented, one must principally assess the distance between the values of each of the variables included and their position in relation to the axes. The way in which they contribute to the interpretation, however, is not entirely a matter of spatial relationships. For a detailed explanation of the method, see Benzecri (1973), Cibois (1983) and Greenacre (1984).

Conclusion

In drawing together these 'ground-clearing' studies of local political participation in Mérignac and Sevenoaks, we wish briefly to highlight five main themes: the sphere of 'local political participation' as an idea and political process; the 'cartography' of activities that comprise it; the linkages between participation and certain sociological, political and psychological traits; participation as a response to issues and problems and, finally, the character of non-participation. We will consider each of these aspects in turn.

On the face of it, as chapter 2 made clear, the local political field is very different in the two countries – 'government' in Britain and 'administration' in France. And yet the evidence, principally on this theme from Sevenoaks, suggests that for the citizenry at least, things might not be so different. For what emerged in that locality was that local issues, and actions taken in pursuit of them, were seen as falling predominantly outside of the 'political arena'. Indeed, only some 38% of the issues and 12% of the associated actions were unequivocally 'political'. By these measures, it would seem, British citizens see their local public affairs predominantly in non-political terms – as 'administration' perhaps rather than 'government'?

And yet, of course, in the French case, this distinction is intended to emphasise the dependency of the local tier upon the national – the periphery as closely tied to the centre. But this, in British eyes at least, is one of the principal ingredients that does seem to 'politicise' actions and issues. For example, those issues that are 'national' in some tangible sense are seen in a political light by the majority of those concerned. Does this mean, therefore, that the local field is viewed as more 'political' in France than in Britain? The evidence, unfortunately, is too incomplete to draw a definitive conclusion. Certainly, there is a very clear sense in the way participants behave in Mérignac that they are moved by national party political parameters. Voting, particularly, is prone to such impulses – as is the case in Sevenoaks. On the other hand, there is also a sphere of local group action, or associational life, which turns out to be very significant in terms of handling problems in the locality. This is seen as largely outside politics – again echoing the British findings – despite the fact that the groups are linked both to partisan institutions and local decision-making processes. What is clear, therefore, is that 'political' life is only a part of the process of building issue agendas and engaging in public action within a given locality in both countries. At least this is the case so far as the citizens themselves see the matter which is, perhaps, a warning to political scientists elsewhere to consider their assumptions on this point more critically and phenomenologically than heretofore.

If, however, we do partake of that kind of 'conventional' wisdom and measure political participation through a range of relatively standard actions such as voting, contacting and protesting, the two pictures that emerge show several common features, as well as some differences. First, it is clear that in both locales, participation comes about through a wide variety of actions, rather than being concentrated in a very limited number. In other words, significant proportions of both populations had taken part in the activities about which they were asked. Perhaps naturally, however, far fewer claimed to have undertaken them 'often' as against 'at least once'. Indeed, in Mérignac as in Sevenoaks, the overall impression is that political participation is on the whole an intermittent and generally minority pastime. Only in the area of voting and signing petitions does a clear majority seem to have been involved. In that sense, neither locality has a very strong participatory culture.

However, it also seems to be the case that the Mérignac culture is distinctly more participatory than that of Sevenoaks. In contacting, group activity and some forms of protest, roughly twice as many citizens in the French town gave positive responses compared with those in the British. Given that the residents of Sevenoaks are, if anything, more advantaged in a predispositional sense, the contrast is very marked. Unfortunately, to unravel the reasons for this discrepancy takes us beyond the confines of our two case studies. For it would first have to be established whether or not this difference was found on a nation-wide basis or was more a product of local circumstances. However, in this connection, it might be noted that from the evidence of the British study as a whole Sevenoaks appears to be, if anything, one of the more participatory of British communities. All we can say here is that there is little within the two towns that might account for such a sizeable difference. Nor, we might add, are there any technical reasons such as question wording or time frame differences (Rusk 1976: 586) that could provide an explanation.

There are strong hints, however, that the actual structure of local participation in the two localities bears some similarities. We can see, for example, that contacting local targets, such as councillors or administrative officials, is about twice as frequent as equivalent actions addressed to national figures like MPs and deputies or departments of the central government. Equally, protest activity declines with the effort or risk involved – although in Mérignac as many as 41% claimed to have taken part in a demonstration, a figure which is many times greater than any otherwise comparable figure from Sevenoaks. Perhaps one may speculate whether such demonstrations take on a more widespread 'expressive' function in France. Furthermore, party campaigning is very thin on the ground in both areas compared with contacting and group activities. But the most striking evidence of a comparable structure comes from the analyses which placed each respondent into one of seven different categories of participant according to the overall profile of their involvement. Thus, we find that the proportions of active and inactive citizens are very similar with about three times as many in the inactive category as in the active. Indeed, this also provides a succinct confirmation of how 'non-participatory' the two local cultures are.

Amongst the inactives, a subdivision between those who 'just vote' and those who are almost totally inert also bears a striking correspondence. In both communities, indeed, the 'just voters' are, at 48% of the total, the largest single type of 'participant'. Equally, the inert are the second largest, with 26% in Mérignac and 23% in Sevenoaks. Amongst the active, again a subdivision into various more particular types shows a considerable degree of similarity. The 'group specialists', for example, who participate principally through groups, form the largest fraction, although they are slightly more numerous in Mérignac than in Sevenoaks (18% to 12%). Conversely, those who confine themselves to protesting or to party campaigning are the thinnest on the ground. Finally, the 'complete activists' who seem to indulge in most of the actions we asked about in the two towns, are also very few in number – a mere 3% in the French case and only 4% in the English. All in all, therefore, the general tone of Mérignac may be more participatory than Sevenoaks, but the structuring of the citizenry, albeit on the basis of a typology that is relative to each local norm, exhibits a remarkable consistency. In that respect, at least, the quality of local democracy in the two areas appears to be rather similar.

The question remains, however, as to whether it is the same sorts of people in both localities that are found in these various strata. Or, to put the matter in another way, do the same sorts of individual traits predispose individuals to be active, or are different imperatives at work? We favour the view that the same forces operate but do so cautiously in that we are faced in some instances with differences of measurement (as in the case of social class discussed in chapter 2). We have also utilised dissimilar multivariate analysis techniques. Nevertheless, the message from both towns seems to be a relatively consistent one. Thus, there are several character-istics which are clearly associated with an interventionist orientation towards local political life. Amongst these, membership of formal groups or associations and a high level of political interest are prominent – findings which, of course, echo patterns established in other research (see, for example, Nie *et al.* 1969; Milbrath and Goel 1977: 110–13). Indeed, involvement in local associational life, consequential formal linkages with the major governing party, and a propensity for collective action are particularly stressed in Mérignac. This syndrome is also visible in Seven-oaks, but our impression is that there, such networks and styles of engage-ment are somewhat less predominant. This may reflect the rather different partisan and class ethos of the two towns.

Other predispositional factors which crop up consistently are the pos-session of high educational qualifications, having a psychological party attachment and not being young. Taken altogether, therefore, there is a significant shared array of political and socio-demographic traits which are associated with activism in both Mérignac and Sevenoaks. On the other hand, they are not entirely the same, particularly in respect to class. Although it is a fairly standard finding in the literature that those in the higher socio-economic classes participate more, in neither location is this consistently borne out. In Mérignac, it is those of 'intermediate' class position who are the most prone to stand up and be counted (though it is possible that this may in part reflect their integration into local Mérignac life as much as their class position, a point further discussed in chapter 9). Similarly, amongst the Sevenoaks citizenry, the 'standard' pattern largely evaporates once the effect of other potentially confounding relationships is taken into account. Clearly, therefore, whatever the role of social class in local activism, here at least it is not the simple linear pattern more typical of nation-wide samples.

When we turn to the complementary analysis of participation, as a response to issue concerns, the particular imprint of each locality becomes, unsurprisingly, much more visible. The apparent discrepancies are further enhanced by differences in the wording of the relevant questions about issues. In the Mérignac survey, the phrasing referred to 'specific problems that seem most important to you . . .', whereas in the English study, a much narrower reference was made merely to '. . . problems in Sevenoaks . . .'. Clearly, this must have had an effect on the sort of issues offered, as well as on the propensity to take action about them. Indeed, evidence that this is so is available from a complementary nationwide British study which asked a question almost identical to that in Mérignac (see Moyser, Parry and Day 1986: 40–3). In particular it shows that, in Britain at least, local issues and problems stimulate far more action than national ones. Hence, the apparent higher propensity to take action on the prime issues, in

Sevenoaks compared with Mérignac seems largely to be explained. Thus, in Mérignac, 59% thought that no action on their part was possible on the concerns that they had mentioned. This is almost the same as the 58% who were found to be in a similar position in the British national study. Hence, the fact that only one quarter of Sevenoaks residents had failed to act seems principally to be associated with the fact that they had in the main offered the sort of local issue which, in the national study, were ones that had occasioned most action. Conversely, the French problems were those which, in the British context, prompted the least amount of action.

Such findings, therefore, underscore just how important is the precise mix of issues in a given locality for understanding the quality and quantity of local participation – and the kind of question asked! Where problems are clearly linked to the national level, then in France as well as in Britain, relatively little action on the part of citizens tends to follow. Conversely, where issues have a local provenance, there is a much greater likelihood that they will stimulate an array of participatory responses.

This contrast is strongly reflected in the sorts of issues that do appear on the agendas of the two towns. In Sevenoaks, environmental and planning issues predominated (principally linked to the building of a local swimming pool), together with transport and traffic problems, and health matters (a local hospital closure). Together these accounted for more than three quarters of the responses. In Mérignac, on the other hand, interviewees, with their wider remit, concentrated much more on economic issues and other matters directly concerned with national political affairs. With these in view, it is not surprising that 'the state' was seen as the authority most responsible for dealing with them, and that only 39% thought action was possible – mainly collective or organised, rather than individual, action. Perhaps in the same circumstances, the Sevenoaks citizenry would have reacted not dissimilarly. Certainly, however, it is clear that the pattern and character of issues on the local agenda play an important role in shaping participation.

We turn, finally, to the phenomenon we have called 'non-participation', represented by those citizens who did not make their voice heard in local political life. Numerically, as we have noted previously, they are far from insignificant. Strictly defined, they represent about one quarter of the respective adult populations but, if we discount voting, which is both occasional and largely non-local in character, then the rates climb steeply to nearly three-quarters of the total. In that sense, the non-participants are the majority and hence form an indispensable element in the political equation.

The reasons which lie behind their inertia can be linked, in analogous fashion to the participants, both to predispositional traits and to issue concerns. So far as the former is concerned, it again seems that a common syndrome, familiar in other national studies, is at work in the two towns. Thus, a lack of political interest, a psychological detachment from any political party, being largely outside local associational life, being young and uneducated, are all factors that tend to de-activate individuals in both localities. So far as issue responses are concerned, again there were shared themes that centred around a sense of powerlessness or inefficacy, sometimes born of experience, and generally reinforced by a lack of knowledge about how to go about taking appropriate action. Together they provide an important basis for understanding why those concerned failed to make their mark in public, especially when (as in Mérignac) the issues were national ones and possibly intractable and perennial features of advanced industrial societies.

However, there was also a second, and in a way more positive, strand to the thinking of the non-participants. In both communities there were those who thought that having elected the appropriate authorities into office, it should be they who should tackle the issues of the day, particularly when they affected (again as in Mérignac) the society as a whole as much as any one individual. Indeed, this general response was the second most frequent in Mérignac, and was also to be found in Sevenoaks, although sometimes only by implication where the respondent said that he or she was 'too busy' to be politically involved.

This general position is, of course, one defended by Schumpeter (1954) as an alternative model of democracy to that espoused by more radical participatory theorists (see, for example, Pateman 1970). It is indeed consistent with some versions of 'democracy' that the role of the citizen might be to control and call to account through periodic elections those who take decisions on behalf of the collectivity, rather than to seek actively to participate in a personal fashion (see also Parry and Moyser 1984). But whether this line of reasoning can explain why the majority in both French and British localities bother to vote and do little else, might be to put too positive a gloss on their thinking. Clearly, part of it has to do with the disadvantages of some categories of individuals in the market and the imperfections of local and national political arrangements. But at least this alternative should not be lost sight of when drawing conclusions about the robustness of local democracy in the two countries.

PART III POLITICAL MOBILISATION

Introduction

In certain situations, individuals organise themselves into groups, elaborate demands and express them in a collective form. They act in concert in order to force the political system to take account of these demands. Groupings which already exist, or which are brought into being for a specific purpose, seek to create or to reactivate a sense of identity and solidarity which is capable of lasting a long time and of being relatively firm. In this sense, political participation is not necessarily a continuous and permanent phenomenon. It can differ both according to the issues which are generated by collective action, and according to the level of decision-making, so that its extent and its intensity may vary considerably.

I A WORKING DEFINITION OF POLITICAL MOBILISATION

As we shall argue, the concept of political mobilisation[1] is not simply a form of participation which has been initiated from outside. Indeed, as a working definition we here take it to mean the processes which are intended to create or to reactivate a commitment or an identification, with the purpose of promoting collective aims. In more concrete terms these aims are to influence public decisions or to put forward new values by means of actions defined according to three distinctive criteria:

(a) A collective dimension: individuals form groups on the basis of common objectives so that their demands will be taken into account in one way or another by the local politico-administrative system. Unlike some approaches to the study of political participation, it is the action of the *group* which becomes the object of study, and not the behaviour of *individuals*.

(b) Organised action: this distinctive feature derives more or less directly from the previous dimension. If political participation is very often thought of as the sum of individual actions, political mobilisation is linked to the development and action of specific structures, and to the elaboration and implementation of collective strategies. The action in question may initially be more or less spontaneous but it almost of necessity becomes organised and structured, without however being systematically orchestrated or manipulated.

(c) An element of conflict: the process of political mobilisation is characterised by the expression of opposition to a public decision, policy or to a normative order. Political mobilisation occurs directly or indirectly in opposition to actors, decisions and values. Conflict is therefore at the heart of the process.

Where there is conflict and there are attempts to influence policy decisions, one normally discovers simultaneous processes of mobilisation and counter-mobilisation – an ascending movement whereby groups organise to oppose or promote policies and a descending movement as the authorities organise their own response. In order, therefore, to understand the phenomenon of mobilisation as a whole, it is necessary to look at the way in which needs and demands are expressed, how they are processed by the politico-administrative system, and the responses which they elicit.

It is in this sense that the processes of mobilisation can be described as 'political'. This is the case irrespective of the way in which they are portrayed or perceived by those involved since these processes, directly or indirectly, affect the way in which the political system functions. They become political from the moment that they entail collective interaction and the demands which they promote start being processed by the institutional political system. Often, political mobilisation may entail very intense but ephemeral actions, that are not necessarily always legal or legitimate. However, such characteristics are not, as will be seen from the case studies, necessary features of such processes.

2 THE METHOD EMPLOYED

The method employed in the two chapters is a qualitative one. It enables us to identify the actors involved, their strategies or attitudes, and to reconstruct the arena of collective action which emerges around an issue. The issue may be more or less specifically local in itself, but is always localised in space. The emphasis in the studies is on the system of interactions rather than on the factors which determine individual participation. The studies also have a diachronic dimension in that they reconstitute in time the processes of mobilisation. The focus is on the effects of collective action on decisions.

In the French chapter, we have looked at four cases in which public decisions were challenged: opposition to the building of a nuclear power station in a rural *canton* (Braud-et-St-Louis) in the department of la Gironde; protest against a traffic plan in an urban commune in greater

Bordeaux (Le Bouscat); conflict over the routing of high-tension power lines in a second rural *canton* (Ste-Foy-la-Grande); and, in another commune (Cenon) in Greater Bordeaux, hostility to the construction of a waste disposal incineration plant.

The British contribution is based upon the study of a small market county town in Wales which, in economic and administrative terms, might be considered fairly representative of this kind of town in Britain. It is the seat of two local government institutions: the Carmarthen District Council and the Dyfed County Council. It has one important distinguishing feature in that more than 60% of its inhabitants speak Welsh. Two cases of local political mobilisation have been singled out. The first concerns a protest campaign mounted by dairy farmers following the imposition of European Economic Community (EEC) milk quotas. The second concerns a more permanent pressure group, the Welsh Language Society, which by engaging in a campaign of action aimed at halting the decline in the use of the Welsh language, is attempting to reactivate a cultural identity. To this end, the Society has been attempting to gain the support of the Carmarthen District Council.

Quite obviously these examples of political mobilisation cannot claim in any way to be representative. The factors which led to their being chosen are relatively arbitrary. They should, therefore, be regarded essentially as illustrations, enabling us to highlight certain mechanisms or dimensions of political mobilisation, but not to generalise unduly.

3 THE LIMITS OF THE STUDY

The French case studies are relatively local in scope, the objective being to assess the potential of the processes of mobilisation to affect the working of the politico-administrative system and the decisions that are taken. These particular studies focus on cases of mobilisation which were reactions against decisions taken by local bodies and which presented especially formidable obstacles to effective protest action. The decisions involved were, in the first place, of a relatively technocratic nature, requiring some degree of expertise in order to assess their effects. Secondly, they raised the possibility of a conflict between the wider public interest on the one side and the various particular interests represented in the protest movements on the other.

Those cases of political mobilisation which relate to a more ideological cause, and which bring into play norms and values and attempt to promote new collective attitudes, are excluded from the field of study, since the effectiveness of these movements cannot be fully or easily comprehended at the local level. These movements may indeed take specific localised forms but, overall, the needs and demands for which they are the vehicles cannot be readily accommodated within the local politico-administrative system. Equally, a whole group of mobilisation movements whose demands are addressed entirely to central government are also excluded from consideration here.

The case studies in the British chapter exhibit a number of special characteristics. The controversies examined differ not only from one another but also in certain respects from those in the French case studies. The first, the protest movement against the EEC milk quotas, is an economic problem. The second, the defence of the Welsh language, is of a cultural nature. The two types of movement also differ in the forms that they assume. The first is of recent creation and is a reactive or protest action, while the demands that it expresses, though based on very local circumstances, are ultimately addressed to central government. The second is an older phenomenon which is more positively concerned with promoting a cause and sustaining a custom and is aimed at a local rather than a national set of authorities. The two examples have also been chosen in order to explore how far the processes of mobilisation may vary according to the type of protest involved.

Whilst there are several differences as regards the specific issues, there are also features which are clearly common to the process of mobilisation in both France and Britain. These include the importance of leadership, the part played by the media, the ambiguous role of the political parties, and the capacities of the authorities to respond. Generalisation may remain difficult but these case studies can and do shed light on the characteristics of local mobilisation in the two countries, characteristics which may have wider resonance in other national contexts.

NOTES

1 This definition is largely borrowed from Chazel for whom

> mobilisation consists essentially in the creation of new commitments and new identifi-cations – or sometimes in the reactivation of 'forgotten' loyalties and identifications; additionally it involves bringing together actors or groups of actors within a framework of a social movement aimed at promoting or sometimes 'restoring' collective objectives, if necessary by direct or, ultimately, violent confrontation with the established authorities ... Mobilisation is carried on through non-crystallised forms of behaviour, i.e. it applies primarily to areas where channels of action are not institutionalised or, at least, have not yet become so. (Chazel 1975: 516)

5

Political mobilisation in France: a study of local protest

PHILIPPE GARRAUD

The processes of political participation that are the subject of the case studies to be examined in this chapter, rest on a number of preconditions which need to be considered, at least in general terms. In the last analysis, it is very difficult to explain why a collective protest movement occurs at a given time and place and a single 'primary cause' is not to be found. Nevertheless, our aim is to discover, first, what forms of action and what kinds of legitimising devices protest movements employ in order to put pressure on the public authorities to take account of their demands. Secondly, we shall seek to assess the effects of the processes of mobilisation on the politico-administrative system in order to discover to what extent they influence its workings.

I THE CONDITIONS FOR LOCAL POLITICAL MOBILISATION

Why, and under what conditions, do individuals group themselves together at a particular moment and organise themselves to oppose a public policy decision? Not every public decision leads to collective participation. For this to occur, the potential negative consequences of the decision have, first, to be recognised; leaders have to establish and organise a collective movement; the relevant interests have to be activated. In this way, processes of mobilisation might be considered to depend on a number of pre-existing conditions which, at least in part, constrain the form which they can take.

This section will, therefore, look at a number of these pre-conditions for a process of mobilisation to develop and, in particular, at the nature of the decisions involved, the role of the activists and, finally, the reasons why the various participants became involved in the movements.

The nature of the decisions and the perception of negative effects

None of the decisions which we have looked at was at a purely local level (in the sense of being a matter entirely for the commune) but involved, variously, the wider conurbation (the construction of the incinerator plant at Cenon and the development of the ring road at Le Bouscat which were the responsibility of the Communauté Urbaine of Bordeaux), the department, or even the national politico-administrative system in the particular case of the building of the nuclear power station. These decisions were the outcome of a relatively technocratic process and were taken by bodies remote from the locality. They were taken, moreover, without the populations concerned being involved in any way, and without the participation of their local elected representatives. Decisions about the location of large-scale projects were made public at the last moment, even though their adverse effects were clearly significant and predictable. In three out of four cases, the completion of the project resulted in a profound disruption of the lives of the local residents, as well as in significant environmental problems, arising from the construction sites, traffic, noise, various kinds of pollution, encroachments on private property.[1] In the end, the decisions were challenged because it was felt that they were arbitrary. The residents directly affected by the decisions could well have believed that the siting of the scheme in their commune or their neighbourhood was the result of more or less hidden pressures and influences which were aimed at protecting private interests. Consequently, the decisions gave rise to a suspicion of injustice.

In such circumstances, the protest movements seem to some extent to have resulted from the inability of the politico-administrative system in general, or of some of its agents in particular, to defend and justify their decisions, and to organise something approaching a consensus about them through the provision of advance information and of arrangements for consultation.[2]

The emergence of conflict was thus a reflection of poor communication between one sector of the local community (a neighbourhood or a district, but also one or more social groups) and the public authorities which appeared incapable of anticipating even the most predictable adverse effects of certain of their decisions. This gulf generated a feeling of disquiet amounting to revolt and this feeling in turn produced a challenge to the legitimacy of the decision and led to a widespread rejection of the public works scheme.

The role of the activists

Every mobilisation movement seems to require leaders who not only devote a large part of their time and energy to the 'cause', but also manage at a given moment to understand and make use of relevant information and thereby assess not only the potential impact of a decision but also recognise the ways in which the different factors involved are fundamentally interconnected. They pin-point the adverse consequences of locating the installation in the particular area and indicate the interests which are likely to be negatively affected. They also identify targets and organise expressions of solidarity. Through their own efforts, such activists amplify and exploit the feelings of anxiety, injustice, discontent and even revolt generated amongst the population resulting from the fact that decisions have already been taken. In doing so, they contribute to a large extent to transforming attitudes which are originally more or less particularised and diffuse into organised, collective action.

In three out of four cases examined, mobilisation was brought about by an already organised core of activists who saw an opportunity for involvement in a new field of interest. This was the case at Cenon where the initial challenge to the incineration plant came from a neighbourhood committee; at Le Bouscat, where opposition to the new traffic plan came from an association of local tradesmen, and also at Ste-Foy-la-Grande. The Braud case was more complex, in as much as, at the outset, a wide range of groupings were involved, such as ecologists and conservationists in the Bordeaux area; wine growers; the tourism lobby in Entre-deux-Mers;[3] radical activists close to the far Left also from Bordeaux; small farmers from the Blayais (the region around the town of Blaye); and oyster farmers from the north side of the Gironde estuary. All of their demands were not, however, identical. Thus in the cases that we have examined, the active 'core' in the mobilisation process was already more or less in place even before any collective protest action occurred.

It appears, therefore, that activists play a predominant role in the emergence of a movement. From the experience and know-how that they have already acquired, their attentiveness to the life of the local community, and the network of relations and mutual acquaintances of which they form part, they are in a sense predisposed towards collective action and are potential leaders. In view of the relative apathy of the local population as a whole, the movement's vitality and activity is a function of these activists' close involvement and strong commitment. On occasion, it takes only the break-up of this small core, for one reason or another, to cause the movement quite rapidly to disintegrate.

Types of involvement

It must be emphasised first of all that participation in local or localised protest movements is, more often than not, informal and not institutionalised. In most cases it is not, strictly speaking, a matter of the membership of an organisation or formal group involving payment of dues or attendance at regular meetings. Rather, the notion of 'mobilisation' covers forms of participation which are not routinised. They typically are occasional or isolated events linked to specific issues.

Among the factors which most strongly motivate commitment should first be mentioned the defence of material interests. At Braud-et-St-Louis, the farmers were essentially resisting the compulsory purchase of the land needed for the power station. The basis of involvement in the canton of Ste-Foy-la-Grande was the same. One of the major issues in these conflicts concerned, directly and importantly, the kind of compensation that the farmers under threat could expect from the legal process of compulsory purchase following the declaration that the land concerned was required for public use. One of the results of the mobilisation movement was undoubtedly to raise the purchase price of land. At Le Bouscat, the traffic plan was challenged first because it was likely to lead to a drop in income for the city-centre traders,[4] and secondly because the planned ring road was a source of environmental pollution for the residents (whether home-owners or tenants) in the area. The same was true at Cenon where opposition to the incineration plant was supported by tenants' associations and co-owners of surrounding blocks of flats. The basic reason for their protest was the fear of a depreciation in the resale value of their flats because of the immediate proximity of the plant.

It is apparent, therefore, that property interests are one important factor in participation. But involvement in a protest movement may also be conditioned by much more ideological motives. In this case, the decision or proposal is challenged in the name of a relatively structured and coherent world view. This type of involvement is especially characteristic of militant ecologists, who were hostile to the building of the nuclear power station in the Blayais and the incineration plant at Cenon. The norms and values which structure their perceptions of what is at stake, lead them to an *a priori* rejection of the proposals, based on their whole image of industrial society.

Finally, a sense of local solidarity may to some extent explain the support which some movements enjoy. Individuals join not so much because they are hostile to the decision, but more because of subtle pressures from the local community. Commitment in such cases is limited and not very strong, merely taking the form of attending a meeting or signing a petition. Thus, relationships with neighbours may lead residents to involve themselves in protest action in order to conform to local pressures out of a sense of community, or a concern not to stand out from the rest, or a wish to give emotional support.

All these types of involvement arose only because of the geographical proximity of the proposed construction site. Except in a few cases

(Braud-et-St-Louis in particular, where the ecologists who became involved did not come from the immediate area of the site), the support enjoyed by the movements studied weakens as one moves further away from the area where the decision would have an immediate impact. Geographical proximity, therefore, constitutes a very important and, indeed, decisive factor leading to involvement in this sort of movement and one, moreover, which severely limits the appeal of such movements and also, no doubt, their impact.

2 STRATEGIES FOR ACTION AND LEGITIMATION

How, and by what means, are attempts made to influence policy decisions? In order to give some idea of the answer to this question, we shall examine in turn the structuring and organisation of mobilisation movements, the forms of action which they particularly favour and, finally, the role of the values and symbols which accompany and give direction to the protests.

The structuring of the movements

The forms of action adopted by the various movements would appear to be relatively similar if not identical. They have, in the first place, an organisational dimension. In all cases, an *ad hoc* defence committee was rapidly formed, which enabled those involved, either as individuals or collectively (in the form of already existing associations or groupings), to unite around common objectives and to attempt to broaden the bases of mobilisation.

In an attempt to establish themselves and achieve their objectives, protest movements give themselves functional structures which allow a degree of division of labour. We have seen previously that these defence committees often stem from a pre-existing association or grouping. To be more precise, they stem from those who control and direct these groups and who thereby attempt to broaden the sphere of action. There is a further aspect to this, in that a clear difference appears, and persists, in intensity of participation and in the running of the movement between activists and rank-and-file. On the one hand, a small group of activists tend to take, and even monopolise, initiatives for action. They almost alone decide the strategy to be adopted. On the other hand, there are the ordinary 'members' of the movement, if indeed this term has any meaning given the fact that their participation is very often purely temporary or episodic. In effect, very often members of this latter type limit themselves to attending one or a few meetings and signing a petition. Only more rarely do they take part in a demonstration or send a protest letter.

However, there are differences in the mode of organisation depending on the nature of the decision which is being challenged, the size of the protest movement, and the duration of the mobilisation process. In two cases, the organisation remained informal and unstructured. In the other two cases,[5] an attempt was made to put them on a formal footing: the movements formed themselves into associations in accordance with the law of 1901, and drew up statutes to enable them to function, if not permanently at least over a considerable period.

Preferred forms of action

The first form of action to be developed generally involved information-gathering. This means assembling the data which are required, and available, in order to try to arrive at a contrary expert opinion which will provide a legitimate basis for challenging the decision or the proposal. The adverse effects are stressed in order to justify opposition. In this way, the protest movements attempt to acquire a degree of credibility both in the eyes of the authorities and of the population as a whole.

In the first phase of the processes of mobilisation, this search for information often occupies a central place in as much as it conditions all the other activities: meetings, demonstrations; petitions; pressure groups, and behaviour towards the public authorities. The subsequent capacity for action displayed by protest movements depends to a large extent on the strategic information which they possess concerning the decision-making processes. It would have been impossible to challenge the decision to build a nuclear power station in the Blayais without first possessing precise knowledge of the sort of reactor to be used; of its cooling system; of the volume of water required; of where the financial resources for it were based; where the line of high tension power cables would be located which would carry the electrical current produced; and about the people responsible for the station and for overseeing the scheme (Garraud 1980). Similarly, no credible challenge to the ring road at Le Bouscat could be mounted without precise knowledge about the route, the width of the road and the amount of land required, the volume of traffic that it was expected to carry and the level of pollution that it would cause.

The second form of action relates to the organisation of support and of pressure. By the use of a variety of means (public meetings, petitions, demonstrations, contacts with the press and in some cases with political parties), the aim is to create a favourable balance of power. Thereby, at one and the same time, the objectives are publicised, a credible and sufficiently broad and representative protest movement is formed, the authorities are challenged, and the demands of the movement are taken into account. In some cases, these moves may be complemented by legal action, but the outcome of this remains very uncertain owing to the disparity in the resources of those involved and because of the complexity of the legal procedures required if an attempt is to be made to challenge, or even to overturn, a public decision. Lawsuits of this sort were pursued, though without success, before the administrative tribunals at Braud-et-Saint-Louis and at Cenon. At Le Bouscat a protest campaign by letter was organised at the time of the enquiry which preceded the declaration that the land was to be offered for public use. The inspector received 571 letters denouncing the plan.

The more the forms of action adopted are radical and involve conflict, the smaller the number of people who take part. Their numbers may therefore vary a great deal, depending on the cost and the constraints of involvement. Hence, for example, 26,000 people in Aquitaine signed the petition demanding that the plan to build a nuclear power station at Braud be abandoned, but only a hundred or so people took part in the violent occupation of the site.

A third form of action concerns the search for allies. The protest movements which we studied attempted to find within the local politico-administrative system, or on its margins, assistance of a more or less institutional kind: elected representatives, political parties, trade unions, who could take up the demands which had been expressed, and promote them through their own influence. This appears to be particularly import-ant in so far as it helps in part to determine the effectiveness of the protest movements and their capacity to influence the initial decision or proposal. In three out of four cases,[6] the groupings which we studied did not in fact manage to find institutional support. When the political system took no account of their requests, the most obvious consequences appear to have been that the movements became marginalised and were disbanded.

The political parties do not appear, as such, to play a very large role in encouraging local political mobilisation. More often than not their action consisted merely of attempting to exploit for their own ends, and with varying degrees of success, the stirrings of dissatisfaction, preferably shortly before an election, by sending out messages of support or adopting positions in line with those of the protesters. To sum up, therefore, we find very little sign of real collusion or close collaboration between the protest movements and the political parties as such. However, at Cenon, the Communist Party and to a lesser extent the RPR (Rassemblement pour la république) did several times vigorously protest against the waste-disposal plant.

This independence from the parties has two main sources. On the one hand the political parties are not really in a strong position to influence controversial decisions and any intervention on their part in the decision-making process could be seen as improper. On the other hand, those controlling the movements we studied seemed to be concerned not to taint their action politically by having excessively close or visible relations with a political party. This latter attitude no doubt reflects their desire to obtain support from, or to promote the participation of, as many members of the population as possible. In these circumstances, it was the elected representatives and also the local press who received more approaches and requests for support than any other person or body.

We need finally to take account of how far the mobilisation processes were purely local in character or, alternatively, had national implications. From this point of view, it is worth emphasising that the challenge to the policy on nuclear power stations was, in a more or less coordinated and simultaneous fashion, both a movement on a national scale and a succession of local protests. Every site chosen for a nuclear power station led to public controversy and local collective action. At the same time a national movement, in the form of a network, was being built up, deriving its strength from local conflicts, whilst in turn reinforcing them, and giving them a wider impact, especially through the national media (Garraud 1979). For all that, the movement was no more effective.

The protest against the incinerator at Cenon also managed very briefly to gain national notoriety, by becoming the subject of a national television programme entitled *La France défigurée* devoted to threats to the quality of life and the environment. This reverberation at national level amounted, indisputably, to a source of strength for the protest movement, adding to its credibility and, by the same token, to the force of its demands. Thrown onto the defensive, the local council was obliged to justify itself publicly and therefore to give some kind of response to the opponents of the proposal.

Access to the media, with the publicity it brings to the cause, clearly emerges as a form of action favoured by all the movements studied. The protesters expect to obtain not only publicity but also, more importantly, legitimacy for their demands (Lagroye 1985) which will help swing the balance of forces in their favour.

The symbolic dimensions

To legitimise their demands, and in an attempt to widen their appeal, protest movements endeavour to establish their symbolic importance as upholders of values. Accordingly, particular interests are overshadowed by values and symbols which have a general significance. Criticism of technocracy and the protection of the environment are the themes which are most frequently advanced by these movements as means of legitimation. Protest movements try in this way to exploit for their own ends significant currents of opinion. They attempt to relate demands, which are basically specific and localised, to broader concerns that are seen as entirely legitimate.

This practice enables them to provide new motives for individual involvement, and thus tends to broaden support. It is also a strategy whose aim is to overcome the limitations of a movement prompted by mere proximity to the threat and to transform it into a more ideological cause which will enable it to include new spheres of action. By widening its concerns to include pacifism, anti-militarism and policies on ecology, for example, the Bordeaux anti-nuclear committee hoped to bring together under one banner struggles which hitherto had been isolated and actions which had been merely episodic and unconnected. This entails resort to an ideology or at least to a set of more global themes. In a more or less comparable way, the movement against the waste-disposal plant at Cenon (which was a purely local and specific conflict) was rapidly transformed into an association for the defence of the environment, with broader, more long-term and permanent objectives. In theory, this sphere of action could then expand to cover several urban communes on the right bank of the Garonne and to environmental problems as a whole.

This symbolic dimension to collective action thus appears to have been one of the conditions for widening the appeal of the movements studied. Such a strategy makes it possible for strictly local or localised protests to be transformed imperceptibly into 'movements of ideas' which are more stable and conducive to sustained action. From this perspective, they constitute a necessary condition for the institutionalisation of the processes of collective action.

3 THE EFFECTS OF MOBILISATION ON THE LOCAL POLITICO-ADMINISTRATIVE SYSTEM

In what way do the processes of mobilisation affect the working of the local politico-administrative system? Political participation is traditionally defined as activity by citizens directed at influencing public decisions, but before we can relate participation directly to decisions, we need to see how the working of the local system is affected in a broader sense. Thus, citizen participation has in all probability no direct and immediate influence on concrete decisions, as certain theories of participation tend to suggest.[7] Rather, action is directed towards a relatively autonomous system of decision-making which obeys its own behavioural logic. In this sense, the capacity of protest movements to influence decisions is very largely mediated by other factors. Amongst these, we propose to highlight the role of the elected representatives and the possible attitudes of the political parties, as well as the way in which the local political arena is structured as a result of the conflict. Finally we shall then seek to assess the ability of protest movements to influence decisions.

The role of the local elected representatives

Once a decision is challenged and an issue arises, the local elected representatives rapidly become involved. Whatever the origin and nature of the decision may be, they are affected and are indeed called upon to state their position on the defence of local interests. They are obliged to act as intermediaries, and are the first to have to deal with the protest movements, whatever their previous role may have been and whatever their ability, in practice, to influence the decision itself. As soon as the available information leads them to recognise or suspect the potentially adverse consequences of the decisions, the activists turn either to the mayor or to the member of the *Conseil Général*, who not only are the nearest actors in the political and administrative system, but also are both known and accessible. The activists first try to inform them about the general concern which the proposal is causing, and then seek to convince them of the necessity and justification of opposing it.

In the two urban cases we studied, an open conflict existed between the protest movement and the municipal authorities, who were held responsible for the decision under attack. At Cenon and Le Bouscat, the (Socialist) local councils were openly blamed for the siting of the schemes even though, in fact, their real role in the decision-making process was much more limited in as much as, in both cases, it was the authority for the conurbation (Communauté Urbaine de Bordeaux) which was at the root of these decisions. This conflict about who should rightly consider demands was closely linked to a political conflict in the partisan sense of the term: local political forces opposed to the incumbent Council lent their support to the protest movement.

At Le Bouscat, the Gaullist deputy and future mayor (after the Municipal Elections of 1983) rapidly took charge of the movement opposing the ring road against the Socialist Council, and several of those controlling the Defence Committee were to be on his list in the Municipal Elections of 1983. At Cenon, the protest movement was led by two sets of individuals. On the one hand, there were former socialist militants who had been excluded from the Socialist Party because of their systematic opposition to the Council and because of their breaches of discipline. On the other hand, the Communist Party took an active role, in particular by distributing a notably violent pamphlet entitled 'Why the Socialist leadership of Cenon resorts to lies and deceit'. To a lesser extent the RPR (Rassemblement pour la république) also rose up against the incinerator proposal, and made great use of this theme in their political and electoral campaign.

In the two rural cases we studied, the attitudes of the local representatives were much more ambivalent, no doubt because of the nature of the decision-making process involved, as regards the building of the nuclear power station and the route to be followed by the high-tension cables. These were both decisions that had been taken by remote bodies. They were also very complex matters in which technical considerations played an important part. The elected representatives agreed initially to express the concern and even the disapproval of the local population, by communicating the demands of the movement to the appropriate authorities. But they then began to distance themselves from it as the movement revealed itself clearly as one of opposition. Finally, and not without some embarrassment, they then began to justify the proposals. This change of attitude was not unconnected with pressures from the central government, which attempted to reawaken the loyalty of the representatives. Faced with opposition, the politico-administrative system reacted by mobilising a counter-strategy which defended the scheme in the name of the general interest.

This occurred in the Blayais and in the canton of Ste-Foy-la-Grande where the half-hearted opposition of the mayors and local councillors was disarmed or neutralised by the concerted actions of the various actors in the administration, involving the prefecture and sub-prefecture, the departmental public works office, the departmental and regional office of Electricité de France, and other regional offices of industry. In a series of meetings and interviews they sought to convince the local elected representatives that the controversial industrial plans were appropriate and well-founded, and finally succeeded in 'bringing them to reason' (i.e., to the point of view of the politico-administrative system).

The attitudes of the elected representatives and their relationship with the protest movements appear to be different in urban and in rural areas, although it is difficult to pinpoint accurately the reasons for this. The explanation may lie in the nature of the issues and the greater or lesser dependence of the elected representatives on the local politico-administrative system. But it may lie also in the greater 'politicisation' of urban areas, and in the specific forms which the political game may take in each case.

The creation of a political issue

The working of the politico-administrative system is also affected by conflict and mobilisation to the extent that these give rise to a public controversy and the creation of a local political issue which political adversaries can exploit and turn to advantage in their struggle for municipal or cantonal power.

This was very apparent in Le Bouscat, where the opposition party in the commune gave considerable support to the local movement and made political capital of the issue. In the canton of Ste-Foy-la-Grande, the protest movement publicly put pressure on the district councillor through the press by threatening to use the sanction of the ballot-box against him. At Cenon, each successive election appeared to be the occasion for calling into question the appropriateness of the incineration plant. By providing an opportunity, or a pretext, for capitalising on the political and electoral effects of local discontent, the image of the elected representatives can be damaged, and hence, the issue may become the source of, or may at least contribute to, political change.

In themselves, the electoral effects are difficult to pin down with any precision, and it is not a simple matter to relate them unambiguously to local mobilisation. However, they appear more clearly in an urban context. This is almost certainly an effect of politicisation (in the sense of the opportunities for party political and electoral exploitation of controversial issues), which is more marked in urban than in rural contexts. But it is also a consequence of the nature of the decision-making processes which are being called into question. For instance, in the case of Le Bouscat, it would appear that opposition to the road proposals may have been partly responsible for the change in the party ruling the Council after the 1983 elections. We can indeed observe a perceptible change in political and electoral opinion in the polling district most affected by the project. Whereas a majority of electors had supported the Socialist list in the Municipal Elections of 1977, the list of candidates of the Right (of the future mayor) made considerable progress in this polling district at the Municipal Elections of 1983. The results in other polling districts in the locality having changed little from one election to another, it appears very possible that the change in the Council which occurred at Le Bouscat in 1983 arose in large part from the changes in voting in the particular neighbourhood affected by the traffic scheme.

While their effects are not always so direct or immediate, the conflicts which give rise to mobilisation movements may be regarded as factors which play a part in the structuring of political opinions and attitudes. Whilst we know that political or electoral behaviour is partly determined by a set of sociological factors, it is also a function of the issues arising in the course of political competition (Gaxie 1985: Part III). It may, therefore, be considered that the processes of mobilisation, by helping to have certain problems put on the local agenda, produce issues which can become, as a result of the action of a few people, significant in political and electoral terms. However, it is then a matter of considerable complexity to determine precisely the extent to which these issues contribute to changes in political behaviour and, not least, the overall result of elections.

The processing of demands and their impact on decisions

The effects of mobilisation processes can be assessed in various ways: the local, and even national, repercussions in the case of the nuclear reactor in the Blayais and of the waste disposal plant at Cenon; the manner in which the public authorities take account of the demands expressed; the capacity to modify a controversial decision or proposal; or the measures of compensation which may be granted in return for acceptance of the development.[8]

In all four of our cases, the protest movements succeeded first of all in gaining a certain degree of publicity for their activities and demands. There was thus a clear public expression of protest and not merely of latent or ill-defined discontent. Thanks to the assistance of the media and especially the local press, the publicity given to the different disputes itself amounted to a form of pressure. The elected representatives and the administration were effectively challenged and placed under an obligation, willingly or unwillingly, to defend themselves. They were then dragged into public controversy, which was one of the objectives of their opponents. The different movements managed to 'get themselves talked about', in one form or another and for varying lengths of time, and this was in itself already one achievement.

Demands are processed in a number of ways. They may be only partially taken into consideration; there may be negotiations or strategies designed to persuade the opposition to make concessions; there may be no compromise, depending on how acceptable the demands are and on the interests at work. At Braud, the demand of the anti-nuclear movement (a straightforward refusal to allow the nuclear power station to be built) was unacceptable. Construction went ahead and today the nuclear power station is in operation. In the canton of Ste-Foy-la-Grande, detailed changes were obtained but the fundamental arrangements for the scheme were not modified. At Cenon, the only tangible result produced by opposition was that some technical specifications were substantially modified, resulting in the incinerator plant having a larger chimney than had originally been envisaged. In all three cases, the protest movements were not successful in radically calling into question the decisions made. Their action led at the very most to greater or lesser delays in the implementation of decisions and projects. Finally, at Le Bouscat, the traffic plan was consigned to oblivion. Here, however, it should be emphasised, the development of the conurbation of Bordeaux, its main routes, and its traffic flows, had made this scheme obsolete, irrelevant and out of date in the ten years since it was first conceived.

At this level, the nature of the problem raised and the institutional source of the decision, almost certainly played an important part in leading to different degrees of pressure being applied. The construction of a nuclear power station, or of high-tension cables, has a logic of its own, in the face of which local bodies (whether elected representatives or protest movements) have only limited powers of action, or none at all. In such cases, the possibilities for negotiation are limited. The politico-administrative system is able to respond with strategies of persuasion which are intended to legitimise decisions, and to drive a wedge between the various elements making up the protest movement.

This is what appears to have happened in an exemplary manner at Braud-et-Saint-Louis where the administration involved (the Prefecture, the planning office, Electricité de France and so on) succeeded eventually in dividing the initial movement and brought about the isolation of the very small hard core of radical ecologists. One by one, the wine growers and those concerned in the tourist industry in Entre-deux-Mers, then the local elected representatives concerned and the oyster farmers from the mouth of the Gironde, and finally the farmers, all seem to have received assurances which led them to moderate considerably their opposition or even to end it.

Furthermore, the fact that it was the site of a major construction project meant that the commune of Braud-et-Saint-Louis benefited from numerous facilities which it would never have obtained but for the construction of the nuclear power station. Hence, the completion of this scheme did not only have its negative side. These balancing positive aspects were strongly emphasised by the various administrative bodies in their contacts and negotiations with the local elected representatives. Undoubtedly, this contributed to rendering acceptable, and indeed ensuring ultimate acceptance of, the decision to construct the plant despite the initial opposition.

We have to assess, finally, the overall effects of mobilisation on the original proposals, and to ask to what extent mobilised protest is able to influence or modify decisions. Here, we must point out that the protest movements which we studied were relatively ineffective. Thus, in three out of four cases, the initial plans were not seriously challenged. In only one case was the opposition effective, not so much in itself, perhaps, as because of the political intervention or support which it generated. In the other cases, the inability of the movements to influence decisions led more or less rapidly to their being disbanded and disappearing, since they were unable to stimulate any long-term involvement or produce any tangible results.

In these circumstances, it is difficult to evaluate in any general way the effectiveness of protest movements in view of the limited number of case studies and of their practical outcomes. However, for all that, we should probably not conclude that collective actions of this sort are necessarily unable to bring about substantial changes in initial decisions. The processes of local political mobilisation are not of necessity ineffective and any generalisation of this kind would certainly be hasty. They always produce some results, however slight and difficult to measure, even if they do not correspond to the objectives initially announced.

The case studies highlight the high degree of integration of the politico-administrative system at every level in France and, in the final analysis, the difficulties local populations concerned face, in consequence, in getting their demands considered.[9] This being the case, the movements studied appear to have much more of an 'expressive' function than a real capacity to change the course of public decisions. Even if an issue is produced which may become electorally or politically significant as a result of the strategies of political groups,[10] the outcome of the issue itself nevertheless tends to remain beyond the influence of the protest movement concerned.

There is also the question of whether forms of political mobilisation exist which, if not specifically local, are partially so. The phenomena studied can be strictly local and only concern a particular population and area: a neighbourhood, a commune or a canton. This is the case when it is a matter of mobilisation prompted by a scheme of public works where collective action is linked to an awareness of common interests and to a feeling of solidarity resulting from geographical proximity. But the anti-nuclear mobilisation was a national, even an international, phenomenon. People not directly affected by the physical proximity of a power station opposed the policy in the name of values and beliefs which created a common cause, with an associated sense of solidarity and identity. In this particular instance, proximity to the plant was merely one factor amongst others making for mobilisation which can, in consequence, assume particularised forms. On some sites, the protest was stronger, more persistent and widespread, and more violent than on others depending on the different local milieus affected, the particular local context and the strategies adopted by the actors involved.

A comparable process can be seen in an entirely different issue area which does not involve a public works policy or decision, namely the defence of the 'independent school' (*école libre*). This originated as a national movement but locally it was capable of assuming a variety of specific political forms. Mobilisation was, self-evidently, stronger in regions with a Catholic tradition. It may have been exploited, therefore, and even stirred up locally, in different ways by local political forces. But in this instance, the determining factor in mobilisation was essentially of an ideological nature not connected with geographical proximity.

It is therefore clear that strictly *local* processes of political mobilisation, as distinct from *localised* processes, only occur where people are living in close proximity to large public works projects. This perhaps explains to some extent the limited, sector-based and ultimately 'ineffective' nature of the movements studied.

NOTES

1 The construction of the waste disposal incinerator plant at Cenon is to some extent an exception, since it was presented as the extension of an already existing district heating scheme.
2 The information and consultation policies developed at the local level seem indeed to be intended first and foremost at justifying decisions which have already been taken rather than allowing the local residents to participate fully in making collective choices within the framework of a genuinely democratic process.
3 A wine-producing and tourist area situated strictly between the rivers Garonne and Dordogne before they join to form the estuary of the Gironde and bounded by the areas producing Pomerol and Saint-Emilion.
4 The major effect of the new traffic proposal was to divert cars from the centre where virtually all the businesses were located. The proprietors feared a marked reduction in business and a loss of turnover.
5 Cenon and Braud-et-Saint-Louis, where the protest movement was certainly stronger and more persistent as it continued for several years.
6 The challenge to the building of the ring road at Le Bouscat is an exception, in that the effectiveness of the movement did not depend entirely on its ability to find support or assistance within the politico-administrative system. This challenge is also linked to the origin and nature of the project. On this point, see below.
7 See Milbrath (1965: 1), Parry (1972: 5), Verba and Nie (1972: 2). For a critique of the notion of political participation, see Memmi 1985: 310–66, who points to the normative presuppositions of some of these studies according to which participation is not only legitimate but also desirable. To the extent that it conforms to democratic norms, it therefore constitutes virtually a duty.
8 Clearly we are emphasising the effects on the politico-administrative system and not the internal effects within the movement itself which, in the absence of genuine participant-observation, cannot easily be demonstrated.
9 The case studies may be compared with other instances of local political mobilisation in France. See Cadène (1983), Hatzfeld (1986), Kukawka (1980), Nayler (1986), *Autrement* (1976).
10 This depends on three conditions: first that those political groupings exist locally, which is not necessarily the case in rural areas; secondly, that these issues can be incorporated into the strategies for gaining and retaining power; finally, that the political groups can rely on the exploitation of such issues to produce electoral support.

6

Local political mobilisation: a case study of a Welsh community

DAVID CLEAVER

This chapter will look at two instances of mobilisation occurring in Carmarthen and its surrounds in order to explore different patterns and styles of mobilisation. The first involves dairy farmers, the second Welsh language activists.

I GENERAL BACKGROUND

The milk quota issue

When the European Economic Community introduced milk quotas in April 1984 as a means of reducing milk production, the British government, which was responsible for the implementation of these quotas, devised a scheme on the basis of an across-the-board quota equal to 1983 production levels less 9 per cent. Over-production was to be penalised by a levy. This method of implementing the quotas was seen as having an especially detrimental effect on the small, rather than the large, dairy farmer. Dyfed's dairy farmers work small family farms and therefore felt themselves to be particularly harshly treated by this system of quota implementation. Many of the farmers took the view that their livelihood was under threat and called for the government both to change the system of quota allocation, and to introduce measures to alleviate the farmers' financial problems. (For the impact of quotas on French farmers, see Naylor 1986.)

The vast majority of Dyfed's farmers, alarmed at the threat to their livelihood, expressed a determination to challenge the government's policy. The farmers' reaction was particularly intense partly because they felt betrayed by their own government. During the late 1970s and early 1980s the British government had encouraged dairy farmers to expand their milk production and, in response to this, many borrowed

considerable sums of money in order to equip their farms with the necessary facilities. However, the introduction of the quotas meant for many
of these farmers that the value of their assets was considerably depreciated.
In addition, they suffered a reduction in their income from milk
sales. Consequently repayments became more difficult to meet; some
farmers even faced bankruptcy. Not only the farmers themselves were
affected, but also the rest of the community. As farming is the back-
bone of Dyfed's economy, the repercussions were viewed as potentially
catastrophic.

An initial response to the introduction of the quotas was organised by
the farmers' unions (these are not trade unions as all the members are
employers, not employees). Most of Dyfed's farmers belong to either the
National Farmers' Union (NFU) or the Farmers' Union of Wales (FUW).
Both tried to influence the government by using their political contacts.
This approach, involving behind-the-scenes discussions and negotiations,
proved a failure. Even the NFU, which has traditionally strong ties with
the Conservative Party, made no headway. Believing that a more dynamic
and open approach was needed to make the government respond to their
demands, a number of disillusioned farmers called a local meeting in the
spring of 1984 with the intention of organising a more vigorous protest. As
a result, an *ad hoc* committee was formed to organise a pressure group to
be known as the Dyfed Farmers Action Group (DFAG). It had a secretary
and a chairman but no official membership as it did not see itself in
competition with the existing farmers' unions. The group's leaders were
not office holders in other local bodies, and its membership was composed
of ordinary farmers, unfamiliar with the role of leadership and the running
of campaigns.

The Welsh language issue

As the 1981 census data show, the majority (61.7%) of Carmarthen
District's population still speaks Welsh. However, back in 1931, as many
as 87% of the population spoke the language. Thus, if present trends
continue, it is calculated that by the end of the century only a little over half
of the population will be Welsh speakers. The language clearly faces a
crisis.

The Welsh Language Society (a translation of *Cymdeithas yr Iaith
Gymraeg*), whose aim is to safeguard the language, undertook a campaign
in 1984–5 to persuade Carmarthen District Council to adopt measures
which would go some way to ensuring that the language remained alive.
To an outsider it might have been expected that local councillors would
take action to support the language without any prompting. However,

according to the protagonists, the local authorities in Carmarthen, both when Labour and Independent-controlled, appear never to have placed the matter at the top of their agendas. Only during the last 15 years have the authorities displayed some concern about the problem, but even in the mid-1980s positive action has only been forthcoming following pressure by campaign groups such as the Welsh Language society. In this sense, therefore, an element of conflict is present as between group and official priorities.

The society's campaign involved persuading the District Council to give planning status to the Welsh language. This means in practice that, when decisions on planning applications are dealt with by the local authority, consideration should be given to any adverse effects planning consent might have on the language. For example, when approval is given to a private developer to build a housing estate in a predominantly Welsh-speaking village, those who purchase the new homes tend to be English-only speakers, usually migrants from England. Consequently, the day-to-day language of the village will change from Welsh to English very rapidly. The society therefore wants to have measures introduced to prevent such developments on the grounds that they will be detrimental to the Welsh language.

The society's specific demands were as follows:

We ask Carmarthen district council to give 'planning status' to the language, i.e. to take a policy decision to give full consideration to the effect of any development on the Welsh language when considering planning applications; limit new housing to meet local needs only, and give special consideration to what happens to the older housing stock; prepare regular reports on the state of the Welsh language as part of every local plan with proposals on how to improve the situation. (*Carmarthen Times*, 14 June 1985)

In order to expound their proposals, the Society held a conference in Carmarthen to which were invited local councillors, local authority officials, representatives of the local political parties and of other local bodies, and the general public.

Unlike the members of the DFAG, those of the society were, in the main, experienced campaigners with a history of successful mobilisation. Since its inception in 1962, the society has been involved in campaigns for bilingual road signs, bilingual official forms, and a Welsh language television channel, to name but a few.[1] All these campaigns involved the use of direct action. Although they were local people, the campaigners in Carmarthen were not members of the local political elite. They were not part of the politico-administrative system. None of them were local councillors, political party officers or local notables.

2 MOTIVES

Both the DFAG's and the society's campaigns were projected in terms of safeguarding 'community' rather than material interests, even though in the case of the farmers economic concerns were clearly at the core. This, more than anything else, seemed to contribute to their successes. But what is meant here by 'community'? Unfortunately there is no generally accepted definition. All that is agreed upon is that the term is commendatory, rarely being used unfavourably (see Plant 1978: 82).

In consequence, perhaps, those associated with the campaigns studied in this chapter use the term 'community' very loosely, making no attempt to define it. When, for example, a Dyfed farmer talks of the local community he may be referring to the whole of Dyfed or simply to the locality in which he lives. That the term is used in such a loose way does not, however, reduce its political value or impact. The farmer or the Welsh language activist is simply indicating through its use that his campaign is directed at safeguarding the interests not just of a section of the local populace but of all the local people. It is interpreted by both the campaigners and the local people as 'ensuring the well-being of all local people'. The term is therefore being used to mean the antithesis of 'sectional'.

'Community' is usually used in this way by campaign groups when there are no marked divisions among the local people. Where such divisions exist the interests of different sections may not be the same or may even conflict with one another. It would thus be inappropriate to speak in terms of 'the community interest' although campaigners may still use the term if they believe it furthers their cause. They may also, of course, take advantage of any community feeling that may exist by claiming to represent the interests of the whole of the locality when in fact they are concerned only with their own particular group interests.[2]

Such a strategy was clearly used by the DFAG when they emphasised the effects the quotas would have, not just upon farmers, but on the entire local area. The farmers advanced the view that, in order for rural communities to survive, a thriving farming sector is necessary; if the farmers were to go out of business, communities would suffer severe hardship and disintegrate or even disappear. The rallying cry of the farmers became 'save our communities'. References to social rather than economic factors became a regular feature of their protests. The support they received was therefore more broadly based but it was still almost entirely local, little being derived from outside Dyfed.

To emphasise the community aspects of its language campaign, the society produced a detailed report for use at its conference in which it used census data, based upon local community council wards,[3] to illustrate the plight of the language. It also attempted to persuade the community councils to participate in the mobilisation process by using their influence to pressurise the District Council. The basic nature of the issue, namely safeguarding the day-to-day language of the majority of the local population, inevitably meant that the issue was seen as one concerning community interests.

It seems, therefore, that both sets of campaigners saw it as vital to project their actions in communitarian terms if they were to achieve their aims. Thus, as will be shown, the whole character of the campaigns and the nature and extent of the support they were to receive was substantially determined by their expressions of concern for community, rather than sectional, interests and values.

3 THE ROLE OF POLITICAL PARTIES

Political parties in their quest for power are inevitably in competition with each other for the electorate's support. All parties therefore search for means by which to win this support. Possibly one of the most obvious methods of attracting votes is for the parties openly to give their support to those groups or sections within the community which are involved in the defence of interests, be they material or otherwise. It could be argued that the greater the number of interests encompassed by a party, the greater would be its support. Therefore, it might be expected that the parties would do their utmost to establish links with, and to participate in, campaigns organised to safeguard specific interests. For example, the rivalry that exists between the Republican and Democratic Parties in the United States in their efforts to represent a wide variety of different interests and groups is one of the most striking features of American party politics (see Eldersveld 1964).

There are, however, a number of factors which may constrain parties and limit their involvement in the processes of local coalition-building. Several of these are apparent from the experiences of the main parties with the milk quota and Welsh language issues in Carmarthen. Collectively, they suggest that the parties may find that their room for manoeuvre in building local group support is limited.

In some constituencies, party competition is very weak. For example, in some South Wales industrial constituencies the Labour Party is so dominant that the other main parties play a generally inactive role in local politics, seeing little to gain from any involvement. In less politically homogeneous constituencies, however, where more than one party has a realistic chance of winning the seat, competition between the parties is often intense. It would appear reasonable to assume that in such constituencies this intense party competition would lead to attempts by the parties to involve themselves in as many local issues as possible.

In doing so, political parties may then perform a key political function, that of acting as an aggregator of interests. However, the parties themselves have to balance the costs and benefits of engaging in such activities when they are designed to safeguard local interests. In this respect, a party's main concern will be to ensure that, as a result of any involvement, it does not suffer at the polls. No party, for example, will wish to be directly associated with a pressure group which holds views or participates in activities that are considered by the general public to be unacceptable. Such an association would prove unproductive in terms of winning electoral support. Another factor is the party's ideology and the nature of its membership. If an issue is such that to take sides would mean coming into conflict with the party's ideology, or offending a section of the membership, thereby creating internal divisions, then a party will in most instances wish to distance itself from the issue. A third factor which can influence involvement is the political label of the party in power. Local branches of the party in government (be it national or local) are less likely to participate in campaigns targeted at the ruling authority than are branches of the opposition parties.

The extent to which such factors influence party involvement is determined by the parties themselves: they weigh up the costs and benefits. There is, however, another factor which determines party involvement in local issues, and one over which the parties have little or no control, namely the attitude or policy towards party involvement adopted by those pressure groups organising local campaigns. Some groups may wish to prevent or discourage all parties, or at least certain parties, from participating in their campaigns.

Among British constituencies, Carmarthen is one in which it would be expected that the parties would be most active in local issues because of the rivalry that exists between not three, but four main parties, namely Conservative, Labour, Liberal and Plaid Cymru. Indeed, this rivalry is reflected in the very close parliamentary election results that have been a feature of the constituency's politics. Yet one of the most striking findings of this study is that party involvement was insignificant in both the farmers' and language activists' campaigns. Why should this be so? What was the relative importance of the above-mentioned factors in determining the extent of the parties' involvement? In looking at these questions each party will be dealt with separately.

Plaid Cymru (The Welsh Nationalist Party)

Plaid's Carmarthen branch considers one of its vital functions to be that of aggregator of local interests. It attempts to associate itself with a wide range of causes. The party is strongly committed to community politics and has a full time district organiser based in Carmarthen. Thus, if Plaid is to practise what it preaches, it is more or less obliged to become involved in efforts to defend local interests.

One group within the community with which Plaid is particularly keen to associate is the farmers. This is because Plaid is determined to try to regain the farming vote it once held in the 1960s and 1970s. To some extent Plaid is a natural ally of the farmers. A commitment to safeguarding the small family farm has always been given a high priority in Plaid's manifesto. When the milk quota issue surfaced, Plaid took steps to involve itself in the farmers' campaign. The issue provided it with a golden opportunity to side with the local farmers in a campaign targeted at one of Plaid's main opponents, the Conservative Party. The party considered the DFAG to be the true voice of the Dyfed farmers. Leading party members travelled to Brussels with DFAG members to lobby the EEC. Plaid also allowed the DFAG to make use of its election manifesto for the European Parliament elections in June 1984 when the milk quota issue was given much prominence. Moreover, they instigated a scheme to transfer surplus milk production from Dyfed to the families of striking South Wales miners as a means of drawing public attention to the farmers' campaign.

Despite its active support for the farmers, however, Plaid was not permitted by the DFAG to utilise the campaign for its own ends. Many of the DFAG members were not Plaid sympathisers and resented the party taking a high profile in their campaign. According to some of the group's members, Plaid was responsible for the DFAG becoming less a farmers' pressure group and more a 'political' group with anti-Tory and pro-nationalist leanings. Indeed, some DFAG activists felt so strongly about Plaid's influence that they resigned their membership. The DFAG was thereby clearly made aware of the dangers of associating itself too closely with political parties.

Plaid also did not take a central role in the society's language campaign in Carmarthen. But in this instance, Plaid's limited role was the result of a conscious decision taken by the party. In the Carmarthen constituency Plaid sees its primary task as that of winning over Conservative voters, and in particular the farmers, if it is to regain the parliamentary seat. The party therefore has tried to play down whenever possible its relationship with 'radical' groups such as the society.

Plaid's decision to adopt only a peripheral role did not raise any alarms among society members. As far as the society was concerned, party support for its cause was of no real significance at least in terms of mobilising support. The society wished to prevent its campaign being associated with only one political party for, if this were to happen, not only might the society have found itself being opposed by the other parties, but it would also have found it difficult to project its cause in terms of community interests. One of the society's aims has been to maintain and foster community life and it has realised that party involvement in its campaigns could lead to conflict and divisions within the very communities it is trying to safeguard. The society was faced with the same problem that confronted the DFAG, namely how to conduct a political campaign without a high party political profile. What is clearly evident is that even a party such as Plaid, which is one of the leading advocates of community politics, will find it difficult to play so much as a minor role in the mobilisation process of any campaign which is projected in terms of protecting community interests. Party politics are to a certain extent anathema to such campaigns, if Plaid's experience is at all typical.

The Labour Party

The Labour Party in Carmarthen, like Plaid, considers one of its main functions to be that of participant in local campaigns, believing that such an approach will contribute to the party's electoral support. It would be reasonable to assume, therefore, that the Labour Party would have tried to play a significant role in the two campaigns under review.

In fact the local Labour Party branch took no part in either. The constituency's Labour MP and the MEP for West Wales both attempted to bring the milk quota issue to the fore in their respective legislatures but they did not have the full backing of their own parliamentary parties. However, Labour's non-involvement at local level in both issues is readily accounted for. Although the local Labour Party would have liked to have supported the DFAG in order to demonstrate its opposition to the British Government's agricultural policy it was unable to do so because the Dyfed farmers distanced themselves from Labour on account of the latter's agricultural policy. And, so far as the language issue is concerned, local Labour Party members, while expressing concern for the language's future, placed the issue well down their list of priorities. One member summed up his party's view on the matter as follows:

The Welsh language is not an issue in the locality as far as we are concerned. We are sympathetic to the language but we do not want it rammed down our throats. We tend to concern ourselves with national issues and not Welsh dimensions here in Carmarthen.

This member is here referring to the Labour Party's traditional commitment to centralism (which of course conflicts with the society's advocacy of community socialism). The Labour Party has never been strongly committed to devolution. It has always been reluctant to examine problems purely from a Welsh perspective, preferring to see things from a national or even an international viewpoint. Welsh Labour leaders, such as Aneurin Bevan and Neil Kinnock, have been strong defenders of this centralist approach.

In concluding, it is clear that (as was found in Plaid's case) a number of factors accounted for the local Labour Party playing a relatively inactive role in the two issues being studied, some of which Labour had control over, some of which it did not.

The Liberal/SDP Alliance

At the Liberal Party's Annual Assembly in 1970 the following resolution was passed:

In determining the organisational strategy to achieve Liberal aims, this Assembly endorses the following objectives as of prime importance:
(1) a dual approach to politics, working both inside and outside the institutions of the political establishment.
(2) a primary strategic emphasis on community politics; our role as political activists is to help people in communities to organise to take and use power, to use our political skills to redress grievances and to represent people at all levels of the political structure. (Liberal Assembly, Final Agenda, 1970, quoted in Gyford and James 1983: 73)

This is still the basic philosophy of the Liberal Party and it has been adopted, if not to quite the same extent, by what were at that time their Alliance partners, the SDP. It is generally agreed that many of the Liberal Party's electoral successes since the 1950s, at both parliamentary and local level, have been primarily due to the party's involvement in community politics (see Cook 1976). However, despite this commitment to community politics the Carmarthen Alliance branches were not active in the DFAG's campaign. This inactivity was partly attributable to indifference or inertia on the part of the branches but, in any case, as was true of Labour and Plaid Cymru, neither the DFAG nor the society expressed any real interest in acquiring Alliance support.

The Conservative Party

Unlike Plaid, Labour, and even the Alliance, the local Conservative Association does not consider one of its roles to be that of participant in local issues. This was confirmed by one of the leading local Conservatives when interviewed. He stated that while the function of the local Association was 'to get a Conservative member elected and to keep the flag flying', this was not to be achieved by participating in local issues or in local government politics, but by attracting a large local membership. This attitude may be the result of a tradition among rural Conservatives that politics is in some ways an unwelcome intrusion on community life and is best left to politicians at the national level. It came as no surprise, therefore, that the association did not attempt to involve itself with either the DFAG or the society.

The Conservative prospective parliamentary candidate for the Carmarthen constituency did, however, vigorously campaign within the party in support of the Dyfed dairy farmers. He publicly castigated his party's national leaders over their handling of the quota issue in a speech at the Conservative Party's 1984 Annual Conference. In it he pleaded with the party to take measures to ensure that no farmers were forced to abandon their livelihood. As he stressed, 'We are very much the national representatives of the farmers'. His efforts appeared, however, to have little impact. In avoiding any direct involvement, the local Conservative Association possibly considered preserving party unity at local level to be of greater importance and the adoption of a non-participatory stance went a long way, so it was believed, towards ensuring that no rifts emerged among its members. They may also have wished to avoid being seen to conflict with their party's national leaders.

From the DFAG's point of view, if there was one party from whom it might have wished to receive active support, it would have been the Conservative Party for it alone among the parties had direct access to the British government and the Secretary of State for Wales. The local farmers realised that Conservative Party support could prove invaluable; they also recognised the contribution that the prospective Conservative candidate had made to their campaign. Yet, while appreciating the potential benefits, the DFAG did not try to persuade or cajole the local Conservative Association to participate in its campaign, and this, possibly more than anything else, illustrates the determination of the DFAG to conduct a non-partisan campaign. They certainly believed that a campaign projected in terms of safeguarding community interests and values would only achieve its aims if it avoided involving any potentially divisive support. And none is more potentially divisive than that of political parties.

In the context of the party system, Carmarthen certainly cannot stand for all British localities. It differs from many in that it is politically very heterogeneous, the four main parties all having a solid local base. Communities which are politically homogeneous, where one party dominates while the other parties are inactive or absent from the local political scene, will probably react differently to partisan involvement in their local issues. In some of the mining villages of South Wales, for example, the Labour Party is seen as the natural representative of the community's interests, and so any campaign projected in terms of safeguarding such interests will be likely not only to involve the local Labour Party but to be initiated and orchestrated by it. The Labour Party's involvement will be unlikely to create internal conflict among the campaigners as it would probably do in a more politically heterogeneous community. Clearly, the findings of the Carmarthen study are of less relevance to politically homogeneous localities. However, one might advance for further investigation the hypothesis that the situation discovered in this case study would find parallels in similar heterogeneous areas. In places such as Carmarthen, where competition between the parties is most intense at parliamentary level, the opportunities for any of the parties to win support by participating in campaigns, which are projected in terms of safeguarding community interests, are less readily available to them than they would be in areas where party competition is not as evident.

4 GROUP INVOLVEMENT IN THE MOBILISATION PROCESS

One of the recurring themes in the pluralist literature relates to the importance attached to coalition-building in the mobilisation process, whereby community groups establish a group network among themselves. The network is not necessarily permanent; it may disband once the issue has been concluded. The purpose of forming coalitions is simply to increase resources and skills so as to improve the chances of success. It might have been expected, therefore, that the DFAG and the Welsh Language Society would have mobilised as wide a range of groups and as big a network of leaders as possible to improve their chances of success. In fact, neither group adopted this strategy: local groups played a very limited role in the mobilisation processes. Why was this so? Was it because local groups did not wish to identify themselves with pressure groups associated with direct action or was it because the DFAG and the society believed it to be in their best interests to campaign alone?

It would be reasonable to assume that some local groups would have declined an invitation to participate in the two campaigns on the grounds that they were strongly opposed to any activities which involved breaking the law. They would not, therefore, wish to have anything to do with those, such as the DFAG and the society, who engaged in this type of activity. Undoubtedly the main reasons for the absence of groups, however, were that the DFAG and the society felt that little could be gained from the involvement of other groups and that it could even have an adverse effect on their campaigns' success. The society, for example, saw no need to seek extensive group support as a means of gaining access to the targeted authority for it had no problem obtaining this access through its own efforts. Equally, the DFAG believed that such support could have a divisive influence upon its campaign.

The need for the DFAG to seek group assistance had in any case been made unnecessary as a result of the Independent-controlled Dyfed County Council creating the Dyfed Joint Liaison Committee (DJLC). The DJLC is a good example of a 'peak group' (see Moran 1985: 126–7). Its purpose was to act as a representative of all the relevant groups and organisations in any negotiations with other bodies or authorities. The DJLC was created as a result of the efforts of leading officers of Dyfed County Council together with the council's chairman, who were concerned about the effects of the milk quotas on Dyfed's economy. The committee comprised representatives of the Farmers' Unions, the Confederation of British Industry, the Country Landowners' Association, and the Dyfed Chamber of Trade and the DFAG. As such it could be regarded as an expression of a concern for the issue which was felt by the community at large rather than by one sectional interest alone. Its purpose was to highlight quantitatively the impact the quotas would have on Dyfed so as to persuade the Secretary of State for Wales to rethink his position. The DJLC, unlike the DFAG, was granted a meeting with the Secretary of State who appeared, according to one of the senior and most authoritative members of the DJLC, to be impressed by its case. He did not, however, agree to meet the Committee's demands.

This experience suggests that the creation of a peak group to coordinate action can be an effective means of extending group participation. The peak association may also be able to increase the impact of the campaign by concentrating effort in gaining access to decision-makers and simplifying any negotiating process. In the case of the Dyfed farmers' campaign, the formation of the peak group appears to have been a viable alternative to the creation of an informal network of groups which may have dissipated efforts. But, notable though these endeavours may have been, the DJLC had no success in terms of achieving a change in policy.

5 DIRECT ACTION

What is strikingly apparent from British case studies dealing with political activity (for example, Newton 1976; Bealey and Sewel 1981) is that the use of direct action as a means of furthering a cause is rarely undertaken. Such action is presumed to be regarded by the vast majority of community members, and especially of decision-makers, as an unacceptable form of protest which if adopted, would alienate its users from the rest of the community (see also Barnes, Kaase *et al.* 1979).

The Dyfed farmers appeared to adopt a policy of direct action without undue deliberation. This was, perhaps, surprising considering that they have not been renowned in the past for their militancy, although in occasional incidents they have displayed a readiness to participate in direct action. The Welsh Language Society did not adopt such methods in its

Carmarthen campaign but the Welsh people generally seem to perceive the society as a direct action group, for it has always been prepared to engage in unconventional activities as a means of publicising its cause. Thus, any support given to the society could be interpreted as, in effect, condoning direct action even if the society has not used such action on the specific issue for which support was given.

The basic aim of the DFAG was to publicise the plight of the dairy farmer by engaging in activities which would be deemed newsworthy and so attract media coverage. To this end it hijacked milk lorries, laid siege to the Minister of Agriculture at a local meeting he attended, blockaded the Ministry of Agriculture offices in Carmarthen with tractors and muck spreaders, and dumped dead cows' heads and udders on the office steps. The activities in which the society members have been engaged in recent years (with members from Carmarthen particularly involved) are of an even more extreme nature: television pylons have been vandalised (in a campaign for a Welsh language television channel), government buildings have been broken into and their contents destroyed, and Welsh Office stands at the National Eisteddfod (Wales' premier cultural gathering) have been attacked by members. As a result some members have been imprisoned. On the basis of experiences elsewhere it might well be expected that groups engaging in such actions in Carmarthen would receive little, if any, support from the local community and would be isolated from local political life. In fact, the reaction in Carmarthen to the DFAG's and the society's campaigns was rather more sympathetic.

Only a handful of farmers took part in the DFAG's activities referred to, but it should not be concluded from this that the majority of farmers and members of the local community objected to the use of direct action. None of the community leaders interviewed expressed unreserved criticism of the DFAG. A few had reservations about some of the tactics, but all agreed that the DFAG deserved at least some credit for publicising the farmers' case. The acceptance of the DFAG and its method of campaigning, by the local community is, perhaps, best illustrated by the fact that it was invited to provide a member of the DJLC. If representatives of such respected organisations as the CBI and the Country Landowners' Association, who both sat on the DJLC, were prepared to work hand in hand with the DFAG it might be justifiably concluded that the DFAG was not being viewed by the local community as a group of outlaws.

The general reaction to the Language Society's campaign was no less favourable. The Carmarthen conference was not boycotted by all the local political elite. Furthermore, among those who did decline an invitation the group's direct action tactics played little part in their decision. The attendance of the District Council's Director of Planning, of representatives from Dyfed County Council's planning department, and of a number of councillors, provides a clear indication that the society was not being ostracised by members of the local political and administrative elite. This was, perhaps, confirmed by the conference's opening ceremony being performed by the chairman of the District Council.

Why were the people of Carmarthen prepared to condone direct action? In a study of attitudes towards direct action in Scotland and Wales, Miller and his colleagues emphasised the importance of the symbolic content of protest actions (Miller *et al.* 1982). These actions were part of the battle for hearts and minds. On this interpretation, the extent to which protesters participate in direct action and the mode of action they adopt are determined by the general climate of approval for direct action methods (Miller *et al.* 1982: 65; see also Muller 1979: 95–100).

The evidence from this study tends to support such a view. The Dyfed farmers neither expected nor received open disapproval of their direct action, whilst the society was also confident that its conference would not be boycotted. There do, therefore, appear to be circumstances where a climate of approval for direct action can flourish. However, this may be principally when direct action is employed to safeguard specific non-materialist interests and values. The people of west Wales seem in general terms to be no more disposed to extreme protest than those elsewhere in Britain. It is only over specific issues that approval for direct action might be given, issues concerned with the safeguarding of certain distinctive features of community life such as the family farm, the Welsh language, and the traditions of religious nonconformity. This in turn may reflect a strong determination to maintain a way of life which has proved both economically and socially rewarding.

Their views are reinforced by features of modern day urban life, such as the breakdown of social order, the relative absence of community spirit, and other attendant social problems, which confront them on television and in the newspapers but not in their day-to-day lives. The potential threat of these social problems to their own lives greatly concerns the people of west Wales. Aspects of their life such as the family farm, the Welsh language and nonconformity help to cement the social fabric and to act as a barrier to the introduction of ideas, lifestyles and other influences which might threaten existing arrangements. The local people, therefore, appear to believe that if the use of direct action can prevent such change then its adoption is well justified and will receive their support.

6 THE SUCCESS OF THE CAMPAIGNS

The degree of success achieved by a campaign can be considered from several perspectives. One may consider how far it gained publicity, how far the targeted authority responded and whether policy changes were implemented as a result. It should be stressed, however, that the aims of campaign groups vary and in some cases groups only had the first and second of these objectives immediately in mind and their success should be measured accordingly. In the case of the DFAG, for example, the campaign was intended merely to publicise the farmers' plight, hoping that changes in the policy itself would be effected more by others through conventional channels. The society's campaign, on the other hand, had much broader aims and all three criteria need to be applied when assessing its effectiveness.

The DFAG set out to bring the farmers' plight to the attention of the public and the British government and it unquestionably achieved its aim. The use of direct action as a means of mobilising support was effective, but only because it involved the media.[4] Direct action without media coverage would undoubtedly have proved futile. The media provided a communication link between the protesting farmers and the British government. It was reported by some of those interviewed that the Ministry of Agriculture requested a copy of a BBC television programme produced by the DFAG in which the farmers' case was vividly portrayed. The farmers' campaign also received coverage on another national television current affairs programme, and in the colour supplement of the *Observer*. That a small group of west Wales farmers attracted such media attention is one indication of its success.

The society's aim, by contrast, was to persuade Carmarthen District Council to take positive steps to safeguard the Welsh language. In the months that followed the society's Carmarthen conference, the District Council abandoned its indifference to the language issue and instructed its Director of Planning (who had been in attendance at the conference) to produce a report. This report, 'Planning and the Welsh Language', made a number of recommendations which met many of the society's demands.

The following recommendations were made:
(1) that in the future preparation of local plans an examination be undertaken of the Welsh language as part of a wider study of social and community issues.
(2) that in the formulation of policies and proposals in local plan preparation and in the determination of planning applications, account be taken of the anticipated impact of proposed developments on the social and cultural fabric of local communities and in particular, there be a general presumption against large scale housing development in excess of identified local requirements. (Carmarthen District Council 1985: 5)

These recommendations were then adopted as policy by Carmarthen District Council in November 1985. They appear to have satisfied the society's local chairman who commended the council's Director of Planning in a letter published in the local press. The society's campaign had clearly succeeded on all three counts: it had successfully publicised its cause; the targeted authority had responded, and policy changes were implemented.

In considering the implications of this case study it needs to be emphasised at the outset that Carmarthen is not a typical British community. It is predominantly rural yet, unlike many other rural areas, marked social divisions are notably absent. Unusually, it also has more often than not a Labour MP. Furthermore, most of its population are conversant with two languages.[5] These factors would have to be taken into account when considering this study's findings in relation to those that might be expected elsewhere.

Nevertheless, it might be cautiously suggested that the patterns of mobilisation and participation uncovered in Carmarthen reflect developments which are more widespread in Britain. Neither of the Carmarthen campaigns sought to achieve its aims by establishing alliances with other groups or by relying on the support of a network of local groups and individuals to forge links with the authorities. Nor did either campaign face concerted opposition. In these respects the experience in rural Carmarthen parallels Newton's findings in the very different context of Birmingham. He found few instances of the direct conflict between opposed interest groups which the pluralist literature of political science has classically anticipated (Newton 1976: 62). Furthermore, he concluded, in a phrase that could with equal force be applied to Carmarthen, that 'coalition building in the world of community pressure groups is not especially common' (Newton 1976: 82). It may be, therefore, that the importance attached to this feature of the mobilisation process in some of the pluralist literature is justified principally when associated with communities in the USA. It may be of less significance when applied to those in Britain.

A possible explanation for the relative absence of party participation from the two campaigns may be that for many nowadays party politics lacks credibility (see Parry, Moyser and Wagstaffe 1987). It may even be that the functions of parties at local level are undergoing a significant change. Parties may no longer involve themselves so fully in local issues: the task of political mobilisation may increasingly be the prerogative of pressure groups. Moran, for example, has made reference to this trend, claiming that 'pressure groups now seriously rival parties in the system of representation' (Moran 1985: 120). He suggests that pressure groups have a much greater attraction to those either wishing to, or compelled to, participate in political activity, particularly in the case of young people:

A generation ago politically inclined young people almost automatically engaged in political activity through a party; now they increasingly do so by supporting a campaigning movement. (Moran 1985: 142)

Campaigning movements were common-place prior to the rise of nation-wide political parties. If the present trend towards pressure group politics continues it could presage a decline of the political party in the twenty-first century.

The evidence from this study also suggests that campaigns claiming to safeguard 'community' interests may be more successful than those concerned only with sectional interests. However, the extent to which a pressure group can present itself in such terms is dependent upon the nature of the specific cause and the character of the area in which the campaign is focused. Both the Dyfed farmers and the Carmarthen Welsh language activists were able to relate their campaign to local community interests and values without difficulty. But in areas where 'communities' are not so easily identifiable or recognisable, those involved in political mobilisation might find difficulty in projecting their cause in communitarian terms.[6]

Areas such as Dyfed, located on the periphery of Britain, are often considered to be at a disadvantage in terms of gaining access to, and attracting the attention of, central government. This point has often been stressed by those advocating devolution of power. Yet it would seem that those involved in political mobilisation in such peripheral areas have some advantages, compared with those situated closer to the corridors of power, in that they can try to utilise their area's sense of distinctiveness and community for their own benefit. By emphasising it they not only generate local solidarity for their campaign but they may also attract greater media attention.

The growth of the media in recent decades has made a significant contribution to pressure group politics. In particular, media coverage has become an important potential resource for local campaigns targeted at national and international government. But the increase in media influence has coincided with the erosion of local autonomy especially in the determination of economic policy. This is partly the result of EEC membership. Decisions are increasingly being taken at national and international level which can adversely affect localities on the periphery. However, the media can provide the people of those areas with a means to protest against higher level decisions. Some might even claim that the media have become the saviour of at least some of the campaigns for without their support little might otherwise be achieved.

NOTES

1 In all instances the government has acceded to the society's demands. Wales, for example, now has its own Welsh language television channel, S4C.
2 See the discussion in chapter 9.
3 Community Councils are grass-roots councils – the equivalent of the English parish council.
4 See Davies (1985), especially pp. 148–60, for the role of the media in pressure group politics.
5 There is no rift or hostility between the Welsh speaking population (almost all of whom are bilingual) and those who speak only English.
6 However, see chapter 9 for two other case studies, including a Welsh locality, where a strong sense of community appears to play an insignificant role in stimulating political participation.

Conclusion

An examination of the two sets of case studies reported in chapters 5 and 6 shows that the difference between them are sufficient to require that one should exercise due caution when mounting comparisons. Nevertheless, whilst these differences may restrict the possibility of a detailed, point-by-point comparison, they also help to suggest certain reflections on the possible links between the process of mobilisation and the nature of the locality.

It should first be noted that the decisions studied are not exactly of the same type. The contribution of the French team dealt with mobilisation movements of a reactive kind, i.e. those which opposed a specific type of decision linked to large-scale public works projects. For its part, the British team studied a protest movement opposed to a socio-economic decision and an organisation whose activity was directed much more positively towards the defence of a cause: the use of the Welsh language.

No doubt this difference in the nature of the decisions analysed goes a long way to explain why, in France, mobilisation against public works was, in three cases out of four, purely local. Proximity to the problem played an essential part, and this may help to explain why the movements studied appealed to so few people. The number of people who were potentially concerned in any direct way was, by definition, limited.

This was not entirely the case in Britain where, whilst the challenges to milk-quotas and the defence of the Welsh language were certainly localised movements, they also had wider implications and dimensions beyond the purely local. The same is true of the anti-nuclear movements in France, where the potential public of those concerned is far greater than is implied by the criterion of whether one lives close to a nuclear plant. Some movements thus have a wider potential basis than others.

However, despite the differences in the decisions and the movements studied in France and Britain, a number of relatively common elements do appear, on the basis of which it is possible to suggest some comparisons.

Protest movements are initially formed, and act, outside the framework of the political parties, even if, in some cases, party organisations attempt subsequently to take over or exploit for their own long-term political or electoral purposes the discontent engendered by some decisions. Hence, it seems likely that protest movements allow the expression of needs and demands which are not taken into consideration in other ways. Their role is to complement other organisations (political parties, trade unions, associations, etc.) in helping to represent specific interests and aspirations. Given the small size of the parties at local level, and the fact that their role is mainly an electoral one, the part played by protest movements in allowing people to participate in the process of articulating their interests is not insignificant, and needs to be emphasised.

Moreover, the movements studied had as their fundamental aim to bring to the attention of the authorities, either at local or national level, an issue judged to be important, and even vital, by the population which had been mobilised around it. The need to take protest action, even of a radical nature if necessary, arose in most cases out of the fact that decisions had been taken, often by authorities outside the locality, without adequate consultation through the established channels. Normal processes having proved unsatisfactory, the local people affected felt impelled to resort to alternative modes of action. Very few were actually ready to act in a violent manner. The extent to which people are constrained by local norms in taking various forms of action is a matter worth further exploration. However, in neither country was direct action excluded as a means of gaining publicity for the local feelings of frustration. The actions which were undertaken were intended to ensure that the problem was placed on the political agenda, since this was a necessary precondition for it to be considered and dealt with by the public authorities. The protest movements managed to achieve this, thanks particularly to the active help of the media, whose role is emphasised in both the French and the British cases.

In order to attract the attention of the authorities, the movements had at their disposal a whole range or repertoire of courses of action, from the most legal and institutional pressure tactics to direct action and even violence which, in certain conditions, appeared to be regarded as a legitimate means of making their voice heard.

Finally, it is worth considering the relationship which may exist between the process of mobilisation and various types of local community (see Oberschall 1973: 118–24). In Britain, the opposition to the establishment of a policy of milk quotas and the defence of the Welsh language both appear to have been rooted in a relatively strong sense of social solidarity linked to a pre-existing identity which is seen in terms of 'community'.

This identity is both socio-economic (a milieu which is still semi-rural and relatively traditional, with economic activity based on the family farm) and socio-cultural. It seems to be the basis of a feeling of belonging to a local community which has quite a high level of integration, a level, however, which is felt to be threatened, and in danger.

This does not seem to be the case in France, where we find sets of circumstances which are largely lacking in any identity able to serve as a reference or basis for collective action. Even in the two rural cantons affected by the consequences of mobilisation, there is no sign of any such feeling of belonging to a relatively well-integrated and supportive community. For various geographic, economic and demographic reasons, these cantons seem to lack any proper identity which can act as a principle binding them together. At the same time, the decisions which cause controversy are not seen as fundamentally challenging traditional activities.

These factors perhaps affect the nature and the intensity of the solidarity developed and in the French cases they give rise to activity of a more instrumental or utilitarian character. Insofar as decisions do not seriously threaten this sense of identity, which is in any event not fully developed and not very intense, local solidarity appears to be less strong. The phenomenon might then help to explain, in the case of France, why, in the absence of any close-knit community or any belief in its role as a mutually-supportive entity,[1] the movements studied tended, more than in Britain, to seek the support of other groups.

The British cases therefore differ in two respects from the French in that there is a conjunction of a relatively well-integrated social milieu and a challenge to decisions which are seen as affecting the very existence of the cultural identity and economic activity of the community.

It should however be emphasised that these specific characteristics may be due to the particular situation and not to any unusual national feature. In all probability, a study of opposition to milk quotas in some more typical departments of France, or movements for the defence of regional languages, would have led to similar, or perhaps even identical, conclusions. From this point of view, though in the context of a different issue area, it seems, for example, that anti-nuclear protest has been stronger, more virulent and more active in regions which have a degree of cultural identity (Alsace, Brittany).

Consequently, where there is a social milieu affected by decisions which are seen as a threat to the very existence of what is experienced as a community, the identity and the cohesion of that milieu (and these may be social, cultural, socio-economic, ideological and even religious in nature) might be factors which favour stronger and more intense political mobilisation, or more active and longer-lasting forms.

NOTE

1 Whether this community does or does not exist 'objectively' is an entirely minor consideration, insofar as the fact that the population believes in the existence of the community is enough to make it a living reality, with the practical results which this produces.

PART IV LOCAL ELITES, GROUPS AND CITIZENS

Introduction

In chapters 7 and 8 we examine the role of the elected local leadership in France and Britain. Local councillors are situated, in both countries, at the point where the various local political forces interact. Councillors play both in democratic theory and, as we shall see, in local political practice a number of different parts.

In the first instance the local council is the body which 'receives' the political demands which are generated in the locality by individuals and groups. Councillors are the targets at which much participatory activity is directed. This may be a matter of an individual contacting the councillor in order to obtain some objective such as assistance with a housing problem or with a building permit. Or it may be a group which seeks to engage the support of the councillor for some project which is for the benefit of the collectivity as a whole or of a particular section of local society. Examples would be campaigns for improvements to the local environment or for the provision of a community centre or place of worship for an ethnic or religious minority.

These are instances of the councillors as recipients of relatively spontaneous demands. Councillors, however, also have more active parts to play in the local political process. They do not merely respond even to these spontaneous demands. They have to act as 'brokers' seeking to reconcile demands which may be in direct conflict with one another, for example if the demand for a religious community centre faces objections from local residents, or more indirectly through competition between projects for financial resources. More positively, councils are themselves actors who initiate policies and set the agenda for the locality. Many of the pressures directed at councillors by individuals and groups will be in reaction to initiatives from the council. Instead of a picture of pure ascending democratic participation, a more realistic representation of local politics would show also a descending process whereby the council in effect shapes the structure of much individual and group activity. This may extend so far as the councillors mobilising groups in support of policies and stimulating them to become active within the local political system.

The councillors are, therefore, centrally involved in the three classic processes of articulation, aggregation and integration. The articulation of demands is normally recognised as the task of groups who express demands and transmit them to the political authorities. However, as has been suggested, councillors play a more complex double role as both receivers and as articulators and transmitters of demands. As the targets and recipients of demands the councillors are involved in the process of aggregating demands into a package of policies on which policy decisions can be taken. In converting policy into practice the councillors (or at least those who play central roles in policy-making) are not merely engaged in a decision-making process internal to the council. They also have to mobilise support and cooperation from the major political forces in the locality – the strategic groups, political parties and the administration which not only puts policy into effect, but also normally exerts considerable influence.

The involvement of groups in the local decision-making process constitutes a part of the process of local integration. The actions of the councillors in responding to groups and also in consulting them and drawing them into the public arena contribute to the accommodation of diverse local interests. This is achieved through the distributive capacity of the council as it provides funds and resources to promote the objectives of certain groups and denies them to others. The councillors, of course, play a political role in this process. The distribution of resources is in part intended to channel support towards the councillors and their political groups and to divert challenges to their authority. In this manner the decisions of the council (what is 'supplied' in response to the 'demand') form one of the factors which determine the future balance of power in the locality and this in turn feeds back into the formulation of new demands.

In both France and Britain a variety of groups – social and sporting groups, trade unions, charitable groups handling welfare problems, associations of parents of school children – act as intermediary bodies between the individual and the local authority. The chapters will look at the processes by which they bring their interests to the attention of councillors, and the extent to which they can claim to be influential initiators of local policies. One way in which group interests attract the attention of the councillors is through interlocking memberships of groups and council. Councillors can be integrated into the political scene through their linkages with the local groups. These linkages help to root the councillors in their local ground, thereby reinforcing the connections which they may have with the local population by virtue of their length of residence or of their sharing similar social and economic experiences through occupation or social class.

The nature and extent of these social and group linkages with the community may be expected to affect the capacity of the councillors to understand and to reflect local needs and demands. The two chapters look at the 'agendas' of the population and of the councillors in this light. However, the councillors' views are also affected by other factors. The local government administration shapes policy, partly as a result of its statutory responsibilities and partly as a consequence of its own direct contacts with the public in day-to-day dealings. Councillors can also be moved by national and local party considerations in formulating their priorities. These factors influence the extent to which the agendas of the councillors will reflect those which emerge from local individuals and groups. As both chapters seek to show, councillors are not merely representative of local forces; they also seek to reconcile forces and to create a greater degree of integration.

Each chapter rests on two case studies of local authorities combined with a study of a wider sample of local councillors. One of the localities in each study is situated within a larger conurbation and has a council elected on party lines; the other is a smaller town with a non-partisan council. The town of Cenon within the Communauté Urbaine of Bordeaux has a population of 23,500 and contains areas of both private housing and of less expensive high-rise flats. It faces acute social problems and difficulties over the quality of housing. The council is a stronghold of the socialists and the parties of the left are deeply rooted in the network of local groups and associations. The counterpart in the British study is an inner part of the borough of Rochdale within (at the time of the study) the area of the Greater Manchester County. Rochdale itself is a town of around 98,000 inhabitants which grew up with the cotton industry of the nineteenth century but which has in recent years suffered severe industrial decline, with consequent unemployment. Chapter 8 concentrates on the area known as Spotland which is near the centre of the town. Like Cenon, but to a much greater extent, the area includes a substantial population of immigrants and their locally born families. Apart from attracting employment the prime problems concern the quality of housing. Politically, Rochdale was, at the time of the study, controlled by an alliance of Conservatives and Liberals, although the single largest party on the Council was Labour. Spotland itself was represented by Liberals.

The other pair of localities are the towns of Blanquefort near Bordeaux and of Oswestry near the Welsh border. Blanquefort has a population of just under 10,000. It has been an agricultural area with market gardening and vineyards but has grown rapidly in recent years by attracting new industry, notably a Ford factory, to its industrial estate. Its main problems are those of developing both the infrastructure and the superstructure of cultural and leisure provisions to meet its rapid expansion. The council is apolitical in the sense that only five representatives declare a party allegiance. The council is nevertheless opposed to the left. Oswestry is similar in size to Blanquefort with a population of 12,000 which, however, has remained very stable. It differs in being isolated from any large urban centre. It is a typical market town serving the agricultural area which surrounds it. It was formerly also a railway centre but, with the closure of the railway and of a large nearby army camp, it has been faced with the need to attract employment to the new industrial estates built by the council for light industry. As in Blanquefort, the council in Oswestry is largely non-partisan with 18 out of the 29 councillors describing themselves as having no affiliation to national parties, though for the most part they would be Conservative sympathisers.

The French study rests primarily on 55 semi-structured interviews with councillors in the two communes. In order to place these in context the chapter also draws on materials from a much wider sample of councillors. Similarly, whilst chapter 8 makes particular reference to the two areas of Spotland and Oswestry, it depends heavily on a wider body of materials from lengthy, structured interviews with 60 councillors (50 from borough or district councils and the rest from county councils, town and parish councils) in six localities in England, Wales and Scotland. The councillors form nearly a fifth of a wider sample of local leaders in the six areas, enabling some comparisons to be made between the experiences of councillors and non-councillors.

Whilst the French research was more qualitative in tone and the British investigation more quantitative there were important affinities resulting from the use of a number of comparable questions in both sets of interviews. Although comparisons cannot be exact, nevertheless the fact that there were elements in common in the methods employed and some resemblances between the localities studied enables patterns to emerge which can be considered together.

7

Councillors, issue agendas and political action in two French towns

RICHARD BALME

In their ordinary day-to-day political life, communes reflect three essential features. First and foremost, they form discrete territorial areas in which a number of social, economic and cultural activities take place. The communes also provide administrative services, through which they interact to a greater or lesser degree with the various areas of their environment. They are, finally, a political arena in which the parties are increasingly competing in order to gain positions of influence. These aspects are similarly manifested in local policy-making. This is conducted in the name of a constructed and identifiable local entity, and provides a certain number of services, thereby defining the various sectors of the communal administration. It is also guided by party political ideologies which, indeed, can structure the general pattern of local political activity.

The role of the council in the integration of the local community can be analysed along three main dimensions of its activity. In these terms, one can distinguish here between a territorial dimension (representing the commune and its various socio-spatial zones); a functional dimension (the various tasks for which the council is responsible and which are formalised by the professionals); and finally a more partisan dimension (involving the representation of different views and the formation of strategies for action along party political lines). It is the combination of these key dimensions which enables conflicts to be settled, and the divergent interests resulting from the effects of local council policy to be reconciled.

What is the respective importance of these three areas of action, each with its own inherent logic? And how are they articulated in a concrete sense in the daily work of the councils? In the present study, we shall use essentially two levels of analysis to deal with these questions:
- by what criteria and by what means are individuals recruited on to the council? What principally motivates them, and how do their motives come to be what they are?
- how do the elected representatives subsequently carry out their political

task of taking account of the demands of the population in the decision-making process?

In analysing the types of involvement of councillors, we need to distinguish 'objective' factors, such as social characteristics, membership of organisations and recruitment procedures, from more 'subjective' ones, such as how involvement is motivated and conceived. Taken together, both these sets of factors will then enable us to characterise the process of political socialisation that is in operation.

Means of access to the council

A social profile of the councillors. We can situate the social position of the representatives through a number of characteristics. In terms of gender and age, the majority of councillors are men (43 men to 12 women) and of mature years (the average age is 49). They have also lived in the commune for a long time (on average 23 years). Their level of education is relatively high – 64% have qualifications equivalent to the *baccalaureat* or above, and 42% have had higher education. Most also have family responsibilities (75% have at least one child) and belong to political parties (62%). In Cenon, all the councillors were members of political parties whereas in Blanquefort we found only five in this position. Conversely, those who practise religion were concentrated at Blanquefort (56% of the councillors). We can, therefore, already see here two rather different models of local political socialisation emerging: a 'political' model controlled by a party political apparatus and a 'parochial' model in which religious commitments appear, alongside other factors, more important in providing the avenue to council positions. Finally, it should be noted that the turnover of those involved is relatively high. Indeed, as 58% of all the councillors interviewed were elected for the first time in 1983, there was a considerable change in council membership in both localities. However, the same majority party or grouping remains in power.

Analysis of the socio-professional origins of the councillors brings out a further set of tendencies, as shown in table 7.1. Thus we can see that two social groups are over-represented in relation to their size in the working population at large, the first being the managerial staff and higher intellectual professions (38%) and the second, the 'intermediate' professions (33%). Conversely, councillors who are workers (7%) and employees (11%) are very few relative to their position in the wider social structure.

Table 7.1. *A socio-professional analysis of councillors and citizens (%)*

Socio-professional category*	Councillors in Cenon and Blanquefort (N = 55)	Working population in the Communauté Urbaine (N**)
1 Farmers	3.6	0.7
2 Artisans, businessmen, factory managers	5.4	7.4
3 Managers and higher intellectual professions	38.2	9.6
4 Intermediate professions	32.7	15.2
5 Employees	10.9	22.7
6 Workers	7.3	34.4

* As defined by the revised (1982) scheme of the Institut National de la Statistique et des Etudes Economiques, Paris. For example, the 'managers and higher intellectual professions' category covers professions such as engineers, teachers, journalists, and business managers; the 'intermediate professions' refer to junior school teachers, nurses, technicians; and 'employees' include salesmen, public officials, and office staff.
** Census information.

The concentration of participation and office-holding at the higher end of the social scale therefore clearly indicates the skewing effect of social status.

However, this 'vertical' bias does not operate on its own. It also intersects with a 'horizontal' bias based on the sector of employment. Councillors are disproportionately employed in the public sector. There is a further tendency for participation in the council to be more particularly marked among those working in the public sector who earn average or higher salaries.

The examination of a broader sample of local representatives taking in nine communes (as in the third column of table 7.2) enables us to develop this analysis.[1] The tendencies which were noticed previously are confirmed since the group showing the greatest over-representation compared with its size within the adult population at large (in table 7.1) is that of the managerial and higher intellectual professions category with a three-fold increase (30.1% as against 9.6%). This pattern is somewhat less pronounced in the case of the intermediate professions (26% compared to 15.2%) and is even lower, though still positive, in the case of artisans, businessmen and factory managers (8.7% to 5.4%). Conversely, employees are only two-thirds the size amongst the councillors that they are in the working population at large. However, it is the workers who show the greatest drop in representation between the two levels: their 10.3% share of elected individuals is less than a third of the 34.4% for citizens.

Table 7.2. *The socio-professional make-up of councils in relation to the political orientation of the municipality (%)*

Socio-professional category*	Left-wing municipality (N = 177)	Right-wing municipality (moderate group) (N = 65)	Overall sample (N = 242)
1 Farmers	0.0	4.6	1.2
2 Artisans, businessmen, factory managers	6.8	13.8	8.7
3 Managers and higher intellectual professions	27.8	36.9	30.1
(a) *Public sector managers in civil service, intellectual professions*	15.8	13.8	15.3
(b) *Private sector factory managers*	6.8	21.5	10.7
4 Intermediate professions	26.0	26.1	26.0
(a) *Public sector teaching, health service or civil service*	11.3	7.7	10.3
(b) *Private sector technicians*	6.8	13.8	8.7
5 Employees	17.5	9.2	15.2
6 Workers	14.1	0.0	10.3

* For definitions see table 7.1.; remaining cases to 100% not classified

The way in which this broader sample is made up enables us also to compare the composition of the councils according to the partisan complexion of the municipalities[2] (see columns 2 and 3 of table 7.2). A comparison of these two distributions brings out, first, a marked difference in the social profiles of right-wing and left-wing communes. The one exception, however, is social category four, the intermediate professions, which are almost exactly the same. Otherwise, in right-wing communes, the 'higher' social categories – including farmers, but also artisans, businessmen and factory managers, and managers and higher intellectual professions – record higher proportions compared with the overall average. Equally, in the same type of commune, categories 5 (Employees) and especially 6 (Workers) are clearly less numerous. Conversely, in left-wing communes, there are more employee and worker councillors than in right-wing areas, while numbers in the higher categories are distinctly lower. In other words, while there is a higher representation of the upper strata in right-wing municipalities the opposite is the case for left-wing councils.

If we now examine in more detail the sub-divisions within categories 3

Table 7.3. *Councillors, employment sector* and partisan orientation of the municipality*

	Left-wing municipalities		Right-wing municipalities (moderate group)		Overall sample	
	%	(N)	%	(N)	%	(N)
Public/para-public sector Managers and intermediate professions	27.1	(48)	21.5	(14)	25.6	(62)
Private sector Managers and factory technicians	13.6	(24)	35.3	(23)	19.4	(47)

* Socio-professional categories 3 and 4 only (see table 7.2).

and 4, we find that there is a difference according to employment sector (see table 7.3). Thus, the public and para-public sector professions[3] are rather better represented in left-wing than in right-wing municipal councils. On the other hand, those working in private industry seem much more likely to get elected (or to stand) in right-wing municipalities. In fact, they are nearly three times more numerous in conservative than in socialist communes.

The effect of social status in distorting patterns of elite participation as compared with citizens is, therefore, further influenced by the partisan orientation of municipalities. In the case of left-wing communes, particularly, the bias towards upper status councillors is partially, though not entirely, off-set. But, equally, the matter is further complicated by the employment sector. If considered as a source of elite socialisation or recruitment, those individuals working in the public or para-public sector clearly rise to greater prominence in left-wing councils. Similarly, there is a linkage between right-wing involvement and the private sector.[4]

Previous group membership as a factor in councillors' socialisation. Councillors obviously do not come into being overnight. They acquire and develop a willingness to become involved in council matters as a result of a process of political socialisation. This willingness is based on a growth in their political skills which then leads them to want to take on these offices. This socialisation occurs through previous memberships in political, social, professional or trade-union organisations outside the council.

The most common form of membership is in interest groups and associations, in which 82% of councillors in Cenon and Blanquefort were involved. More than half of them (53%) stated that they had belonged to at least two such associations. Recreational clubs were mentioned most frequently (including sporting and cultural associations such as festival committees and similar groups organising local events). Their importance in building up networks of local influence is something which deserves to be emphasised. Next in frequency come parent–teacher groups and associations for extra-school activities. This demonstrates the importance of the school in local life as well as its political relevance. After these we find, in order, associations for social assistance and for supporting the aged; associations for the defence of residents' interests (tenants and home-owners); and finally, at the bottom, associations of veterans and of former deportees.

The work of these associations demonstrates that they have several functions. They perform a socialisation function (for example, in the case of school-based and recreational groups); they offer collective solidarity (as in voluntary social work and support for the aged), they also have an expressive role (organising events which display local life and activity); and they play an essential integrating role in the community, giving it a basic identity. The extent of participation by councillors in these associations is in itself proof, therefore, both of their keenness to be involved in organisational life, but also of their attachment to the local community. Moreover, these associations are also the place where councillors can gain an apprenticeship in the power structure of the community, where, indeed, they make their first contacts with elected representatives, where they come to identify the local power-holders and the networks which they have built up, and where they learn about political procedures and issues. These associations are, therefore, an important element in the socialisation process. It is largely through them that councillors build up their first impressions of the political map of the town.

Membership of a political party is also very important, involving in the two communes, 64% of the councillors. We should note, however, that the figure varies enormously between the two – 100% at Cenon as against only 25% (or 5 cases) at Blanquefort. Finally, 58% of all the councillors belong to professional organisations, most often as members of employees' trade unions (50.9%), but also, in four cases, of agricultural or employers' organisations.

The most characteristic feature, however, is, without doubt, the extent to which councillors accumulate these various memberships. (The instances where councillors are involved exclusively in a single organisation enable us to isolate 'pure' types of socialisation. But these are relatively uncommon since they affect less than a third of the total number of councillors.) On this general basis, we can distinguish four patterns. First there is a type of 'relational' socialisation (the one case of a councillor with no involvement in outside bodies, but who knew the mayor personally). Secondly, we can define a form of strictly party-based socialisation (2 cases). Thirdly, there is an equivalent process of strictly trade union socialisation (2 cases). This particular 'pure' group, however, is outnumbered by the fourth type – socialisation through interest groups and associations (12 cases). This last type provides a pattern of recruitment to the council which is almost entirely locally-based.

In total, 20 councillors, or 36% of the sample, are involved in nonpartisan groups. Despite the apparent extent of such non-party social participation we must, however, be circumspect in interpreting it. For, even if councillors are not necessarily party activists, there is at least a minimal interaction with the partisan dimension of politics, leading them to take up policy positions by reference to the stance of the parties.

Political parties, therefore, play a considerable role in creating this willingness to become involved in council politics, and party membership (involving 58% of councillors) is, in most cases, additional to other forms of activity. The significance of this partisan involvement may, however, vary a great deal. At Cenon, the party is almost entirely merged into a wider network of social activity which the local associations have set up in the various neighbourhoods of the town, and which forms a pre-existing framework for action. Thus, involvement in social life and involvement in the party tend to become one and the same thing. Yet membership in a party remains virtually a requirement for election to the council. Furthermore, it is through the party that the council's resources are mobilised. Equally, involvement in a party and the wider network of social organisations enables the councillor to develop relationships with the local citizenry at a personal level. Such memberships, therefore, are both instrumental and communitarian, the two aspects often being linked in an intimate way. For example, one councillor who belongs to an association justified his party membership by his feelings of friendship and solidarity with other leading elected representatives. His social activity was transformed into a political engagement largely out of a sense of solidarity with the elected representatives resulting in his joining the party after his election to the council.

In Blanquefort, on the other hand, only the minority socialists espouse overt party political commitments. For them, involvement in a party depends more on non-local factors and hence takes on largely an expressive function. Indeed, in comparing Cenon with Blanquefort, we might argue that the more thoroughly partisan a council is, the more party membership itself takes on a local, instrumental and communitarian character. Conversely, where few members of the council have partisan affiliations, the more such ties take on an extra-local character – and the

Table 7.4. *Circumstances of initial involvement in the council by type of organisational membership (%)*

Main membership outside council	Initial form of involvement		Total
	Approached	Volunteered	
Party	6	18	24
Social club/association	15	4	19
Trade union	2	0	2
Professional	3	4	7
Total	26	26	52

more party activity in the town hall fulfils purely expressive needs. Thus, as in the latter case, adherence to a party may be simply a way of showing support for one or another of the national political parties. At the other extreme, on the other hand, it may instead form part of an instrumental strategy in the locality in order to defend the interests of some pressure group. In all of this, the mayor and his personal network have an important role in determining which of these alternatives holds in his or her particular commune.

The analysis of the immediate circumstances which lead councillors to involve themselves in politics enables us to characterise more precisely their participation in the work of the council itself, and to assess the main factors which encouraged them or created difficulties. As is shown in table 7.4, the circumstances surrounding the decisions of future councillors first to get involved in running for office may in fact differ considerably. In this respect, we can distinguish between those whose involvement resulted from approaches from outside and those whose decision to stand took a more voluntary form – a result of the councillors' own interests that arose either from some position they held within their local party or simply from their own personal aspirations. The overall numbers in each of the two basic types are the same.

The extent to which council involvement originally resulted from an outside approach or alternatively was largely self-initiated varies according to the kinds of organisations, apart from the council, to which the councillors belong.[5] Of those 24 councillors whose main previous organisational experience occurred within a political party, as many as 18 (or 75%) were mainly self-motivated. Conversely, 71% (or 20 ex 28) of those who had held office in clubs and interest groups and unions (or to a lesser extent professional bodies) were brought into the council as a result of an outside approach. Furthermore, where the elected representatives tried to encourage people to put themselves forward as candidates, many of these efforts were directed at non-party activists.

The numerical importance of such approaches puts into perspective any overly democratic view of participation at local level. There is little competition from would-be councillors for places on the lists of candidates for the council elections.[6] As further evidence of the relative lack of people willing to stand for election at this level, as many as 16 councillors (29%) stated that they had hesitated before agreeing to put their names forward.

Several councillors also mentioned attempts to dissuade them from standing for office. Most of these were made by their families or by professional colleagues. But some also had a more political origin in that candidates from the other party on occasion tried to 'see off' the future elected representative. The most flagrant case was that of a councillor who held office in one of the communes, and who was pressurised by the head office of his firm. The initiative in this instance was local (coming from the opposing party), but the pressure was then relayed through an elected national representative and the management of his firm in Paris. Besides having an anecdotal interest, this also illustrates how national resources can be mobilised to bear on a local political matter, and how the professional milieu of the representative may be used to restrain his or her political activities.

The reasons given for finally deciding to stand for office were primarily the feeling that the councillor was pursuing a previous history of public activism to its logical conclusion. It was hence a matter of extending that activity in a new direction. However, the persuasive efforts of existing elected representatives or other party activists were also explicitly acknowledged.

These factors taken as a whole, therefore, bring out the range of factors operating as agents of political socialisation for these activists (especially a party background and personal relationships with elected representatives). But it is also important to note that organisations do not seem directly to have exerted their socialising influence on councillors. Rather, they rely on the networks of formal and personal relationships whose effects in stimulating activism appear to be a necessary counter to the restraints and pressures arising from the private, family and professional spheres.

Motivations and perceptions: subjective factors in the participation of councillors

If there are certain organisational conditions leading councillors to stand for office, there are also more subjective interests and values that are significant. When questioned as to the main reasons which, in their view, made council work important and worthwhile, councillors expressed their answers in a variety of local, personal or party terms. An interest in local non-party matters was the most frequently mentioned (43%). Amongst these we can distinguish those responses that were mainly instrumental in character (30%), such as promoting social or associated activity; representing a social category (workers, farmers or factory managers); helping with the problems of specific groups of people (the young, the aged); and carrying out specific projects. The other type of answer was couched in more general terms and concerned their role in helping to develop the whole locality (13%) through economic expansion.

Another way of looking at motivation is the distinction between collectivist as against personal modes of expression. Thus, in 20% of cases, the councillors saw their involvement in terms of party-based activity, such as achieving party objectives, implementing the ideals or ideology of the party and representing the party, or opposing the majority party, on the local council. In contrast, more individualistic motives were mentioned in 37% of the responses. These related essentially to a desire to achieve personal fulfilment (an interest in running the council, the possibility of making contacts with other elected representatives or with residents). However, there were also more clearly altruistic factors such as being useful to the community or helping the local population, and those that were perhaps idealistic – demonstrating personal convictions, for example, or translating them into practice. Overall these latter individual and non-party rationales seemed much more important than partisan considerations in prompting a continuing interest in council work.

Such attitudes, however, have to be set in the context of the motives which the councillors claimed had originally led them to seek active involvement in running the affairs of the town. This allows in turn a more detailed analysis of their views as to their subsequent outlooks on their work. The most powerful initial motive turned out to be a desire to become part of the power network on the council (i.e. the mayor and his team). This was mentioned by 41% of the respondents and was therefore more important than factors associated with specific issues and problems (34%), or even the simple desire to get involved in politics (25%). Such evidence, indeed, is a measure of the importance of networks of personal relationships, and of personalised forms of interaction, as influences on recruitment into local political life.

Involvement in the council can either reinforce activism by adding further to an already established accumulation of offices or limit it by restricting the number of these organisational memberships that the councillor feels he can take on. One measure of the extent to which council work precludes these other activities is the number of councillors who chose to give up their previous commitments. In fact, this was the case for only a minority of councillors (25%), and it applied even less to those who were involved in party political work (a mere 2 out of 12). On the other hand, 37 councillors (or 67%) chose to retain their previous commitments.[7] Moreover, of these, 21 councillors (or 38% of the total) also said that their involvement in the town's affairs had led them to take on additional external commitments. Thus, those councillors whose official work led them to maintain, or to take on further commitments were far more numerous than those who were led to restrict such activities. This was particularly the case for those whose involvement in the council arose from party considerations.

The new commitments undertaken after joining the council involved, in nine cases, responsibilities in local social clubs and associations. In this way, taking an active part in running the town strengthened social participation within the locality. We also found two cases where the councillors in question joined a party subsequent to becoming a member of the council. But it was above all within the wider local political system itself that these new commitments were taken on. These included becoming assistants to the mayor (*adjoints*), or councillors in the Communauté Urbaine, or holders of other similar official positions. In this way, membership of the council led to further personal involvement at both higher and lower levels within the local political and governmental apparatus.

2 FROM THE AGGREGATION OF DEMANDS TO THE INTEGRATION OF THE COMMUNE

How do councillors process demands on a day-to-day basis? To examine this we shall look first at the structure of the local political agenda and the way it is shaped by citizen participation. We will then consider the various ways in which demands are aggregated and handled and see how the processes of integration in the local community are in consequence affected.

The shaping of the local political agenda

The local political agenda covers the whole range of questions which are defined as problems requiring attention by the local politico-administrative system. The approach followed by Verba and Nie (1972) puts the emphasis on the degree of congruence or agreement between the views of the councillors, the activists and the population at large as to which are the important local issues. Here, however, we have chosen an approach which focuses more on actual behaviour. The shape of the local agenda is established by ascertaining the views of the councillors as to the most important categories of problem facing the commune, but also the fre-

Table 7.5. *The shape of the local political agendas[a] in Cenon and Blanquefort (%)*

	Agenda of problems[b] (n=119)	Agenda of contacts[c] (n=59)	Agenda of involvement[d] (n=46)
Social problems	26.1	27.1	15.2
Social security	*16.8*	*20.3*	*6.5*
Young people	*5.9*	*1.7*	*2.2*
The old	*3.4*	*5.1*	*6.5*
Urban problems	25.2	23.7	32.6
Unemployment and jobs	18.5	18.7	13.0
The local economy	10.1	0.0	2.2
Educational problems	8.4	13.5	13.0
Leisure, sport, culture, social life	7.6	16.9	17.4
Law and order	4.2	1.7	0.0

[a] The responses are expressed in percentages; several responses were possible, and only the first three items mentioned by each respondent are shown in the table.
[b] 'What, in your view, are the most important problems in your commune?'
[c] 'As a local elected representative, on what matters in particular is your help sought?' (Frequency of approach)
[d] 'Can you give an example of a problem in which you are personally involved in trying to find a solution? (Try to offer a significant example.)' (Frequency of involvement)

quency with which they are actually contacted about these problems by the population at large and, finally, the frequency with which the councillors become actively involved in seeking solutions for the problems.

This approach offers two particular advantages. It is based essentially on the 'formal' agenda (Cobb and Elder, 1972),[8] and provides a possible measure of the degree of congruence between the actual work of the representatives and the active concerns of the participatory elements within the population. It thus provides us in a more direct way with some estimate of the effects of participation on the decisions made by the local political authorities. Furthermore, when we compare the issues over which the elected representatives have become actively involved with those which they say are particularly important, we can identify the nature of their contribution to, and their influence in, the running of the commune.

When we consider the policy priorities of the councillors, as set out in the first column of table 7.5, the most significant issues were the social problems of helping the underprivileged (26.1% of responses). It was also about these problems that they were most often contacted (27.1%). These problems were, however, less often mentioned when they were questioned about those they were personally involved in (15.2%). Undoubtedly, one reason for this is the important role played by the welfare services and the existence of regular administrative procedures for tackling such problems. This leads the elected representatives to work on the basis of a division of labour and to specialise in particular policy areas.[9]

Second in importance, according to the councillors, were urban problems (housing, highways, transport, amenities), with 25.2% of the responses. The representatives were also equally often contacted about these matters (23.7%). But, in terms of their actual involvement, these problems were the ones in which they claimed to intervene most frequently of all (32.6%). Similarly, the problems of leisure, including sports, culture and social activity, moved up from sixth place (7.6%) on the councillors' list of important issues facing the locality, to second place in terms of the frequency with which action was taken (17.4%). Thus, in comparison with the place they occupied in the minds of the representatives and among the demands expressed by the citizens, residential problems as a whole (urban issues, leisure and education) seem to have been 'over-represented' in terms of councillor activities. Conversely, employment problems, which come relatively high on the councillors' list of priorities (18.5%), and about which they are as frequently consulted (18.7%), were somewhat less often the subject of action on their part (13%). In this sense, therefore, they were not perhaps treated as fully by the council as might have been expected. If this is a fair inference, the reasons may be that, in the first place, such problems are difficult to handle at the local level and, secondly, that there are obvious difficulties in dealing with individual cases of unemployment, which thus limit the councillors' capacity to act.

Two points, in particular, might be made about the way certain problems get onto the agenda. The first concerns the local economy – the problems of revenue and of the development of local resources. Although these questions clearly concerned the councillors (10.1% in table 7.5), they were not, it seems, the object of a single approach by local citizens, and only a very small proportion of the elected representatives indeed were actively involved in finding solutions for them (2.2%). This would suggest that problems affecting collective goods (such as the future of the local economy) are dealt with by a relatively small group of people centred on the mayor. The absence of citizens' demands in this sphere underlines by contrast the private and divisible character of goods which are more typically the subject matter of their participation at the local level.

The second point relates to the problem of law and order. The level of concern amongst the councillors (4.2%) was again not related to the number of contacts on the issue (only 1 case) nor did it provide a single instance of councillors getting involved. This is almost certainly an example of agenda-building 'from above'. In other words, the prominence of the issue in national politics leads councillors to take up symbolic positions on the matter even though they have no relevance to the actual concerns of the locality and its population.

These two types of issue thus appear on the council's agenda without there being any apparent interaction concerning them as between the elected representatives and the population. For this reason, approaches to the study of political participation which focus on the passage from individual citizen participation to the collective political agenda and, thence, to the production of decisions, seem to represent only a part of the complex reality of the local political process.[10] Such a focus does nonetheless have the merit of making clear that participation is essentially associated with obtaining individual and divisible advantages, for the sorts of reasons presented in discussions of the 'free rider' or 'collective action' problem (Olson 1971). It also highlights the particularised nature of the interests which are often expressed through the processes of local participation.

As indicated in table 7.5, the shape of the political agenda is marked by the prominence of social and urban problems.[11] However, as the active involvement of councillors was more pronounced in the latter area, it seems that their role in integrating society within the commune is dominated by their role as representatives for their particular area. This may well result from a combination of different factors. It is affected, first, by whether the matter falls within the responsibilities of the elected representatives, the communal administration, or other local authorities. Secondly, it arises from the varying degrees to which problems are amenable to treatment at the local level. Finally, it is affected by the differential ability of individuals in each issue area to express their demands.

It should be emphasised, however, that there is an overall congruence between the priorities of the elected representatives and the frequency with which they are contacted about problems. In other words, the issue concerns of those who actively participate, and the priorities of the elected representatives, are relatively close to each other. On the other hand, there is only a much looser fit between the councillors' actual involvement in particular issue areas and the demands that citizens express. Thus, social problems and unemployment receive a lower level of councillors' attention than would be implied by the pattern of demands from below. On the other hand, in the cases of leisure activities, urban problems and education, a relatively high degree of citizen participation leads councillors to become more involved than their own perceptions of priorities would lead one to expect. In short, the effect of mass participation differs according to the issue areas under consideration. But in understanding the divergences that do exist, we must be aware, as will become apparent, of the importance that organisational and other structural constraints have in shaping council activity and, not least, in limiting the council's capacity to act.

The processing of demands

Besides the factors which shape the political agenda, we need also to look at the processes whereby citizen demands are considered and needs assessed within the political sphere. First we can look at the way in which demands are articulated by analysing the circumstances or sources which led to action by the councillors. Three types of such circumstances can be discerned.

The most frequently mentioned source of personal involvement by the representatives was an approach from an individual (19 examples). This would include people looking for a job or seeking advice on social security problems. Similarly, residential problems, such as housing and road maintenance, come under this heading. Even some strictly collective problems may be expressed in a particularised way through individual initiatives, for example safety at school exits, the need for a crèche or for a supplementary bus service. Finally, councillors are sometimes contacted as a last resort, to obtain the reversal of a decision, such as a building permit previously refused, or an exemption from a town by-law – for example, one governing opening hours for business premises.

A second, and much smaller, source is an approach by a group (6 examples). Associations play a special role in expressing demands which articulate collective benefits such as the building of a sports hall or making available a place for religious worship, or setting up a day-nursery. However, their activity may also sometimes take the form of mobilising opposition. For example, in one case a plan to close some classes led the pupils' parents, in the absence of support from the local council, to 'occupy' the premises of the Académie.

But the third, and perhaps most striking feature, is the extent to which the action of councillors results mainly from their own personal initiative (16 examples). In these instances, their objective may be either of an individual or a collective nature. They may seize the opportunity presented by a government programme (a public utility project, for example), or respond to a suggestion by the mayor or one of his assistants (to study the problems of library provision), or they may make common ground with one of the concerns of the Civil Service (such as the official sent to the commune by the Inspection Académique). But councillors seem chiefly to assess and identify problems on the basis of their own presence 'on the spot' and of their contacts with the local population. In this way, they select those concerns in which their intervention appears both feasible and desirable. Of particular importance, in this respect, are their associational or professional memberships. Such groups enable them in many cases to anticipate a demand, and even to formulate it in cases where it otherwise might not be openly expressed (as, for example, in the case of battered wives). Their involvement in the social life of the locality is thus fundamental to their capacity to articulate demands and often provides them with a better understanding of such demands than would result simply from the approaches of which they are the targets.

Once demands have been expressed, the way in which they are then processed by the local governmental system and converted into a decision depends both on the form in which approaches are made and the kinds of benefits or goods which are aimed at.

Individual goods, such as people asking for work or help with housing problems, sometimes lead councillors to invest a great deal of personal time and effort in the case. One illustration of this involved a woman councillor who voluntarily took charge of collecting and distributing firewood for underprivileged families. In most cases, however, the councillor plays more of a brokerage role, relaying the demands to the various decision-making bodies. This may mean the mayor or the local government service or even private organisations (for example, company managers in the case of employment problems). Thus, those bodies which have the capacity to solve, or at least to intervene in, the problems under consideration may often be unconnected with the town hall itself.

The activities of councillors in relation to these individual goods consist mainly in mobilising secondary resources to deal with the demands through established administrative procedures, whether by giving backing to a request or by getting something done about it when there is no statutory provision for dealing with the matter. Citizen participation in these matters is relatively frequent, but is mainly a means of obtaining exceptions to established procedures which in turn enables the bureaucracy of the commune to work with a degree of flexibility.

Collective goods are generally more a concern of groups, but their degree of formal organisation can vary greatly. They may be religious or ethnic communities concerned, for example, with the problem of finding a place for worship (in Cenon), or facilities for accommodating migrant populations (at Blanquefort). They may also be occupational groups with well-defined interests, such as farmers or shopkeepers. Equally, they may instead be groups with more loosely-knit interests involving questions of housing for tenants or accommodation for recreational associations. Finally, there are the more nebulous groupings with no formal organisation, like public transport users and, in the most problematic cases of all (such as drug addicts and battered wives), those with no capacity at all to express their collective demands. In these instances, decision-making may follow more complex lines inasmuch as, in most cases, it requires a high degree of councillor intervention, and also involves money, personnel and sometimes even the establishment of new procedures.

The most common reaction among councillors to requests they receive is to set up a committee under council auspices.[12] In this way, the problem is discussed directly with the appointed assistant (*adjoint*) and the person responsible for the relevant department. Both the political and the administrative channels within the town hall are thus jointly brought into play. Minor problems are dealt with by the departments concerned, while more important questions are debated, as circumstances require, by the local council, though previous preparatory work on them will have been done by the mayor and his close advisers. However, the local council is not the only place where decisions are taken, for its activity as an 'honest broker' may be directed towards the Communauté Urbaine or even departments at national level.[13] But we should note in this respect that the involvement of other levels of decision-making may, in some cases, then be used by the local council as grounds far not taking a decision themselves. It enables them to put the file 'on ice' for technical administrative reasons.

The political integration of local society

Political action in the commune is to a large extent constrained by statutory bodies, the officially-established procedures which they must follow, and the financial resources at their disposal. The mechanism of demand aggregation is, therefore, in the last analysis, of marginal importance to the process of decision-making. In advance of the decision, information-gathering procedures are established, sometimes through the distribution of a questionnaire to members of the public who may be affected, or more often through contacts with the professional and voluntary charitable bodies involved in the problem. Subsequent to the decision, forms of concertation and participation are developed, very often, by the creation of consultative committees and associations. These may, for example, be in conjunction with the residents of a district in the case of a housing problem, or with social workers in organising a refuge for battered wives. Local intermediary groups are closely associated with this activity which is an important element in the integration of local society. Not least is this the case in that it increases the capacity for conflict resolution within the commune over issues involving the council.

Whereas groups rarely initiated contacts with the elected representatives, as we saw, nevertheless, associations did intervene in more than half of the issues mentioned by the councillors (24 examples). They participated in decision-making by sitting on committees, or by forming *ad hoc* groups. This was the case in Blanquefort, for example, where, in the sphere of cultural activities, the elected representative responsible for such matters found himself surrounded by a number of associations that mobilised themselves in order to become more actively involved in the life of the commune.

Councillors may try to encourage the participation of groups in decision-making for two main reasons. In the case of groups established before a given decision is taken, they are a source of information, of contacts and, indeed, they are often a means whereby official action on the issue can be taken. As such, they constitute a resource which the council can utilise in developing and initiating its policy. Such concertation between the two reduces not only the probability of failure but also the overall 'costs' of the decision.[14] For example, it enables the council more easily to anticipate possible tensions, and consequently to avert the emergence of open conflicts and public challenges to the council's authority. Concerted action thus both mobilises and channels support for the local authorities.

At another level, councillors quote 32 examples of the involvement of bodies specially established to deal with a particular issue and which reflect a problem-centred approach. More often than not, these are structures which bring together the local councillors, representatives of relevant associations, and professionals (for example, from social security offices, socio-cultural and sporting agencies, or local employment offices). These organisations in turn tend to formalise or institutionalise participation in a relatively standard pattern, notably through a tripartite membership arrangement involving elected representatives, voluntary workers and professionals, and using the concept of a 'preparatory working party'.

Finally, political parties were mentioned 25 times by the councillors as having played a part in solving the particular problem under consideration. These responses arose, for the greater part, amongst the Cenon respondents, and can be grouped into three categories. First are the relations maintained between the parties and the population through daily contacts and grass-roots action, and through attempts to mobilise voters during elections. The second type revolved around the party's role in the search for extra funding at other levels of the politico-administrative system, and in the implementation of governmental measures. Here, the party was not so much involved in expressing local preferences as in providing a network within the political system facilitating the mobilisation of resources.

Significantly, the third, and most frequent, references to the involvement of parties in the decisional process related to the positions they took up in the council following the work of its party groupings. Sometimes these stances were a way out of a set-back which the minority party had suffered in committee. Council debates, at which the press is present, are often a means through which the various parties can develop strategies to highlight their differences. Thus, in dealing with local problems, the parties usually play the role of a 'tribune' in stirring up controversy about the council agenda. But this activity is not necessarily connected to any priorities expressed by the citizenry at large. Rather, it reflects the political need for publicity about council action, and here the 'systemic agenda'[15] becomes one of the intermediary issues in political competition. One illustration of this is provided by 'the opposition's exploitation of a purely technical paper for party purposes', to quote the time-honoured phrase employed by majority groups in order to reject the grounds on which their decisions are challenged (in one local case we looked at, it was a matter of the cleansing of the swimming pool having been postponed on the mayor's decision). This combination of technical and political argument is a good example of the strategies used in the construction of an agenda. For the opposition, the point is to raise issues which can cause sufficient controversy as to shake the local council. From the standpoint of the controlling group, the object is to limit any controversy over problems which they either cannot solve or do not want to handle. The simplest strategy in such cases is to control (and quite often to prevent) access by the opposition to the files of the administrative services or even to membership of committees. The appearance of problems on the political agenda can therefore be very far from being the direct result of participatory activity. Rather, it may be the effect of agenda control – the second face of power. Seen from this point of view, the parties appear more actively in structuring preferences than in expressing demands.

Party factors remain secondary, however, compared with the importance of sectoral, social and economic or territorial influences when it comes to the process of dealing with local needs. Cenon appears, in fact, to be a commune where the dominant party can channel the expression of demands because it has become implanted in the social life of the district over several decades and has become virtually identified with the local council. Conversely, Blanquefort lacks any equivalent 'party machine' without, however, suffering as a consequence any major conflicts, or any special problems in taking account of the views either of local activists or of the population at large.[16] Indeed, an opposition councillor in Cenon emphasised that the parties of the right play little part in considering demands because the commune was regarded as 'unwinnable' by the national party and thus not worth the political investment. He was thus giving expression to an essentially strategic element in local party activity, and consequently to the primacy of social and territorial considerations over party considerations in the handling of demands.

Although participation is not crucially important in terms of its influence on decisions, it is, by contrast, essential to the structure of power within the commune. Indeed, it integrates the various social networks into that power structure. The cooption of leaders, and especially those who are leaders of associations – the eternal 'associates and rivals' of the elected representatives on the council – and the incorporation of groups in decision-making, together legitimise the actions of the council in issue areas where otherwise grass-roots social forces might have challenged its authority.

The importance of intermediary organisations in the decisions which have been studied emphasises the extent to which the procedures for participation have become formalised. Everyday political action depends less on the expression of demands which have arisen in a spontaneous or informally organised manner than on cooperation between the local elected representatives, local authority employees, the staff of the public services and volunteers who run associations. This collaboration permits the assessment of 'needs', of what are the critical sectors of local social life, and of the areas in which the council is expected to intervene. Such linkages, therefore, provide an information-gathering function, which is an important first stage in the decision-making process.

Through this learning process, ideas and relationships are developed which help to define appropriate action for the local public or para-public services. These procedures also enable the professional and voluntary workers concerned to participate in the working out of council decisions. As well as being a source of information, their participation provides some assurance that tensions can be anticipated, and that possible conflicts with the more established groups can be kept within bounds. Equally, they complement, and even act as a substitute for, the mediating role of the political parties themselves in the context of local politics. These elements together then help to institutionalise local participation and, not least, support for the power structure of the commune. In doing so, they serve to limit the emergence of more spontaneous forms of participation which might challenge the legitimacy of the local authorities. The organisation of participation into such institutionalised forms plays an important part in promoting the integration of the whole community.

NOTES

1 This sample is made up of the communes of Cenon, Blanquefort, Saint-Medard-en-Jalles, Mérignac, Villeneuve d'Ornon, Bègles, Gradignan, Pessac, Talence, all forming part of the Communauté Urbaine de Bordeaux.
2 The data for the broader sample relate to the local councils elected for the period 1977–83. They are divided up politically as follows: Councils run by the union of the left and of socialist tendency: Cenon, Mérignac, Villeneuve d'Ornon, Pessac, Talence; Communes run by the Union of the Left and of

Communist tendency: Bègles. Saint-Medard-en-Jalles and Gradignan are communes classified as 'moderate groupings', belonging to the RPR–UDF coalition in the council of the Communauté Urbaine.

3 The para-public sector is made up of the institutions and organisations whose management and finances are controlled by the state or local authorities, but whose organisation is regulated by private law. In this category can be placed, for example, social security offices, or the associations set up by the public authorities to deal with social and cultural matters. Public enterprises are, however, in the public sector proper, although the two have been combined in table 7.3.

4 The left–right division is a short-hand one here, and hides the distinction between partisan and non-partisan. We must therefore be somewhat cautious in interpreting the figures. Nevertheless, such an apolitical stance was not untypical of councils which were in fact linked to the parties of the right before 1983.

5 Where there were several non-council memberships, the most important one was identified on the basis of three criteria: the reasons given by the councillors for their involvement; the length of membership; and the order in which the groups were joined.

6 This shortage of people wanting to stand for election is especially noticeable in small communes where one often finds an absence of competition, and the presence of candidates from only one list. It also helps to explain the rate of turnover, since councillors are not always sufficiently motivated or available to want to stand again.

7 The majority of councillors justified this view in terms of the need to maintain contact with the population and to acquire experience through participation in organisations other than the council. This position was, however, frequently subject to two qualifications. The first emphasised the danger of political control of organisations which could result from an improper extension of these practices. The second criticised the leading elected representatives for accumulating an excessive number of positions.

8 Roger Cobb and Charles Elder distinguish the 'systemic' agenda, which includes the whole range of controversial issues, and the 'formal' or 'institutional' agenda, which are items the authorities have under active consideration (Cobb and Elder 1972). This distinction has the advantage of emphasising the gap between the forum in which public debate takes place and the more restricted arena in which decisions are actually taken. We shall see later that the systemic agenda is sometimes used as a strategy in appeals for items to be placed on the formal agenda, and to challenge the leadership of the council.

9 In contrast to Britain, French councillors tend not, in practice, to be involved in all the decisions of the locality. Such powers are mainly concentrated in the hands of the mayor who then turns to particular councillors for advice according to their specialised skills and interests.

10 On the place of 'off-cycle' decisions in the establishment of local government policies, and for an overall treatment of the problems of studying local council agendas, see Jones 1983.

11 'Social' problems refer here to optional and mandatory social security payments (for the handicapped, medical care, financial assistance), and the problems of specific categories of people such as the young, the aged, battered wives. 'Urban' problems, as noted in the text, refer to problems of housing, accommodation, public works and transport.

12 These committees are set up by the council and may include outside spokesmen such as the leaders of interest groups. Although they provide a platform for outside bodies, the committees depend on the mayor and any recommendations have to be approved by the council.

13 Decision-making points mentioned in the survey were preponderantly those inside the town hall (36 examples). Amongst these, the committees were in fact most often approached by elected representatives ending, according to the normal procedures, with final deliberation by the council (13 cases). Alternatively, the mayor was contacted personally (8 examples), or the *adjoints* (7 examples), or those directly in charge of the local services (8 examples). The Communauté Urbaine was approached in another ten instances cited, principally through its service agencies. The other decision-making bodies (18 examples) were scattered through the central Civil Service or public service enterprises (such as public transport, EDF, SNCF, HLM associations, and Agence Nationale pour l'Emploi). Yet another category of less official targets were local associations or volunteers from the commune (the users of the social centre, volunteer librarians, the parish priest) (13 examples). Finally there were three cases involving private citizens, landowners and a factory manager.

14 Richard Rich emphasises under this heading the role played by groups in the articulation of demands, as well as the production or co-production of services they may then undertake (Rich 1979).

15 See note 8.

16 Jones also argues that the role of intermediate groups depends on whether the party is firmly established or not. In his study dealing with Chicago, associations were to some extent in competition with the party machine in considering local demands, and mobilising the loyalties, of the citizens (see Jones 1981). The example provided by Cenon is, however, less extreme, the party controlling what the associations did rather than denying them any expression whatever.

8

Councillors, citizens and agendas: aspects of local decision-making in Britain

GEORGE MOYSER and GERAINT PARRY

The focus of this chapter is on the process by which issues and problems are raised in local government and the roles which councillors play in that process.[1] This entails a consideration of how councillors fit into the social and political milieu in which they operate and how they perceive that milieu since these perceptions will shape their own conduct. Councillors, central as they are to local government, are not the sole group with political influence at a local level. Accordingly, the analysis makes a broad but essential distinction between councillors and other elite individuals with influence in local affairs. They, in turn, are also collectively contrasted with both the groups and private citizens who comprise the local grass-roots populace.

We begin by examining a number of social and political characteristics which throw light on the degree to which elites and citizens differ in background or in the extent of their integration into local life. We then move on to consider similarities and differences in the perceptions of local issues possessed by councillors, other influentials and by the population at large. Finally, the chapter will look at the kind of role councillors play in reconciling and integrating the various groups and forces operating in local political life.

I THE SOCIAL AND POLITICAL LOCATION OF COUNCILLORS

In order to examine the role of councillors in the management and processing of demands we must first locate them, and the citizenry, within a common framework of significant social and political characteristics. In this way, we can then begin to understand the patterns of formal and informal linkages that connect representative to represented, the nature of the social influences that flow between them and, ultimately, the extent to which the community itself is integrated into the local political system.

Personal characteristics

The councillors in our survey are, on average, middle-aged, male and relatively highly educated. In these respects they are not dissimilar to a representative sample of councillors from throughout England and Wales (England 1986). Over half of the councillors (53%) were aged between 45 and 64, as were our set of other local influentials. Compared with the population at large the younger generation are under-represented. No councillor was under 25 and only a third were below the age of 45. Labour councillors are few in our sample but they are on average younger than the population at large, whilst Conservatives and Independents are a decade older than their Labour counterparts.

Women, though a majority of the British population, are strikingly under-represented amongst the councillors. Only 32% of our councillors were women, which is higher than the national figure of 19% (England 1986: 19). This, however, conceals some variations. In the most remote rural area there were no female councillors in our sample whereas in Conservative Sevenoaks near the metropolis they were quite numerous. Both Spotland and Oswestry are very typical of the country as a whole.

Educationally, councillors, like other leaders, differ markedly from their constituents. Nearly a quarter (23%) were university graduates – a rate some four times that for the population in the six areas as a whole. This difference also appears in all the political parties suggesting that educational qualifications are a common factor in their selection procedures. However, Independents who are not subject to the same kind of formal selectorate and who may be elected for reasons not associated with educational skills are relatively less highly educated.

Economic and residential characteristics

The occupational and residential patterns of councillors' lives are factors which, potentially at least, affect the extent of their integration into the locality. Two thirds of councillors were in either full-time or part-time work, a proportion substantially higher than the 49% recorded for their constituents. Only 5% were unemployed – less than the rate for ordinary citizens. Of those who were economically active, around two-thirds of both councillors (59%) and ordinary citizens (67%) were employed in the private sector – in both cases principally in medium to large businesses. Only some 10% or so were in small local businesses, with a slightly larger number being self-employed. Among the large minority in the public sector, again the distributions roughly corresponded.

Within both these two broad sectors, not unsurprisingly, councillors, like other members of our samples of local leaders, have occupations of relatively high status. Thus, in terms of an eleven-fold conventional grading scheme (see A. Heath *et al.* 1985: 25) over half (53.2%) were found in the top two categories (professional and managerial), although twice as many were in the latter than in the very top professional stratum. As such, they did not quite attain the overall status profile of other local leaders, 63.3% of whom were either professionals or managers. On the other hand, they were clearly more of a piece with their group than with the rank-and-file only one fifth of whom (21.8%) had high status occupations. Conversely, very few councillors, under 15% in fact, were drawn from the ranks of the working class. This is only a small fraction of the 29% of ordinary citizens who held jobs of that general character.

These patterns are repeated in broad terms in each political party. Two-thirds of Conservative councillors, but also over half of their Labour counterparts, could be described as sharing middle class backgrounds, although other findings indicate that Labour representation is drawn more from public sector than from private sector occupations – in short a different middle class (see Moran 1985: 158).[2] Even the Independent councillors held relatively high status occupations, although only a quarter were of the professional/managerial variety, perhaps reflecting their lower levels of formal education.[3] Clearly, therefore, councillors are at some considerable social distance from the majority of their constituents.

This social distance may to some extent be mitigated, however, by the length of residence established by leaders in their localities. Just over half of the councillors, as well as of the other leaders, actually lived within the immediate confines of our research sites, and very few of either lived at any great distance. Furthermore, the resident councillors had, on average, lived in these areas for over 33 years, a figure substantially in excess of that for other elite individuals (20 years). Perhaps more importantly, it was also greater than for the mass of citizens (24 years) or for those among them who were politically active (21 years). In other words, councillors may have different educational backgrounds and occupations from their constituents, and be of a slightly different generation, but they have been in the locality for a long time – much longer than could be accounted for merely by being somewhat older. They are, in other words, rooted relatively firmly in the life of their area (see also Grant 1977: 19).

Again, this generalisation seems to hold good in both Oswestry and Spotland although, in the latter case, there is evidence of greater residential mobility among both leaders and ordinary citizenry. This no doubt reflects their respective locations, Oswestry being a rather remote and traditional rural community whilst Spotland is part of a much larger conurbation and includes an ethnically mixed population with all the mobility and flux that such a context often entails. As for party differences, all had generally the same lengths of residence (about 29 years). The Independents, however,

Table 8.1. *Social group linkages of councillors and other respondents (%)*

| | Elite | | Non-elite | |
Group category	Councillors	Other leaders	Whole population	Politically active
Religious/church	55.9	41.2	19.2	25.2
Trade union	55.9	49.4	25.2	37.2
Civic/community	40.7	39.7	5.6	11.7
Voluntary service	39.0	35.4	6.5	12.0
Social club	35.6	32.3	22.3	30.9
Hobby/sports	23.7	41.2	22.1	30.7
Political club	18.6	6.6	2.9	6.6
Professional societies	15.3	38.9	6.2	14.2
Cultural	13.6	21.0	4.5	10.1
Self-help	11.9	15.2	2.6	6.8
Armed forces	6.8	6.6	3.7	5.3
Feminist	3.4	4.3	0.4	0.9
Evening class	1.7	21.4	8.1	14.5
Average no.	3.22	3.54	1.35	2.19
N	59	263	1,618	372

had a substantially higher record (nearly 42). The problem, of course, is in deciding whether this reflects their political status as independents, or the more rural and traditional milieu in which they are predominantly to be found (see Grant 1977).

Group linkages

Perhaps the most explicit indication of the extent to which councillors and others are integrated into their communities and, also, of the degree to which social groups are linked into elite networks is the nature of local group memberships.

To examine this we devised a scheme whereby groups could be divided into a number of mutually exclusive categories. We then recorded, for both mass and elite respondents, the proportions who were members of at least one group of each type. The results are displayed in table 8.1 and show that councillors have connections across a wide spread of formal groups, but that the strength of those connections varies considerably. Thus, over half are attached to religious groups and trade unions, and over a third to civic or community societies, voluntary service organisations and various types of social club. These would seem, *prima facie*, to represent the most prominent aspects of organised community life. Conversely, councillors are very thinly represented in groups associated with the armed forces, feminism and evening classes. However, these are probably groups which have less impact on local public life. Overall, as can be seen at the bottom of table 8.1, councillors are on average associated with over three different types of group. About a fifth, indeed, are to be found in as many as five.

By comparison the other leaders are still more strongly connected with local group life. These other leaders include council officers, police chiefs, churchmen, head teachers and office-holders in local interest groups. Many, but not all, of these persons will, by the nature of the case, belong at least to the one group through which they attained local leadership status. Hence the interest lies in the fact that they tend to belong to other types of group in addition. Their profile of membership differs somewhat from that of the councillors. Not quite so many have an association with those groups, at the top of table 8.1, that seem most central to community life. Instead, they have more specialised preoccupations such as professional societies, hobby and sports clubs.

The ordinary citizenry, in clear contrast to both elite categories, are far less formally linked to local institutions. The largest category, that of trade unions, sweeps in a quarter – or just over a third if one looks only at the politically more active citizens. Figures for trade union membership may, however, be somewhat inflated by the fact that for many people joining a union is seen as an essential concomitant of their job rather than as a purely voluntary act. Even so, union membership amongst the citizens at large was half the equivalent figure for the elites. Where the voluntary element is clearer, the discrepancy grows. Thus religious associations among the citizenry, for example, are only a third of those for elite individuals, and the attachments to civic or voluntary service groups are some six or seven times fewer. The general picture, therefore, is clearly one in which councillors and other local leaders are relatively well-linked to local groups. It is the citizenry, not the elites, who are comparatively poorly integrated into such formal networks.

Not only is this repeated in both Oswestry and Spotland, it is also reinforced by attachments to parties. Thus whilst 83% of our councillors (but only 9 out of 13 in the largely non-partisan council of Oswestry) had formal partisan commitments, a mere third of the other leaders and a tiny 6% of ordinary citizens were so affiliated. Furthermore, office-holding is yet another factor which accentuates the contrasts. In the parties, for example, nearly one third of councillors hold office, compared with 14% of others and the merest handful of ordinary citizens. Indeed, in Oswestry, where only 3% of the citizens claimed a party membership, precisely two

Table 8.2. *Perceptions of local political influence (%)*

	Councillors	Other leaders
Political stratum	*58.5*	*55.5*
Councillors	31.8	31.5
Local government officials	13.8	13.4
Central government, elected and officials	4.8	4.4
Other elite individuals, e.g. MP, police chief	3.9	2.9
Political party	4.2	3.3
Formal Groups	*38.2*	*40.7*
Economic, e.g. firms, trade unions	9.0	10.8
Residents, e.g. civic associations	14.3	11.8
Other	14.9	18.1
Mass	*3.3*	*3.9*
e.g. as general category, or informal group		
Total	100.0	100.0
N Responses	456	2,367
N Individuals	60	323

said that they attended a party meeting even once a year. Office-holding patterns within social groups, however, are not quite the same. There is still a massive differential between councillors and ordinary citizens. But office-holding amongst other members of the elite (who, admittedly, include group leaders) is higher than for councillors. Thus overall, most elites including councillors, are well placed in the institutional network of their localities.

Figures such as those cited earlier showing the differences between leaders and led in their social and economic backgrounds have been often employed to call into question the representativeness of elites. Against this it can be argued that any gap between councillors and constituents will be attenuated by the integration of elected representatives into the group life of the locality. This can be the source both of political pressure and political communication, albeit sometimes selective or partial depending on the social and political character of the groups in question.

Political location

Important though personal characteristics and institutional linkages are, ultimately it is within a framework of political power that councillors, groups and ordinary citizens must be located. Only then can the character of mass-elite relationships and the nature of local decision-making be properly assessed.

To elicit elite perceptions about the exercise of local political power we asked all those concerned to nominate up to four 'individuals, groups or organisations' whom they thought were particularly influential in general decisions about three different major policy areas in their locality. Across our entire set of elites (some 383) well over 2,800 responses were made. These were then sorted into a number of different categories, separately for councillors and other leaders, as laid out in table 8.2.

The opinions of these two elite groupings, as can be seen, show a remarkable degree of agreement as to the general distribution of political influence across the six localities. The general balance, in both instances, gave preponderant influence to various types of actor from within what might be called the 'political stratum'. Most centrally placed, in their view, were the councillors who, as a single category, received more support as 'receptacles of power' than any other. Indeed, their third share of all responses was about double that for the next largest category. As this perspective is shared equally by both councillors and other leaders, it at least indicates an important point of consensus within the local elite culture, if not necessarily 'reality' itself (see Dunleavy 1980: 143–4).

Across the 'political stratum' councillors (who were incidentally nominated almost entirely in the collective, rather than as individuals) far out-rank any other. The nearest are local government officials with less than half the representatives' 'votes'. On this evidence, it seems, officials are indeed more the servants than the masters of local government. On the other hand, the impression is equally clear that although the councillors may form the 'central circle' (Kadushin 1968) of local political power, they are seen as not exercising it in any exclusive manner. Not only local officials but, albeit to a much lesser extent, central government and local political party machines, also play a significant role. Thus, to the extent that elite autonomy is implied here, it seems to apply in a broad sense rather than to councillors alone.

Support for such a view can be gleaned from elite perceptions about local forces which operate essentially from outside the immediate policy-making arena. Collectively they are seen as having lower, if significant, levels of influence. Least important among them are the general public – either *en masse*, or in informal categories or groupings. Clearly, the elites' vision of local decision-making is one in which the ordinary citizen counts least of all. This is also a vision held as strongly, it would seem, by elected representatives as by those with other bases of prominence. More importance is given to organised groups whose variety we have already discussed. Those specifically mentioned vary from policy area to policy area, but the two most frequently mentioned were residents' groups, such as civic associations, and those of a more strictly economic variety like trade unions or chambers of trade. This shows, therefore, that 'the community' is seen as being influential in the local political process principally through formally organised groups. Local residents as individuals, or in amorphous groupings, do not count, but when organised into a pressure group they do. Not even then, however, do they seem to count enough, in the eyes of our elites, to be major, still less dominant, actors within the decision-making process.

Again, broadly speaking, the overall pattern is repeated in each locality, including Spotland and Oswestry. There are, of course, variations in precise percentages, but the ranking is approximately the same. Thus, councillors receive just over 40% of responses by other leaders in one community, and as few as 24% in another (Spotland). Similarly, the civic association in Sevenoaks and the tenants' association in Stockwell were fairly prominent. But, even in these two cases, and certainly in Spotland and Oswestry, the balance of perceptions was not greatly different. Local elites in all areas, it seems, put themselves, and councillors in particular, at the centre of the political stage. It is their views, their perceptions, their political agendas which are seen as carrying most weight, although not without at least a modest input from the groups 'out there'.

2 DEMANDS – AGENDAS AND PROCESSES

Local issue agendas

One of the prime virtues claimed for local democracy is that it produces government which understands the particular issues and problems of the locality. Such an understanding is presumed to arise, in large part, from the extent to which those working in local government are integrated into the area they run. It has been shown that the extent of such integration varies with the indicator used. Whilst there is social distance between representatives and electorate, this is compensated by the length of residence of the average councillor and by the significant degree to which these individuals are linked to local group life. The question then arises as to how far this integration is reflected in the capacity of councillors, as compared with other local leaders, to recognise and reflect the interests and priorities of the local electorate. At the same time it must be recognised that there are many factors other than the current demands of the local residents that affect the councillors' priorities. Councillors may claim to be taking a longer term view of the collective needs of the locality rather than responding to current, particularised needs. They may also be influenced by their party position and ideology as well as by the policy recommendations of the local officers (see England 1986: 64–86). Some divergence between leader and citizen agendas is thus entirely explicable. However, this cannot be taken too far without undermining at least some principles of democratic representation.

The 'issue agendas' of councillors, of other leaders and of citizens were constructed by asking them to list the local issues, needs and problems which had affected their areas over the past five years. The very many issues mentioned were then grouped into a number of 'families'. It is also necessary to bear in mind that these agendas are not static, nor are they independent of one another. Thus, not only can one properly expect that councillors will be influenced by their constituents but the reverse may also be true. Ordinary citizens react, positively and negatively, to what those with authority or power do and think. Equally, political leaders, by their decisions, can shape the environment in which citizen agendas are formed, not least through their access to the means of communication. Hence the proximity between the priorities of leaders, elected or unelected, and of the ordinary citizens, may be due as much to elite influence on citizens as to the impact of the people upon the leadership. To establish the degree of proximity between issue agendas is not therefore to make any claim, necessarily, about the direction of causality.

As might be anticipated, councillors had little difficulty in nominating the major issues and problems facing their localities. The 60 councillors put forward nearly 250 issues.[4] Looked at overall, two families of issue dominate as can be seen in column A of table 8.3. Almost one issue in three (31%) was concerned with 'environment and planning', rather under a fifth (17%) were to do with housing. Both sets of issues fall, of course, firmly within the responsibilities of local government. Environment and planning covers a broad range of areas including applications for, or objections to, grants of planning permission, town development, conservation of buildings or of the rural environment. In four of the six localities, including both Spotland and Oswestry, the most frequently cited issues were of this type. However, this conceals the true extent of local variations. In some localities problems of refuse collection were the main component of the environment family whilst elsewhere it was the provision of sports and leisure facilities. Thus, in Spotland, where a third of the councillors' issues belonged to this family, the focus of concern was on the programme of housing conservation undertaken in the locality, whilst in Oswestry, with environmental issues constituting 44% of councillors' issues, planning matters formed the main element.

Housing, although the second highest issue overall on the councillors' agenda, was more a matter of concern to the conurbations and the pit village. The Stockwell councillors placed housing at the head of the agenda with 30% of the total issues mentioned. Spotland and Oswestry provide

Table 8.3. *Local issue agendas (all six localities)*

Issue categories	A Councillors		B Other leaders		C Citizens		D Councillors' expectations of citizens	
	% Mentions	(Rank)	% Mentions	(Rank)	% Mentions	(Rank)	% Mentions	(Rank)
Environment, planning	31.3	(1)	22.2	(1)	26.7	(1)	21.6	(1)
Housing	17.3	(2)	13.5	(3)	12.2	(3)	18.9	(2)
Unemployment	14.5	(3)	13.9	(2)	6.0	(8)	12.6	(4)
Economic (not including unemployment)	9.2	(4)	10.6	(4)	7.8	(4)	11.6	(5)
Transport	8.0	(5)	9.1	(5)	14.5	(2)	13.7	(3)
Health	4.4	(6)	5.2	(9)	7.4	(5)	4.7	(7)
Education	4.0	(7)	3.8	(10)	3.1	(10)	3.7	(8)
Youth	3.2	(8)	5.8	(7)	7.1	(6)	2.6	(9)
Elderly	2.4	(9=)	1.8	(12)	2.2	(11)	2.1	(10=)
Ethnic	2.0	(11)	1.9	(11)	1.0	(12)	1.0	(12)
Law and order	1.2	(12)	6.4	(6)	5.7	(9)	2.1	(10=)
Other	2.4	(9=)	5.7	(8)	6.1	(7)	5.3	(6)
Total	100.0		100.0		100.0		100.0	
N Issues	249		1,018		2,872		190	
N Individuals	60		262		1,101		60	

the appropriate contrast between densely urbanised and rural areas. Whilst housing problems constituted 6% of the councillors' issues in Oswestry, ranking fifth, in Spotland housing came second in the order with almost a quarter of the issues raised.

The agendas of councillors have a privileged status, being those of elected leaders with authority to transform at least part of that agenda into action. The agendas of other notables are significant partly because some may have exceptional access to councillors and others in authority and partly because their leadership status arises from possession of political, economic or social resources of their own in the locality. Clearly they will view local issues, needs and problems from many different standpoints, but all could be said both to speak with some knowledge of the area and potentially to provide an alternative perspective to that of the councillors.

In the event, column B of table 8.3 shows that there is not a great difference, in aggregate, between councillors and other leaders. Taking all six communities as a set, the average difference between the proportions of each family of issues raised by councillors and by other leaders is a little over 4%.[5] Similarly, whilst Spotland (4.7%) and Oswestry (second highest at 5%) both could be said to display a higher than average discrepancy between the view of the two leadership groups, the difference is not truly significant. It is the overall degree of consensus which should more properly be stressed, although, for reasons stated below, this does not necessarily extend to solutions.

Oswestry and Spotland are very typical of all the localities, in that both display elite consensus with differences only of emphasis rather than in the rank order of issues. In Oswestry, environment and planning provide 44% of the councillors' issues compared with a quarter of the issues of the other leaders – a 19% difference. A similar situation also arose in Spotland where there was also a smaller, but significant, gap (7%) between councillors and others, arising from the greater emphasis the former placed on educational problems.

In broad terms, therefore, there exists a notable degree of elite consensus on defining the important issues. This is not to say, however, that a consensus also exists on the solutions to the problems. To establish this for over 1,250 issues represents too great a task, important though it is in principle to understanding local leadership. It remains, nevertheless, for us to examine how far this consensus on issue priorities deviates from the agenda of the ordinary citizens and whether the elected councillors are any closer than other leaders to public opinion.

A comparison between the councillors' agenda and that of the citizenry across all localities (column C of table 8.3) reveals a difference of 5%.[6] Given that there are few similar studies of discrepancies between leaders and citizens, there may be disagreement over interpretations of such a figure. But on the surface the difference would seem relatively modest. In this instance, however, the discrepancy conceals greater differences as to the rank ordering of issues. As ever, environment and planning is in first position on both lists. Housing is also high on both agendas. Thereafter there is greater deviation. Most striking is that, for councillors, unemployment appears in third place whereas it was, surprisingly, only eighth on the citizens' collective agenda. A possible explanation is that whereas the ordinary person considers unemployment as more a national than a local issue (Moyser, Parry, and Day 1986: 47), councillors believe that some responsibility lies on them as local leaders to alleviate the problem in their own area. Oswestry councillors, for example, spoke of the importance of developing the town's industrial estate as a potentially successful policy which the local authority could undertake, even though the underlying problem of unemployment was a central government responsibility. As one councillor put it,

I think the ultimate issue must be decided at Whitehall in adopting a more expansionary economic policy. Locally the Council are doing what they can by setting up small industries by buying and developing industrial land.

The differences in rank orderings are arguably less significant than the extent of agreement between citizens and councillors on the issues. Unemployment apart, there was no difference on any family of issues greater than 5%. Moreover, the six localities do not differ markedly from one another. The most consensual is Sevenoaks, the greatest gap is in the rural area of the Machars. Oswestry is closest to the average whilst Spotland shows a fractionally greater discrepancy.

It remains to be tested to what extent there is any closer relationship between the people and their elected representatives than there is between the people and other community leaders. A comparison of the citizens' and the community leaders' agendas suggests in fact that the gap is narrower than that between citizens and councillors. The relationship holds true in both Spotland and Oswestry. In Spotland, for example, the other leaders are closer to the citizenry than are the councillors in a majority of the issue families. Even so, the rank order of the issues does not differ radically. Moreover, on certain issues, both elite groups depart from the citizen agenda in the same direction. Councillors and other leaders in Spotland are much more likely to think of ethnic issues as important than is the population at large. Issues connected with ethnic groups were at the bottom of the citizen agenda, whilst they were third and fourth among councillors and other leaders respectively. In part, this may be accounted for by the under-representation of ethnic minorities in the citizen sample despite their being an important factor in Spotland social life. On the other side, the ordinary person is more likely to stress both law and order and transport and traffic than do the leaders.

It might appear from this that locally elected leaders are less able to reflect opinion than other leaders – a disconcerting finding for local democrats. However, it is possible that this outcome is at least in part a statistical artefact resulting from the relatively small number of councillors compared with the set of other leaders.[7] The councillors are less likely to encompass the whole range of issues raised by the population as a whole and will, rather unjustly, appear to fail to reflect opinion accurately.

According to certain conceptions of the function of representation, councillors quite properly develop their own sets of priorities which do not necessarily correspond with those of their electors. Their agendas constitute their perception of community needs about which they may claim to be better informed than the average citizen. Councillors may, indeed, be aware that they deviate from public opinion. Accordingly, councillors were additionally asked to suggest what they believed were the matters which most concerned the local population. In fact, the councillors made only slight rather than radical changes to their original agenda (column D of table 8.3). The main alteration lay in anticipating that the public would place rather less emphasis on environment and planning and somewhat more on problems affecting transport and traffic. In other words, the councillors were relatively confident that their own priorities were shared by their electors.

The councillors in general proved shrewd assessors of opinion. The agenda they imputed to the population was in every locality, bar one, still closer to the citizens' estimate of the issues than was the councillors' own list. The average differences between the councillors' anticipation and the actual outcome was 4%. In two communities the councillors were, on average, within 3% of the result. In Spotland the councillors overestimated the frequency with which citizens would raise housing matters. This largely explains the rather higher than average discrepancy. In Oswestry there was a similar tendency to exaggerate the likelihood with which unemployment would be mentioned by local people.

All in all, councillors could be said to be well in touch with what their populations considered to be the leading types of issue. It remains possible, however, that this relative consensus arises not so much from the responsiveness of councillors to citizens as from the ability of councillors to set agendas which shape the priorities of citizens. There are reasons for giving some credence to this suggestion. We shall see below that, as in the French cases, councillors believed themselves to be, within various structural constraints, more initiators than reactors. But the extent to which they could in addition shape citizen attitudes requires a more complex analysis of concurrence on agendas across a wider range of localities. The study of opinion formation is a major exercise in itself. Nevertheless, when it came to acting on the agenda 60% of citizens said that they had taken the initiative themselves and only a handful had been activated by a councillor, which may be an indirect measure of the self-consciousness of the citizens' agenda. In that event, the convergence of citizen and elite agendas could be regarded as not unsatisfactory in democratic terms.

Processing of demands

The simplest model offered of the processing of demands in a political system pictures those demands emanating from individuals and groups in the society. These demands are, next, articulated, also in part by groups, and then aggregated or packaged into policies by political parties. Elected representatives then engage, along with officials, in transforming such policies into action, resulting in 'outputs' (see Easton 1965, for a classic statement). The model is, in this form, essentially an example of what Nordlinger has termed a 'societal' explanation of politics (Nordlinger 1981). Public actors respond to individual and group agendas. An alternative stresses the extent to which public actors, including elected representatives, can exercise initiative both in setting agendas and in shaping solutions. (Nordlinger 1981 is the best statement, echoing the classical elitist tradition.)

Reality tends to be more complex than either model would suggest, particularly as politicians have their own conceptions of the proper role of representatives. The extent to which councillors perceive themselves at the interstices of group and individual pressures, or, by contrast, as having a degree of independent initiative is likely to vary by type of issue, according to the particular local government resources and the general political and economic climate. Thus, our local representatives emphasised the severe constraints under which they operated, as a consequence of central government policy, whereby local autonomy was being gradually restricted (see also England 1986: 82–4). Such constraints, considerable as they now are, merely reinforce a number of longer-term trends which have resulted in local decision-making being strongly influenced by a range of extra-local political and economic forces. Within councils, moreover, the scope of initiative varies, with often only the inner circle of leaders, especially in party-controlled councils (which are of course the norm), being able to make strategic policy decisions. This leaves the rank-and-file councillors frequently with only residual influence over very localised matters (Dunleavy 1980: 140–3; Jennings 1982). Nevertheless, even back-bench councillors have to be seen as proximate decision-makers and, as such, are, as has already been noted, viewed by other actors in local politics as central figures in the processing of demands.

With this in mind, councillors were asked about their involvement in some of the major issues facing their localities, concentrating primarily on the one in which each was most involved. Although councillors are, of course, generally well aware of the activities of groups in the area, very few of those issues in which the councillors were most involved were prompted either by group or by individual pressure. Out of the total of 57 issues studied, in only 12 was involvement stated to be, even in part, the result of a request by some other person or body for assistance. Moreover, some of these were requests from other councillors rather than generated from outside. Of the remainder, the decision to get involved was seen as the result of a personal initiative by the councillor (21 cases) or to have arisen simply in his or her normal course of duties as a councillor (24 cases).

Some allowances must be made for the possibility that councillors may have a natural tendency to cite as the issue in which they were particularly involved the one over which they were most able to take a personal initiative. Nevertheless, the impression remains that councillors feel that, on the important issues, the stimulus to action comes from themselves individually or from the council as a whole – to the degree that local independent action remains feasible. Moreover, when asked which body had put most effort into tackling the issue the commonest reference was to the council itself. The emphasis is, once more, very much on the autonomy of the elected council, coupled sometimes with the officials.

In both Spotland and Oswestry most councillors described their involvement as arising in the course of their normal official duties. Furthermore, in several instances, they indicated that 'normal duties' implied a strong element of collective or individual initiative. Indeed, none suggested that action was a response to pressures from local groups. For most the issue was recognised as one of the key problems facing the area. In a sense they did not need to be activated from outside. Typical are remarks about the attraction of new industry and enterprise and the solution to urban regeneration, problems common to both Spotland and Oswestry:

I think it is the most important issue today . . . It is clear to me that things have to get done.

I felt it to be one of the key interests in the town at the moment.

In these ways the council itself is seen as the positive force in policy-making.

Notwithstanding this, councillors cannot but recognise, as we have seen, the world of local pressure groups, and their potential influence on decision-making. Around 40% of councillors said that 'a lot' of groups contacted them over the previous five years about an issue, need or problem. Another 45% spoke of being contacted by 'a few groups'. Variations across the six localities were not marked (except that Oswestry councillors reported rather fewer group contacts). By far the most contacts were by residents' associations. Just under half of the councillors said that they had been contacted at least once by such a group. If one adds the 20% of councillors contacted by a tenants' association (acting for council tenants only) one can appreciate the prominence given to housing matters in group contacts. In the environmental and planning areas almost a third of councillors had received approaches from local civic societies or amenity groups. Voluntary service groups, such as 'Help the Aged' or 'Women's Voluntary Services', formed the only other category mentioned by a large number. The remaining groups ranged from trade unions (mentioned by only 8% of councillors) to churches (mentioned by 3%).

Councillors were also ready to go to the groups to mobilise support on an issue. In some instances they went further and sought to assist in the process of the very articulation of demands. Thus some councillors in Spotland sought to involve still further the active local Residents' Association in expressing their views on housing renovation. One councillor described the association as 'helping' to deal with the issue by 'organising street meetings and voicing their opinions through me, and themselves to the Council.' In Oswestry a councillor who had seen himself as an initiator of a policy of town centre conservation had been active in re-founding the civic society which he described as 'the best pressure base outside the Council'. Another Oswestry councillor described his initiatory role in the policy of attracting new industry as one of realising that 'while we had the ingredients of a sound industrial base, we had to sell it.' The council and existing industrialists were then involved in a campaign leading to an exhibition of local products. The councillors were in these instances playing two roles simultaneously. Individually, they were themselves articulators of issues, needs and problems which, collectively, they would, as members of the council and, in some cases, of party groups, have to aggregate and convert into action. At its strongest the councillor acts as a 'facilitator', helping groups or individual citizens to express their demands more effectively. One Spotland councillor described how he had helped a newly formed pressure group to campaign for a community centre: 'I showed them the means of succeeding in the campaign by using the example of other areas. I showed them how – and to whom – to write letters and the people to meet and helped draft the application in the first instance.'

As we have hinted, one distinction sometimes drawn by councillors is between those groups which have been 'helpful' and 'unhelpful' – a means, in the view of critics, of legitimising or de-legitimising certain types of group (Newton 1976: 131–4; Saunders 1979: 232–6). Our councillors, however, found most of the groups with whom they had dealings to have been, on the whole, very helpful. But this may have arisen through liaising primarily with groups which they anticipated would be co-operative. Equally, it makes tactical sense for groups to approach those councillors who are most likely to be sympathetic to their point of view.

In any event, some of the groups were regarded as more effective in putting their message across than others. Civic societies and residential associations in Spotland received the most commendatory rating of all categories. At the other end of the scale, ethnic groupings clearly had some difficulties in communicating with councillors, although these were confined to Spotland and Stockwell. Also rated as ineffective were those informal groups lacking such organisational features as a membership list. Organisation and perceived effectiveness do seem to go hand in hand, a common characteristic, it is often alleged, of pluralist politics (Newton 1976).

Councillors also play what has been called the 'tribune role' by taking up the grievances of the individual citizen (Gyford 1976; Jennings 1982; Byrne 1985: 132). In some respects they perform a task closer to that of the social worker, helping individuals through the labyrinth of local government regulations and welfare benefits. An Oswestry councillor, for example, had run a welfare benefits market stall for two summers to advise individuals in addition to the regular councillors' 'surgery'. Across all the localities, 60% of councillors said that they were contacted 'very often' by individuals. Again, there are variations between localities, with councillors in the pit village of Penrhiwceiber and in Stockwell reporting the most frequent contacts. The rural areas of the Machars and Oswestry reported rather lower levels. These figures correspond fairly accurately to those reported by citizens, since the fewest contacts with councillors occurred in the two rural localities and the highest in the mining community.

The most frequent topic of such contacts was housing. Indeed, almost 90% of councillors gave this as one of the chief matters raised by individuals. The other major concern of individuals was over planning matters which might affect themselves or their community. A quarter of councillors had been consulted by individuals about such matters. The broad 'family' of environmental and planning issues (including conservation, refuse collection, provision and leisure facilities as well as planning) was listed by 68% of councillors — very much the bread and butter of council work.

These kinds of problem are the typical subject of what Verba and Nie (1972) termed 'particularised contacting', a form of participation which is concerned entirely with the needs of the individual and his or her family and which is only in the public realm to the degree that it is directed towards a public figure. Over half the councillors (58%) did view personal contacting as dealing generally with matters entirely of private concern to the particular individuals involved. However, a quarter considered such contacts to involve wider matters, whilst 16% recognised a mixture of the general and the particular. This is perhaps typical of many environmental issues which can affect both the individual and the community. Individual contacts thus form one significant level of councillors' work. They also contribute to the flow of information concerning the needs of the constituents. Despite a commonly held view that citizens are not well-informed or articulate, 65% of councillors thought that individuals put their message across either 'very' or 'fairly well'.

3 INTEGRATION OF THE LOCALITY

The way in which local demands and problems are processed is one which involves a mixture of, on the one side, activation or mobilisation by councillors and other leaders and, on the other, of participation by groups and individuals. It is a pattern in which, in the view of our local leaders, the council plays the most prominent part by way of initiating action. At the same time, this picture of the relative autonomy of the local politician has to be set against a background in which the typical councillor is comparatively well integrated into the locality through extended and strategic group linkages and the experience of long residence in the area. This combination of autonomy and integration is enough to establish a reasonably high level of appreciation of what the population sees as the major local issues. It remains to be ascertained whether the outcome of this general process produces a wider integration of locality in the sense of a reconciliation of interests and forces or at the very least a high level of satisfaction with outcomes.

The range of specificity of particular issues and problems makes a direct analysis of levels of satisfaction with the specific decisions impractical. More indirect measures of reactions to the process of decision-making are, however, available and pertinent. Across the six localities two-thirds of the people considered that local government did understand the needs and problems of the locality. (The authorities in Spotland and Oswestry both received better than average ratings.) Despite this, only a third of citizens, compared with two-thirds of councillors, had a favourable view of how local government works. The larger body of the population (45%) were neither favourably nor unfavourably inclined. It would seem, therefore, that it is not enough to understand needs but that there must be signs of action upon them.

Nevertheless, where people had acted, whether individually or through a group, to raise a local issue, the level of satisfaction with results was high. Two-thirds of contacts with councillors and also with town hall officials were described as producing a result. Of these, over 70% were said to be satisfactory. Clearly, there is a level of dealing with problems where councillors have the scope to act and the power to produce recognisable results. It might be objected that such satisfaction may be more with the manner in which the problem was handled than with the outcome itself. This objection, even if warranted, fails to recognise, however, that responsiveness may in itself be as crucial to generating support, of a diffuse nature, for local government as the capacity to gratify particular demands.

Generally, people displayed an element of realism in believing that the prospects of influencing councillors were greater for groups than individuals. Whilst the majority in every area, with the exception of middle-class Sevenoaks, agreed that persons like themselves had no influence on councillors, 68% considered that groups could be influential. In other words, people tend to differentiate between the rationality or political efficacy of individual as against collective action (Goodin and Dryzek 1980). Furthermore, they are right to do so, it seems, given the way in which councillors themselves perceive the influence of organised groups compared with that of informal groups or of citizens in general (see table 8.2 above).

This does not mean that people anticipate that political outcomes do, or perhaps can, promote consensus. According to the citizens there are winners and losers. Indeed, some groupings are seen as regular victors and victims. The winners are 'the rich' or 'better off' (15% of respondents). The losers are 'the poor' (9%) or, with somewhat more precision, the 'unemployed' (8.7%) or 'the elderly' (9.4%). Councillors, too, recognised winners and losers in most of the issues they handled. Thus, in Spotland there were people who had benefited from the renovation of housing and others who had been net losers because their properties were beyond improvement. But overall, from the perspective of the councillors, there was no consistent pattern of winners and losers. Tenants' groups, for example, appeared as frequently on the lists of 'winners' as on the 'losers' lists. Hence, councillors tended to regard such outcomes as reflecting the swings and roundabouts of normal political life.

In many instances the outcomes of the decision-making process are, particularly when controversial, the prelude to new participation. This is, however, as we have seen in chapter 3, typically a minority reaction among the population. In part its extent may be affected by a local culture recognised by the citizens and leaders alike. Thus, Stockwell and Penrhiwceiber councillors perceived their constituents as potentially very active about issues. This impression is borne out at least in that the number of protesters was rather higher in these areas. Near the other end of the scale were the Oswestry councillors who considered that the locals tended to accept things as they are – a view confirmed by 71% of Oswestrians, the highest for any community. Opinion in Spotland was evenly divided amongst both councillors and population as to whether the locality was best characterised as active or inert.

The relatively low level of participation to be found in all localities is notoriously open to a variety of interpretations from being evidence of 'consumer satisfaction' to an indication of either apathy or even alienation. Our evidence, however, lends little support to those who suppose that the population at large is antipathetic to local government and its practitioners. Only around a fifth of the population in the six areas thought unfavourably of its operations. On the other hand, satisfaction was muted. Across the localities just over half the people considered that their area was well provided for by the council with both Spotland and Oswestry giving distinctly favourable assessments. Similarly, a small majority of our populations believed that generally councillors could be trusted to do what was right, the rural areas of Oswestry and the Machars being the most supportive.

It is not to be expected by the nature of liberal-democratic politics that all political forces and interests will be fully reconciled and integrated by the process of decision-making whether national or local. If, however, a general measure of satisfaction can be taken as an estimation of the success of an institution and its leaders, then local government receives qualified support from a sceptical population. Since the 1974 reforms, there appears to have been little consensus amongst opinion leaders that the new system has reconciled the efficient provision of services with an adequate response to local needs and issues, as repeated partial reforms and centrally-imposed restrictions evidence. In a highly imperfect political world the citizens in our study rated local government as having performed no better, but no worse, than the parliamentary system itself and better than such other institutions as business, trade unions or the social services. Like national politics, local government and its councillors only receive two cheers but that may be, as E. M. Forster said of democracy itself, 'quite enough'.

NOTES

1 The councillors surveyed in this chapter were drawn from all six of the localities covered by the British Political Participation Study, selected as contrasting areas each broadly typical of different social, economic and political milieus within Britain. Four are in England: Stockwell in the London borough of Lambeth, Spotland – a small area of the northern industrial town of Rochdale, Sevenoaks – an affluent commuter town outside London, and Oswestry – a small market town near the Welsh border in the West Midlands. The fifth was Penrhiwceiber,

a mining village in the Cynon Valley of South Wales, and the sixth a collection of rural villages and hamlets in South West Scotland collectively known as the Machars. (On Scottish councillors more generally see Martlew 1988.)

2 Equally, a national sample suggests that working class representation amongst Labour councillors may be rather higher than in our six localities (see England 1986: 38).

3 In this instance, our sample seems to understate the extent to which Independents have middle class occupations. National results suggest that they fall between Conservative and Labour councillors in this respect, and come closest to the Liberal profile (see England 1986: 38–40).

4 Some issues have more than one aspect. Thus transport for the elderly is partly an issue of transport and in part an issue for the elderly. Such issues have been counted as two issues, at a maximum. This procedure makes very little difference to the overall pattern.

5 Within the constraints of the two distributions, the maximum possible average difference is 16.5% or nearly four times the figure actually recorded.

6 This is the average of the six individual community figures. Again, the maximum was 16.5%.

7 This results in some issue categories for councillors being empty, a circumstance which may affect our measure of discrepancy.

Conclusion

These two chapters have been concerned with processes which are common to all political systems – the articulation and aggregation of demands and the integration of society through the reconciliation of interests. In both Britain and France local councillors play an essential part in these processes. They facilitate the expression of demands as well as being receivers of demands from individuals and groups, thus performing a double role. On occasion they are in effect the initiators of action. By a process of downward mobilisation they themselves activate groups in the local population to put forward demands.

The capacity of councillors to reflect priorities and also to bring about reconciliation of interests is partly related to the extent of their own integration into the locality. One indirect measure of integration is the degree to which councillors are socially representative of the local population. This is not an entirely satisfactory measure since it does not follow that councillors who are drawn from a similar background to the electorate necessarily mirror the views of the population nor that they are the best advocates of the views of the local population. The background of leaders is, therefore, often more an indication of social opportunities. Nevertheless, any social 'bias' in the composition of councillors may reflect the capacity of political institutions to activate different sectors of the local population.

Comparisons between countries are here beset with difficulties arising not merely from the differences in social structure itself but also from the different ways in which occupations and social groupings are categorised in standard schemes of classification. Bearing these reservations in mind it is nevertheless possible to indicate similarities between British and French councillors. In both the French and the British localities the councillors were drawn disproportionately from outside the working class. In Britain 79% of councillors had other than working-class occupations compared with 55% for the population as a whole. The comparable figures for France were 75% for councillors and 43% for the local population. Given the difficulties in comparing classification schemes it is not possible with any safety to suggest that 'over-representation' of the middle class is greater among councillors in one country rather than the other. Similarly, the level of such 'over-representation' amongst left-wing councillors would appear to have gone equally far in both countries. There is also a very comparable tendency for councillors in the Labour Party and on the French left to be employed in the public sector. At the other end of the spectrum it might be noted that neither in the French nor in the British localities was there a single councillor from a manual working class background representing a party of the Right. In Blanquefort and Oswestry there remains a level of non-partisan, and in some sense 'de-politicised', local politics which is likely to decline still further in both countries. Here councillors are also from relatively high-status occupations but rather fewer had the formal educational qualifications which political parties seem more inclined implicitly to require. Rather, their claim to office rests more on their prominence in local social or economic life.

There are, therefore, social disparities between councillors and the local population in both countries. Such social distance as there is, however, may be compensated by other integrating factors. Long residence is *prima facie* a good basis for familiarity with the area's circumstances and for a high degree of social involvement in the locality. While councillors in the British sample certainly filled this requirement with an average of thirty-three years residence, the councillors in the two French communes had resided on average only twenty-three years in their areas. This may reflect the more particular circumstances of these areas which had seen a considerable turnover in population, particularly in the case of Cenon.

Possibly the most significant form of integration, however, is through membership of groups active in the locality. In both countries the vast majority of councillors belong to at least one group and on average to well over two. There are, nevertheless, some differences in the patterns of membership. In France councillors are most involved in the various groups representing leisure and cultural activities. These leisure, sporting and cultural groups provide an important opportunity for the councillors to demonstrate their commitment to community life and to establish contacts with the electors and with local networks. In Britain, councillors are less involved with such associations. Rather, this is the realm of those local notables who were not councillors, as well as the source of most group activity amongst the citizens at large. Yet the substantial engagement of British councillors in civic and community groups concerned with the environment, with voluntary service groups dealing with welfare, and in social clubs, performs a similar function. Their activity in this direction matches that of the non-elected leaders with whom they are thereby brought into close contact.

Despite the classical pluralistic picture of groups as the prime movers of political action, neither in the British nor in the French cases did they appear as giving impetus to involvement by the councillors. Rather, it was the councillors themselves who sought to activate groups in the solution of problems. In some instances, indeed, councillors virtually brought the groups into being. Whilst groups were certainly regarded as influential – at least in comparison to the ordinary individual – their importance lay almost as much in promoting the integration of the locality, if only at leadership level, by involving them in the decision-making process. In the French case this amounted to a process of cooption of leaders who might otherwise tend to rival the elected representatives for authority. The network of groups could even be virtually integrated into the political system by penetration of groups by the parties, constituting a mechanism of political control. The British studies, by contrast, did not suggest this degree of integration. Perhaps the tradition of voluntary groups ensures a certain distance and autonomy from the political sphere, although the situation may be found to be different in the inner cities.

In both France and Britain councillors perceived themselves as possessing a considerable degree of initiative and citizens were in broad agreement with them about the issues facing the locality. But the major actions which they took were not in the main prompted by citizen demands. This suggests that councillors conceive of themselves as possessing an element of political autonomy. There would appear to be a level of routine problems and demands which councillors face in each country. Beyond that are the areas where councillors can take more of an initiative and which they are more likely to cite as the sort of problem in which they have been particularly involved. To a certain extent the problems which are raised by individuals are in the nature of divisible private goods. They concern the particular needs of individual and family, with housing high on the agenda in both countries. The councillors' job in this respect is partly that of 'social worker' caring for the welfare of individual 'clients' and partly that of 'broker' who passes requests on to the local administration or who seeks to solicit support from other councillors in order to obtain a more rapid and effective response to demands.

Councillors have, however, other dimensions to their office. They supervise the provision of local services and promote the interests of the locality in the country at large (by, for example, competing with other local authorities to attract industry). In these ways they are also concerned with the provision of local public goods, and their active involvement may reflect this aspect of their function rather than action in response to demands. It is arguable that by its nature the study of local participation places its emphasis on the responsive role of councillors and under-estimates the more general, governing aspects of their work which some councillors may consider more important. There is, in other words, more to local politics than merely the accurate reflection of the needs and problems of the local residents. The councillors are not merely delegates whose opinions should mirror those of the voters and whose actions are guided by their wishes. The councillors act as traditional 'representatives' mediating between voter and government. In one sense they are imposing their will over that of the electorate, but the councillors themselves may tend to think of it as the legitimate use of their own judgement concerning the collective interest. Certainly in Britain councillors were more prone to think of their task in this way than the general population who over-whelmingly believe that councillors are in office in order to reflect the opinions of the electors.

Particularly in their concern with decisions affecting collective provision for the locality, the councillors are influenced by their position within the structure of local government and administration. The internal forces within the town hall are not the focus of the present study of citizen participation and its effects but should nevertheless be kept in mind as a factor of considerable importance. The local bureaucracy is itself far more than a neutral administrative force, particularly in the large cities. In the British study local officials were ranked by the non-councillor leaders as second to councillors in influence on decision-making. In partisan councils the party programme necessarily affects the perception of priorities, of appropriate solutions, and the degree of freedom councillors may have to act. Moreover, the chapters have not sought to distinguish the agendas of those councillors at the centre of power – those closest to the mayor in France and the holders of the crucial committee chairs in Britain. Finally, councillors' actions and priorities are shaped by the statutory powers of the local authority, its resources and the decisions of the state. These various internal forces would lead one to anticipate a discrepancy between the agenda of councillors, who are subject to a particular process of political socialisation, and that of citizens, and also a different set of priorities for action. The fact that the discrepancy was relatively small in both countries is perhaps some evidence that the local administrative and political systems are at least reasonably effective in communicating mess-ages, whether from citizens to leaders or in the reverse direction.

A number of factors have to be taken into account in explaining the particular configuration of the issue agendas. Clearly the local context is significant. One must also bear in mind the statutory responsibilities of the local and central authorities in the two countries discussed in chapter 2. The point at which responsibility is established, as well as the sense of where responsibility ought to lie, would be expected to affect the directions in which political pressure is applied. The local economy receives much the same level of attention in the two countries. Problems of housing are also in the forefront. More generally there are signs that in Britain problems affecting the provision and consumption of urban services receive greater prominence whilst in France social issues such as education, the problems of youth, and of the elderly and social assistance are, taken together, higher on the agenda.

The evidence from both sets of case studies suggests that of the two roles of receiver of demands and initiator of action it is the latter that means most to councillors. As far as demands are concerned, the agenda of issues outside election times is concerned with the area which the councillor represents or with the problems of particular social sectors (the homeless, the unemployed) rather than being of a party nature. Beyond this is an area of relative autonomy (Nordlinger 1981) in which the council is able to exercise initiative and even, where it perceives the need, to mobilise and channel support for its priorities. In the relations between citizens and elected leaders the descending relationship would appear to be at least as significant as the ascending.

PART V COMMUNITY OR LOCALITY?

Introduction

Most political participation is conducted on a local stage. Even in our mobile, modern society, relatively few people pursue their affairs, whether social or political, beyond the boundaries of a particular locality. One of the characteristic features of 'political professionals' is precisely that they escape the gravitational field of the locality.

However, to say that most social and political activities are carried on in one single place does not necessarily imply that these activities are themselves locally determined. Many will be local instantiations of nationally determined practices. People vote in local constituencies in national elections whose outcomes are largely settled on the basis of national or international issues. Equally, they may campaign in local sections of a national pressure group, or contact the local official of a central government department about a problem. Moreover, social structures which have so powerful an impact on patterns of participation are commonly produced by forces which regulate the whole nation, its culture and its economy. Few localities in modern life can remain isolated and idiosyncratic, as the film *Heimat* by Edgar Reitz vividly illustrated.

Indeed, there are many political scientists who would argue that local policies on major issues are for the most part the outcome of non-local forces which may include nationally based economic and professional sectional interests (Dunleavy 1980: 98–133) as well as, in Britain, the increasingly centralising pressures mounted by national government (Newton and Karran 1985; Goldsmith and Newton 1983). It is the operation of these national factors which explains the extent to which changes in local authority policy and practice can occur virtually simultaneously across the country despite the apparent political autonomy of local governments and the powers of local politicians.

Nevertheless, there is a host of activities prompted by issues and problems which have a local dimension. People campaign to keep their local hospital open or they complain about the state of the local roads. These issues are specific to the locality even if it is the case that, partly because of national factors, they have their counterparts elsewhere. Hospital closures are to a significant degree a reflection of policy decisions about the operation of national medical services. Accordingly, wherever such closures are threatened it is likely that certain alignments of sectional interests will emerge such as medical specialists or public sector unions. For this reason, a full study of participation at local level has to take account of both exogenous and endogenous forces. The very notion of a 'local politics' is taken up again in the concluding chapter.

We may accept, therefore, that local action may well occur within a larger national context and will frequently bring to the forefront elites and activists representing local branches of national interests. But, it still remains an open question as to how far the population in general is led to participate as a consequence of its very locality in addition to such factors as class, education or gender which were discussed in chapters 3 and 4.

In pursuit of this question, the British study in chapter 9 focuses on two local areas – Penrhiwceiber in Wales and Stockwell in inner London. As is explained more fully at that point, these represent contrasting instances of how locality can form the basis of political action as well as shaping individual political outlooks. The French materials, reported in chapter 10, are again drawn from Mérignac, whose characteristics were described in an earlier section of the book.

There are, in the British and American literature on local societies, two broad accounts of the way in which political activity might be expected to be shaped by locality – the 'community-identification' theory and the 'social interaction' theory (Putnam 1966; see also Rossi 1972). On the basis of either theory, it could be expected that participation would be increased to the extent that individuals were highly integrated into local life. They differ in the manner of the integration described.

According to the community identification theory, where inhabitants of an area have strong affective ties to it and a sense of solidarity with its inhabitants, one would expect that these attitudes might motivate individual and collective action which would sustain the distinctive quality of local life. The interactionist approach suggests that residents will have a greater propensity to take local political action if they also interact socially with other individuals and groups in the area. Unlike the community identification theory, the interactionist view does not stress the psychological attachment to the area.

Whilst these theories have some affinity to the contrast drawn by Weber between 'communal' and 'associative' relationships (Weber 1947: part 1, section 9, 136–9), the correspondence is not exact. The community identification theory does, like Weber's theory of communal relationships, emphasise subjective and affective ties with a 'community'. However, the interactionist perspective does not assume, as does Weber's idea of an associative relationship, that local involvement is entirely instrumentalist, concerned with the rational defence of interests. Instead, the theory is agnostic about motivation. Local political action could stem either from processes of competition and compromise between conflicting individual and group interests or from involvement with more consensualist forces. For these reasons, the two approaches are not polar opposites, as they are in Weberian theory. Instead one should anticipate, as Putnam pointed out (Putnam 1966:641), that psychological attachment and social interaction would be related, whilst being logically and, hypothetically at least, also empirically distinct.

The empirical investigation of the community identification thesis is fraught with difficulties. In the first place, 'communities' are not solely identifiable by political and administrative boundaries marked on a map. Whether any given area is a community in this sense depends on the attitudes prevalent amongst the population. Secondly, the attributes of any area which lead to its being characterised as a community are highly contestable (Plant, 1978). 'Community' is, at one and the same time, a descriptive and an evaluative term. When people describe a town or a village as a 'community' they generally ascribe to it qualities which they value highly and which are connected with their outlook on life or their ideological stance. For a conservative, the social life of a community could be organically inter-related, deferential and hierarchical. The socialist would regard such arrangements as incompatible with a genuine sense of community which could only arise where individuals consciously and freely provide mutual support to their fellow citizens as equals. Hence, even when one succeeds in identifying an area as being, in the minds of its inhabitants, a 'community', it still remains to be established what are the characteristics which lead to this designation. Moreover, although the communitarian hypothesis suggests that participation should be enhanced as a consequence of community attachments, it is also apparent that the patterns of participation by classes and groups and, perhaps, of what are perceived as being important issues, could vary according to the conception of community which prevails.

The interactionist perspective sees political participation as a reflection of engagement in the social processes of the locality. It does not face the same methodological problems of defining a particular manner of interaction as 'communitarian'. Interactions may arise in the course of either conflictual or consensual processes. With the 'decline of community' which has been so widely alleged to be a feature of the modern world, it may be that the interactionist theory would explain the effect of locality on participation more fully. The community identification theory would then only apply in certain residual outposts of solidaristic sentiments. Reality may, however, be less extreme than the rivalry of theories supposes. Participation may be activated in one and the same area both by communitarian sentiment and by involvement in social existence.

Comparisons with France introduce new problems of a conceptual nature in addition to the problems of institutional and cultural comparisons germane to all such studies. In France, the notion of community carries connotations which differ in certain significant respects from those which it possesses in Britain, complex as these already are. Indeed, for a long time now in France, the vocabulary of the social sciences has feigned a lack of interest in the idea of community as it is understood in the sociological tradition (Tönnies 1963; Nisbet 1967). The concept has been more or less banished, following the disputes which occurred during the 1970s. This is not the place to describe the somewhat heated debates which took place at that time (for a general view of the debate, see Ritaine 1979). The emphasis placed on identifying at the most general level of society the socio-economic processes most closely tied to small territorial units, had the effect of discrediting for a time the search for interpretative systems based on a degree of local political autonomy, and based to an even greater extent on the idea that there could exist socio-political systems which were sufficiently self-contained to justify their being described as communities (Jollivet 1974). Nowadays, when the tide of 'grand theory' has receded, the renewal of interest in localised phenomena is being expressed more through a 'revival' of the notion of political culture, which is often supported by the highly ambiguous notion of 'identity'.

For these reasons, it will be appreciated that the chapter contributed by the French team could not make such confident use of the notion of community. It is referred to only very occasionally. And yet, this hesitation as to the academic use of a word ought not to hide the fact that our approach is primarily a comparative one. If, on this question, French and British investigators are separated by a semantic divide, should they inflict the consequences on the populations which they are trying to describe? In other words, should the differences between the concepts favoured by the two groups have repercussions for the analysis?

Yet again we face the question of nominalism, which, despite the use of a unified vocabulary for the social sciences, still has some pitfalls. Fortunately, we have the data collected by the survey. But here, too, even when those involved have been allowed to speak, there is still a risk of labouring under an illusion: to ask Welshmen, Frenchmen and Englishmen whether the local society in which they live is a 'real community' may mean that we run the risk of regarding as of equal value answers which have fundamentally different connotations in each place. The vocabulary of daily life is even less unequivocal than that of political science. It is not self-evident that a 'community' has the same meaning in a Welsh mining community as a '*communauté*' in a suburb of Bordeaux.

However, these objections do not pose insurmountable difficulties. This is because, in the first place, the specificity of language is one of the forms of closure found in symbolic systems: the significance of the community is probably not the same among the senior managers of Sevenoaks as among the miners of Penrhiwceiber. The same observation would also apply in France, and we would have needed a much more varied sample in order to investigate the possible correlations which might exist between populations whose socio-economic situations remained comparable through several generations, and to assess the part played by 'social', 'linguistic' or 'cultural' factors in keeping different societies apart. After all (though this cannot be confirmed), the significance and meaning of community may be closer in two mining villages on each side of the Channel than in two districts of the same town. This, at least in France, is what many investigations have shown (Ledrut 1973a, 1973b; Chombart de Lauwe 1965).

What is more, the extent to which investigations carried out in Britain and France can be compared depends more on looking for objective indicators than on differences in belief systems. In the following chapters, emphasis is placed on an attempt to test hypotheses concerning the effects of cohabitation by individuals within limited territorial areas. The minimum definition and basic concept is the 'locality', and not the community. By 'locality' we mean simply that processes take place within the same spatial area, and we do not prejudge any system of integration which this unit offers. If the community defines one type of social grouping, the locality describes only the surroundings, and does not specify any one type of social relationship. A desert island is a locality, though it does not greatly interest the political scientist. If people start to live there, they may found a community; but it is not impossible, either, for them to live in isolation from one another, every man for himself, maintaining links only with the mainland. This fanciful situation is not so far from describing what has actually happened in many residential suburbs (Chamboredon and Lemaire 1970).

Starting from territorial areas defined in terms of local government and administration, our aim was not to discover those spatial areas possessing the relevant sense of social solidarity, as in the approach adopted by some geographers (in France, Lacoste 1986). Our investigation was concerned only with the significance of the more visible territorial boundaries, namely those which serve as the basis for local political institutions. This was a deliberate research decision. In these circumstances, the relatively low levels of participation as measured by our various indicators should not necessarily give rise to a sense of disillusionment.

Clearly a study of non-spatial institutions whose function is to channel political participation, either in the narrow sense (political parties and party activists) or in the wider sense (associations and their members) would have provided different results. It is even conceivable that there are other forms of territorial area which are now more relevant to political participation than the commune or the local government district. Thus, the policies of school catchment areas which have been in operation for some years both in Britain and France, have had the effect of changing the composition of the areas of towns, as parents search for a 'good school', for their children. Since we know that all kinds of cultural or sporting activities can grow out of parents' associations, a dynamic process may develop which structures participation on the basis of a sort of partial spatial community (since not all those who live in the area are members), whose territorial limits have been set by the local authorities who determine the catchment areas.

Again, this type of process is not peculiar to the urban context. In the countryside, organisations such as cooperatives for processing and marketing agricultural products (wine-producing cooperatives, for example) often provide support for a 'quasi-community' structure; they encompass activities going beyond the initial objectives and are in a privileged position in talking to the local political authorities. These organisations stretch over areas of land paying no attention to administrative maps, and involve not only communes and cantons, but also departments and regions.

The two chapters which follow cannot claim to provide a definitive falsification or confirmation of the existence of a distinctively local or community dimension to political participation. Rather, they constitute explorations of the nature of the phenomenon in the two countries. Being based on the present state of community attitudes in the various localities, the studies cannot provide evidence as to the 'loss of community' which has been one of the well-established themes in the sociological analysis of the impact of the industrial revolution on communitarian relations and social integration, as exemplified in different ways by Durkheim or Simmel. It is indeed possible that the social attitudes and relations found in the present studies reflect the dissolution of previously existing communities. However, even if more historically oriented research had revealed the existence of past communities, this would probably not have significantly affected the picture of social relations as they are at present.

An alternative vision which is sometimes offered is of what has been termed the 'community saved' (Wellman and Leighton 1979) – the idea that neighbourhood community has survived as a primary tie and serves as a basis for political participation. However, as will be seen, our studies offer little support for this contention. Even if one can establish that a sense of neighbourhood community has been retained and that it provides a significant measure of sociability and mutual aid, nevertheless it would appear to have only a weak influence on the propensity of individuals to take action and seldom serves as a basis for purely local political mobilisation. It remains possible that it will ultimately be through a third notion of community – what Wellman and Leighton call the 'community liberated' – that political participation is related to community. Like the 'loss of community' theory, this view accepts that there has been a weakening of traditional community. However, it shares with the theory of 'community saved' the idea that primary ties have remained viable and important. New communities have, on this analysis, arisen but they are rarely based entirely on neighbourhoods or on spatial proximity. Community has been 'liberated' from the confines of neighbourhoods by the effects of a more mobile society and may come to rest on networks of social or professional ties or based on a shared concern over issues, any of which can activate members of such communities politically.

Thus there are various ways in which participation may relate to structures of community which themselves are not in reality always sharply distinguished one from another but which may overlap as people belong to both spatial and non-spatial communities. The study of the relation between local, spatial community and participation, whilst crucial to some fundamental understandings of community, does not necessarily exhaust all the political possibilities of community identity.

9

Community, locality and political action: two British case studies compared

GERAINT PARRY and GEORGE MOYSER

There is a long-standing theory, of which Tocqueville and John Stuart Mill are joint progenitors, that local government is the school in which political understanding and participation is learned (see Parry 1972: 3–38). Knowledge of local problems and interest in their solution would enhance local participation, with beneficial effects for both individual and society. Despite the longevity of the theory and its popularity, particularly amongst those radical democrats who favour de-centralisation, the empirical evidence in favour of the link between locality and participation is scanty and contradictory (Verba and Nie 1972: 229–32). To some degree this state of affairs arises because of uncertainty about the central terms in the discourse (Rossi 1972) and about the way in which individual participation is mediated by locality.

According to one view, participation will be enhanced to the extent that individuals live in 'communities', which are, at a minimum, localities characterised by a certain sense of solidarity and common identity. In such 'communities' residents are likely to have 'an intention . . . to act in certain ways towards one another, to respond to each other in particular ways, and to value each other as a member of the group' (Plant 1978: 89). Such intentions are actualised, it is hypothesised, in higher levels of local participation. The major problem with this 'community identification' theory arises from the deep ambivalence of the notion of community which is a prime instance of the 'essentially contestable concept' (Gallie 1955–6) in that a person's notion of a community is inextricably related to that person's ideological stance on a range of other values. Thus, the attributes of a community will be significantly different for a person on the left compared to someone on the right (Plant 1978; McCulloch and Parry 1986). Potentially, this should in turn affect the types of issues and actions taken in pursuit of community values.

A second view of the relation between locality and participation perceives locality as the setting in which individuals interact particularly

190

intensively in the course of their economic, social and domestic lives. This 'interactionist' perspective would hypothesise that local participation would be greater among those who were highly integrated into the local society – at least to the degree that the promotion of individual and group interests was affected by local decision-making. This view does not suppose that those who interact frequently at a local level necessarily think of their area as possessing any of the solidarist characteristics of a 'community'. Such persons may look upon their locality in entirely instrumentalist terms, and the extent to which local integration and a sense of community-mindedness are related is, in principle, a matter for empirical testing.

It remains, of course, a possibility that locality and community are entirely irrelevant to the modern era. It is certainly arguable that people are moved by interests that transcend locality, such as class, status or profession. Indeed, some may regard these as non-spatial 'communities'. Thus academics, or church-goers or chess-players may be viewed as communities. It must be a matter for investigation whether participation at a local level is a product of local integration or community identity, or is to be explained by such factors as class (Verba and Nie 1972: 229–47).

I THE RESEARCH SITES

The two areas focused on in this chapter were chosen because of the potentially contrasting ways in which community and social interaction might affect political participation. Thus the two localities differ in significant respects. Features in their social life and even in their physical location constitute key factors in explaining the interconnections between community and politics. One locality is the traditional Welsh mining village of Penrhiwceiber. Homogeneous in employment and in social class, it is a small, very compact village, its terraced houses facing one another across narrow roads, with a more recent council estate higher up above the main village. It is adjacent to the small town of Mountain Ash in the Cynon Valley. It has suffered severely from unemployment (male unemployment was already 17% by the 1981 census and rose subsequently) and has some of the poorest housing conditions in Britain (Cynon Valley Borough Council 1984). The time of the survey coincided with a national miners' strike during which the miners gave almost unanimous support to their union. The local authority is dominated by the Labour Party. According to the great majority of those answering the survey, Penrhiwceiber is a 'community'.

The other locality is Stockwell which forms part of the Labour-controlled London Borough of Lambeth. The area is, to outsiders at least, less geographically distinct from its neighbours than is the pit village. Socially, it has lost much of the homogeneity it may once have possessed. Though largely working class (about 40% in the Borough as a whole), the residents also include some middle-class professionals, many of whom work in the area. Like other inner London areas it contains a substantial number of people with a West Indian or Asian background. The area suffers from unemployment (15% across the Borough) but, by contrast to Penrhiwceiber, is not dependent on one form of employment. Stockwell is at the opposite end of the scale from Penrhiwceiber in the relatively low proportion of the population who regard it as a community.

There are, therefore, differences between the areas in the degree of social homogeneity, the extent to which there is a dominant single work-experience and in their physical distinctiveness – all of which have been at times regarded as affecting the sense of community and the degree of integration into a locality. At the same time both areas have certain common aspects. They are primarily working-class areas which have, in much of the literature on the topic, been associated with a particular type of solidarist community (Young and Wilmott 1957; Frankenberg 1969). Such a working class community is sometimes seen by Marxists as a source of resistance to capitalism although its existence is itself an effect of what is regarded as exploitation (Plant 1978: 93–5). In popular imagery this kind of community is noted for a sense of equality and for mutual discipline and support, often in the face of adversity.

These two case studies cannot, of course, encompass the range of possible connections between participation and patterns of local social relationships, such as might occur in isolated but heterogeneous towns or in more scattered rural areas or in affluent suburbs. Taken together, however, the two case studies permit an examination of the variations in community identification and in social interaction which can exist within one particular, working-class, sub-culture.

2 THE MEASUREMENT OF LOCALITY AND COMMUNITY

In order to test the community identification and local interactionist models, we have constructed indices of both community attachment and local integration. In this section we examine the empirical characteristics of these measures and the patterns they form in our two chosen localities.

Community

The community index is composed by combining a cognitive and an affective indicator – whether the respondent believes the area to be a community and whether he or she is strongly attached to it. On the first of these, Penrhiwceiber residents were much more likely to think of their locality as a community than was the case in Stockwell. Nearly 90%, in fact, agreed that Penrhiwceiber was a 'real community' compared with under half (44%) in Stockwell. Equally, nearly twice as many felt a 'very strong' or 'fairly strong' attachment to Penrhiwceiber as did Stockwell respondents about their area (72% to 38%). In short, the sense of community is very different between the two. It was on this basis that they were selected for a detailed comparative analysis in this chapter.

To explore further the nature of that difference, we also examined the relationship between the belief that the particular area was indeed a community and other opinions about the characteristics of the locality. These were designed to identify whether criteria associated with particular theoretical conceptions of community are in fact associated empirically. For this purpose, we asked respondents about five such attributes, one concerning spatial boundedness, and four related to 'communality' (McCulloch 1984: 437–50) – the sharing of similar needs, problems and interests; the extent of mutual support; the treatment of each other as equals; and the sense of togetherness and fellowship in the locality.

In all of these, as perhaps might be expected, the views of Penrhiwceiber residents were much more 'communitarian' than those of respondents from Stockwell. The pit village was seen, for example, as having 'clear boundaries' by 85%, whereas in Stockwell the figure was significantly lower at 48%. A similar discrepancy was also observed for all four communality items. Thus, 85% of Penrhiwceiber residents felt that 'people treat each other very much as equals', compared with only 53% in Stockwell. In general, therefore, the widely held belief in Penrhiwceiber that it is a community does seem to go hand in hand with a relatively strong presence of other qualities traditionally associated with a feeling of communality. We might, indeed, say that Penrhiwceiber is a place where both community and communality are strongly to be found (see also McCulloch 1984: 438).

Thus it is not surprising that we also found a positive individual level association between the sense of communality and of community. However, the strength of that relationship varied quite sharply across the different measures. Strongest of all, in Penrhiwceiber, was the association linking the belief that the area formed a community with the view that residents treated each other equally ($r^1 = .48$), followed closely by mutual support (.46) and the sense of togetherness and fellowship (.43). These were also the traits that proved the sharpest discriminators in Stockwell. At the other end of the scale, by far the weakest correlation in Penrhiwceiber concerned the sense of the area having clear boundaries ($r = .10$). Why this should be so is, frankly, puzzling. For although it is not a measure of communality, as the others are, it does have a clearer spatial ingredient which might arguably create a stronger linkage with a sense of spatial community. Furthermore, in Stockwell it does have a somewhat stronger association (.25) than the sense of sharing similar needs (.18). But even here, the connection is obviously still rather weak. The average strength of relationship for all five measures, however, is the same in the two areas – .35 in Penrhiwceiber and .36 in Stockwell. On this evidence, therefore, community and communality are empirically related to a moderate degree, but no more where their aggregate presence is high than where it is low.

When examining communitarian sentiment, as it is manifested in a particular local area, it is necessary to consider whether one might be measuring a more general propensity of people to think in communitarian terms. This might be displayed in two ways. People might, first, think that a number of social groupings which transcend local boundaries (such as those who share the same sort of work, the same religious or political views, the same social class or leisure interests) could also be described in communitarian terms. If those who consider the local area to be a community also thought of those other groupings in communitarian terms one would be faced with a broader attitude of mind rather than with a distinctive sense of spatial community. In the event, however, there was no general association in either locality between the sense of spatial and non-spatial community. But one important relationship did emerge. In Penrhiwceiber a markedly stronger view existed that individuals sharing a common occupation or social class form 'communities'. It therefore seems that Penrhiwceiber's spatial communitarianism is buttressed by solidarities based on a common occupation, mining, and hence on a shared class. The experience of community in Penrhiwceiber is thus both spatial and social.

A second broader form of communitarian thinking might arise through individuals who identify their locality as a community also being prone to think of other spatial aggregates as communities. In this instance there was indeed a tendency in both Penrhiwceiber and Stockwell for strong attachments to the locality to be related to similarly positive sentiments about other areas – from neighbourhood up to 'Europe as a whole'. In other words, loyalties or commitments to a spatial entity at one level are, in the British context at least, complementary to rather than incompatible with, those at another level (see also Inglehart 1977: 337). Further evidence that this is so can be gleaned from the fact that the pattern of associations is much stronger in Penrhiwceiber than in Stockwell. However, in both places the strongest link was between locality and neighbourhood (r = .54 and .37). In short, we found that the broader and more 'remote' levels generated weaker associations with local attachments. Indeed, in Penrhiwceiber these formed a descending scale so that, for example, the correlation with district, county, Wales and 'Britain as a whole' were, respectively, .32, .26, .19 and .08.

In order to establish that the composite community index[2] did indeed discriminate between respondents in relevant and predictable ways we examined its relationship with two other variables which, in the literature, are regularly associated with most conceptions of community. First, respondents were asked how important it was to them to have a sense of 'togetherness and fellowship' – typically solidaristic sentiments. One would clearly anticipate that respondents who thought this 'very important' would score more highly on the community index than those who thought it 'not important'. In fact, this is precisely what was found, the correlation being .36 in Penrhiwceiber and .25 in Stockwell. Put another way, four times as many who thought fellowship 'very important' fell into the 'high' category[3] of our community index compared with those from the 'not important' group (in Penrhiwceiber, 50.2% as against 11.9%).

The second measure, length of residence in the locality, suggests an equally obvious empirical hypothesis, namely, that long-term residents would be more community-minded than new arrivals. In this case, however, the actual patterns were rather more complex. In Penrhiwceiber, the relationship was broadly linear – the longer the residence, the higher the community score. Indeed, for those living in the area for two years or less, only 17% fell into the 'high' community index category, compared with 84% of those resident 60 years or more. The net effect, however, of residence over the range seems gradually to diminish, with the steepest rise in the index being in the very early years.

In Stockwell, on the other hand, the pattern matched Penrhiwceiber's only up to 20 years of residence. Thereafter, so few respondents were identified in our sample as having lived in the area for the relevant length of time that calculations become very uncertain. But, to the extent they suggest anything, it is a falling off in community sentiments – a feature confirmed by statistics that allow for non-linearity.[4] The reason for this seems to lie in the different social and economic location within the community of the very long-term residents. The evidence suggests that it is because they are white, relatively poor, uneducated and typically no longer active in the workforce. This syndrome of marginalisation and withdrawal associated with old age is supported by our finding that such individuals have very significantly lower levels of social interaction within the locality. In any event, perhaps what is more important here is the fact that, in Stockwell, there are so few long-term residents who are still active enough to support community life. Indeed, if we look, for a moment, at the community index scores in the other four localities in the British participation study, there is a very clear aggregate relationship between average length of residence and average community score. Localities with large numbers of longer-term residents, in other words, seem most conducive to community spirit, as we measure it, and floating, unstable population patterns are most inimical.

Locality

Our locality index is intended to measure degrees of individual integration into the life of the area and levels of interaction with fellow residents (see also Rossi 1972: 95). One ingredient consists of the number of group memberships, weighted according to how active the particular individual is in each one of them. This might, therefore, be construed as tapping the extent of integration into formal networks within the locality. In both Penrhiwceiber and Stockwell nearly half our respondents (48%) claimed no such affiliations. In this sense they form a major stratum effectively detached from local institutions. A further quarter in Penrhiwceiber, and 18% in Stockwell, reported membership of only one group in which, moreover, they took little or no active part. This left merely 29% of Penrhiwceiber respondents, and 34% in Stockwell, who were at least quite active in one association, or held multiple memberships of differing sorts. Overall, therefore, the tendency in both areas was for very little formal interaction amongst the ordinary citizens (see also chapter 8). But, such as it was, there seems to have been somewhat more in Stockwell than in Penrhiwceiber.

The pattern thrown up by the second component of the index, intended to tap informal networks, was in this respect very different. When asked 'How many people would you say you know well in (the locality)?', over two-thirds (68%) in Penrhiwceiber claimed to know 'many' of their fellow residents, with only 2% saying that they knew 'almost none'. In Stockwell, by contrast, just under a quarter (23%) thought they knew many, with slightly more (24%) saying that they knew 'almost none'. Clearly, there-fore, localities can differ as to their patterns of formal and informal interaction reflecting varied mixes of personal and communal character-istics. Hence, both elements are needed for an overall assessment of the topic. Indeed, this view is clearly reinforced by the fact that, in Penrhiw-ceiber and Stockwell, the correlations between the two are both remark-ably low (.16 and .11 respectively).[5]

When the index is created, the large differences between the two areas on the informal interaction measure produces a distribution in Penrhiw-ceiber that, as with the community score, has a significantly higher average than in Stockwell. The figures show, however, that the discrepancy is entirely to be found in the 'low' and 'intermediate' range[6] rather than at the top end of the scale. Thus, the proportions in the latter category are about the same – 23% in Penrhiwceiber and 24% in Stockwell. But those who had virtually no interaction with their fellows constitute over a third in

Stockwell (38%) compared with a mere 14% in Penrhiwceiber. Broadly speaking, therefore, our two localities stand in the same relationship to each other on both our main indexes. Penrhiwceiber not only is a case of high community spirit, it is also one in which comparatively high interaction can be found.[7]

To look briefly into the patterns formed by the locality index, we again examined its relationship with length of residence. In some contrast to the community situation, however, the correlation in both Penrhiwceiber and Stockwell was very weak (albeit positive at .09 and .03 respectively). But, such as it was, it again seems that it was the first five years of residence that made the greatest difference. Thereafter, further increments were small.

Finally, we looked at the relationship between the locality and community indexes themselves. In both Penrhiwceiber and Stockwell they were positively, albeit weakly, associated. Furthermore, the relationship was again stronger in the former than in the latter (.24 versus .07). In short, locality and community represent empirically very distinct characteristics of the corporate life of different areas. But where one aspect is present there is some mild tendency also to find the other.

The character of their relationship in Penrhiwceiber and Stockwell is set out in table 9.1 where respondents are located according to their scores on both factors. The table shows that there are substantial differences between the two areas. Six times as many Penrhiwceiber respondents, for example, score highly on both indexes compared with those in Stockwell (12.3% to 2%). Conversely, the 'low' combination in the pit village is only one-third the size (1.6% to 5.9%). Nevertheless, it has to be said that in both more people are to be found in the middle ranges of the table. To that extent the contrast represented by Penrhiwceiber and Stockwell is one of tendency or degree than of two ideal types – shades of grey rather than black and white.

3 SOCIAL BASES OF COMMUNITY AND LOCALITY

The patterns revealed in the previous section suggest that the possession of a sense of community, or being well integrated into the locality, are not matters of chance but reflect systematically the different experiences and social locations of residents. One example already discussed is their association with length of residence. Here, however, we wish to extend this analysis, to consider in detail the extent to which communitarian views, and individual integration into the area, have particular social, economic or political bases in each locality. In other words, is it the case that individuals from certain socio-political segments of the local population exhibit stronger community sentiments, or higher levels of integration, than those from other quarters? We might expect, for example, that those

Table 9.1. *Distributions of community and locality indexes in Penrhiwceiber and Stockwell*

Penrhiwceiber	Community Index (C)			
	Low (0–1)	Intermediate (2–4)	High (5–6)	
Locality Index (L)				
Low (0–1)	1.6[1]	10.4	2.2	13.9[2]
Intermediate (2–4)	1.3	35.8	26.6	63.6
High (5+)	0.8	9.0	12.3	22.5
	3.6[3]	55.1	41.4	100.0

Index Means 4.12(C); 3.57(L)

Stockwell	Community Index (C)			
	Low (0–1)	Intermediate (2–4)	High (5–6)	
Locality Index (L)				
Low (0–1)	5.9[1]	25.9	23.1	37.6[2]
Intermediate (2–4)	8.8	25.2	5.5	38.8
High (5+)	1.5	22.1	2.0	23.6
	16.5[3]	73.1	10.4	100.0

Index Means 2.69(C); 2.99(L)

[1] Percentages sum to the corner of the table
[2] Column percentages
[3] Row percentages

closer to the 'centre of gravity' of the locality, in social and political terms, might exhibit a stronger community spirit and be more integrated into the area than those more on the margins of local life.

On the face of it, Penrhiwceiber would seem an appropriate case for such a model. It is a locality with a predominantly working-class population and a strong Labour-oriented political ethos. In short, it is a relatively homogeneous place with one dominant socio-political focus. We might anticipate, therefore, that in such a strongly 'mono-pole' locality, those with manual occupations, or who identify with the Labour Party, would be more in the vanguard of local communitarian zeal than those with non-manual jobs or 'deviant' partisan sympathies. Stockwell, on the other hand, might well present a more complicated picture. We know that community sentiment is, on average, much lower in this area than in Penrhiwceiber. This may be associated with the presence of more than one social centre of gravity. Thus, although it too has a strong Labour representation, its class base is much more heterogeneous than Penrhiwceiber's. Indeed, those in manual occupations[8] are only one-third of the total sample compared with two-thirds in the Welsh pit village. Moreover, the latter's professional strata[9] are almost non-existent being a mere 2% of the total which is markedly less than the equivalent figure of 15% in Stockwell. Furthermore, whereas Penrhiwceiber is ethnically homogeneous, our London locality is clearly multi-racial in character with some 22% of the sample being 'non-white'. In these ways, therefore, Stockwell may well provide an instance of a 'bi-polar' or even 'multi-polar' locality in which several socio-economic centres of gravity can be identified. To the extent that these provide alternative or even conflicting loyalties, such a situation may well explain Stockwell's generally lower sense of community. Indeed, although we cannot test the hypothesis here in any rigorous sense, 'monopole' localities such as Penrhiwceiber may well be the main repository of those communitarian sentiments that are expressed in spatial terms. Even this hypothesis must be cautiously expressed, however, since the case of Carmarthen (in chapter 6) suggests that a sense of community may be an important political and social value which is not negated by the existence of a multi-polar party system.

Community

We look first at the patterns formed between our community index and ten potentially relevant social and economic factors. These comprise age; gender; ethnic background (in Stockwell only); educational achievement; class; employment status (employed vs. unemployed); public vs. private personal consumption patterns; wealth; employment sector (public vs. private) and party attachment.

In both Stockwell and Penrhiwceiber, these collectively accounted for about 30% of the variation in community sentiment to be found in the two localities. This suggests that there is indeed some systematic patterning, but overall the explanatory capacity of our ten factors is rather limited. In other words, the links between communitarian outlooks and the sort of bases identified here are not all that substantial, and this applied as much to our community test case of Penrhiwceiber as to Stockwell.

Thus, in Penrhiwceiber, our analysis suggested[10] that several characteristics were particularly strongly associated with variations in community mindedness. These included principally educational achievement, party and class, as well as age, consumption pattern and employment sector, but not gender or employment status. Even amongst the former group, however, the detailed nature of the relationships was not always clear. In the case of education, for example, those with no formal qualifications were the one large category with a pronounced communitarian outlook. Insofar as they were also, in educational terms, the overwhelming majority (some 78%) one might take this as evidence in support of our general hypothesis. But this is to some extent offset by the handful (only five) with very high qualifications who were even more positive, and by the group educationally only one step up from the 78% who were the least community minded.

Class too, although a seemingly important element, did not, when scrutinised more closely, throw up a single clear pattern. It is true that skilled manual workers had the highest community scores and the professionals and managers (again only five in number) were clearly on the non-communitarian side of the fence, a pattern that would accord with our expectations. But, once more, other aspects of the class relationship tend to undermine it. In this instance the principal cause was the largest class formation (at 33% of the total), the semi- and unskilled workers, who were also below average on their community scores. Hence, there is no easily interpreted association between class and community sentiment in Penrhiwceiber.

Finally, the partisan link also proved problematic. Here, Labour Party supporters (at 78% of the total) were on the high side of the fence and those attached to their major national rivals, the Tories, were substantially below the norm. However, the clarity of this association is again somewhat clouded by our finding that the handful (nine) of Alliance supporters were the most community-minded and those lacking any party ties at all (eight) were bracketed with Conservative sympathizers. All in all, therefore, there are hints that community spirit is to be found more in certain perhaps understandable quarters than others, but in no case is the linkage unequivocally consistent with our expectations.

In Stockwell, one might perhaps expect a rather muddy picture. For if, as seems to be the case, the sense of community spirit is relatively weak, then it is not perhaps surprising if its social and political roots are equally varied or indistinct. Whatever the case, its empirical pattern does bear some similarities with Penrhiwceiber's, as well as some notable differences. Once again, age, class and party reflect important variations whereas gender, most notably, does not. Equally, it is old people, skilled manual workers and Labour sympathisers who display most of what community sentiment exists, and young, professional Tories who exhibit the least. To this extent, the working-class Labour ethos found to varying degrees in both localities is indeed a basis on which attachments to those localities seem to be formed.

However, as we indicated earlier, ethnicity also plays an important part, in fact the largest part, in identifying the communitarians in Stockwell. The complexities introduced by this dimension are reinforced by our finding that it is the minority non-white population who exhibit the strongest sentiments rather than the white majority. Clearly, this does not follow the pattern of a single centre-of-gravity model. Rather, it seems to be a product of the character of communal life experienced by our non-white respondents. Thus, they, and especially West Indians, claimed to know more fellow residents than was the case for whites. Equally, they saw their neighbours in clearly more communalistic terms, which may in part reflect minority ethnic solidarities as well as being based on a higher degree of class (and, in particular, working class) homogeneity. On the other hand, the complexity or subtlety of the matter is indicated by our finding that the higher attachments of non-whites (again, especially West Indian) to those of the same ethnic background are not translated into any greater sense that ethnicity is the basis for a 'real community'. All in all, therefore, the exact social and cultural underpinnings of the sense of community in Stockwell are less clear, although they seem to be principally a matter of relatively small but intense minorities. No doubt this situation explains, at least in part, why the overall ethos of Stockwell is much less avowedly communitarian than is the case in Penrhiwceiber.

The rather complex, even erratic, quality of the relationships under review is underscored when we look directly at the differences between Penrhiwceiber and Stockwell. For example, in the latter area, the semi-skilled (the largest class grouping at 31%) had above-average community sentiments, like their co-workers in the manual grades. This is at least consistent with our overall expectation whereas the opposite was the case in Penrhiwceiber. Similarly, on party, Alliance supporters in Stockwell sided with the Conservatives rather than, as in Penrhiwceiber, with the more community-minded Labour majority. All of which undercuts any attempt to argue that Liberal and SDP sympathisers have a consistent ideological tendency to view the world in communitarian terms.

Clearly, therefore, one must be very cautious in using socio-economic and political criteria of the sort displayed here to predict where community spirit will most likely be found. There are echoes of a common tune in both localities, echoes that suggest at least some systematic linkages between socio-political bases and community mindedness. But it is equally true that there are sufficient notes at odds with the underlying theme to make any simple or all-embracing account difficult to sustain.

Locality

The same general conclusions can also be drawn from our evidence relating to the locality index. As with 'community', we examined the extent to which individual integration into local life varied systematically with significant social, economic and political characteristics. Our results showed that, in both localities, such factors performed somewhat better in 'explaining' integration, but not to the extent that we could speak of uniformly clear and consistent patterns.

Thus, in Penrhiwceiber class and party again proved to be important discriminators between those who were well integrated and those who were poorly integrated into the locality. Equally, gender and consumption pattern both seemed to make as little difference here as was the case with 'community'. So far as social class is concerned, however, it was not the majority manual workers who were best integrated but that very small group of managers and professionals at the top of the class hierarchy. Indeed, all the working class groupings, whether foremen, skilled or unskilled workers, were below average. This suggests that, in contrast with the community index, integration as we measure it has more to do with high status or prominence than with being notionally close to a locality's social fulcrum. That this is so can, perhaps, be further sub-stantiated by our finding that those with more wealth in Penrhiwceiber were distinctly more likely to be well-integrated than those who were not. And, for what it is worth, the one person in our sample with a degree attained a very high integration score indeed. Once more, however, there were some wrinkles to report. Thus, the few white collar workers[11] (twelve in number) were more of a piece with those in manual occupations than their fellow non-manuals. Moreover, the unemployed were slightly more integrated than those in a job. But, perhaps these are less substantial exceptions to the overall pattern (at least numerically) than was the case with 'community'.

The other main ingredient, party attachment, showed a pattern more consistent with that for community sentiments in the pit village. In short, here too Labour sympathisers were above the local average and the small number of Tories well below. But, once more, it is perhaps surprising that the handful of Alliance adherents in Penrhiwceiber were also seemingly relatively well-integrated – although they too were in this position in regard to communitarian beliefs. Overall, therefore, if local prominence is the key here, it does seem to mean something broader than social status, and possibly includes political criteria, especially where one party is strongly in the ascendancy.

In Stockwell, the substantive relationships had some familiar hallmarks, as well as aspects that once more make the overall pattern at times less than clear. Social class again was an important factor in explaining integration into the locality. Furthermore, it was the professionals who (as in Penrhiw-ceiber) were in the vanguard and the blue and white collar workers who were not. Equally, party preference made a small contribution, with

Labour sympathisers again having above average scores and all others, principally Tory and Alliance adherents, being below the mean.

On the other hand, our suggestion that integration is linked to a broadly defined social status in the locality is somewhat undermined in Stockwell by the wealthy being seemingly less well-integrated. However, we may perhaps speculate that, in so far as 'non-whites' also are somewhat better integrated than their white fellow residents, status or prominence in multi-racial locales may depend on factors that have little to do with wealth or other criteria that typically make for prominence in the country at large. Indeed, wealth may here indicate a life-style which puts those concerned at odds with the bulk of their neighbours in Stockwell. Whatever the case, a broader range of localities and ethnographic materials would be needed to throw sufficient light on the matter.

What we do have, however, is a large body of evidence concerning political values and participation. Indeed it is in this direction that the present discussion is principally aimed. We wish to consider the role, if any, of 'community' and 'locality' in shaping individual political dispositions. It is in this connection that Mill and others argued that the significance of community is to be found.

4 COMMUNITY, LOCALITY AND POLITICAL VALUES

The communitarian thesis would anticipate that associated with a sense of community would be a set of attitudes towards society and the political system which would encourage a participatory disposition. However, it is important to ask whether, controlling for such significant factors as party support, social class, race, gender etc., these attitudes are indeed distinctively associated with communitarian sentiments or whether those who are socially active and prominent (our 'localists') are equally or even more likely to adopt them. We look particularly at views of class conflict, levels of interest and involvement in politics, attitudes of political cynicism and of support for the system. All of these could be expected to be affected by a sense of community.

A communitarian view of the world, of whatever ideological leaning, tends to be contrasted with a conception of society as divided into conflicting classes. Accordingly, people were asked whether they believed that 'there was bound to be class conflict' in society. Whatever the reputation of mining communities for working-class militancy there was little difference between Penrhiwceiber and Stockwell in their general tendency to think about society as divided by class, even though a slightly higher proportion in the pit village (19%) thought that there was a lot of conflict than in Stockwell (16%). But it is important to enter one important note of caution. What was expressed was a view of society in Britain at large

Table 9.2. *The effect of community and locality on perceptions of class conflict, controlling for other background characteristics*

	Score†				
	Low	Intermediate	High	Mean*	SD*
A Community					
Stockwell	+0.45	−0.11	+0.00	1.70	.748
Penrhiwceiber	+0.25	+0.07	−0.12	1.77	.767
B Locality				N*	Range*
Stockwell	+0.04	−0.08	+0.07	211	2
Penrhiwceiber	−0.04	+0.38	−0.04	272	2

† Standardised by local standard deviation (SD).
* Ns and unstandardised statistics for class conflict measure within each locality where 0 = no conflict, 1 = some conflict, 2 = a lot of conflict.

rather than in the particular area in which the respondents lived. Thus one might believe that one's own town was a community but nevertheless think that the country as a whole was divided into conflicting classes.

Possibly as a result, community sense and the degree of local interaction were not, in fact, good indicators of views on class conflict. These were more associated with political party sympathies. The two indexes of community and locality were less powerful predictors in Penrhiwceiber than in Stockwell, with locality and community having much the same effect in the former whilst community was rather more powerful in the latter. The fundamental pattern is, however, similar in the two areas. Given a choice between describing society as bound to experience a 'lot' of class conflict, 'just some' conflict or as capable of getting on without conflict, those with higher community scores displayed a lower sense of conflict than did the less community-minded (see table 9.2). In Stockwell the 'low' communitarian group tended, relatively, to think in the most conflictual terms (with a deviation of +0.45) whilst the high communitarians were typical of the local population as a whole in being more consensual. The pattern in Penrhiwceiber is much the same with the high communitarians here perceiving less class conflict than the average (though the deviation of −0.12 is obviously slight). The locality index, however, shows no clear pattern in either area with the most socially active appearing as likely as the inactive to think in conflictual terms. Social interaction does not, in these areas at least, appear to affect one's tendency to think either conflictually or consensually.

Both high communitarians and high localists might be expected to be involved in politics. The measure of 'involvement' is an index constructed

Table 9.3. *The effect of community and locality on political involvement, controlling for other background characteristics*

	Score†				
	Low	Intermediate	High	Mean*	SD*
A Community					
Stockwell	+0.30	−0.06	−0.10	2.64	2.40
Penrhiwceiber	−0.41	−0.06	+0.12	2.66	2.23
B Locality				N*	Range*
Stockwell	−0.18	+0.04	+0.16	225	7
Penrhiwceiber	−0.14	−0.04	+0.23	289	7

† Standardised by local standard deviation (SD).
* Ns and unstandardised statistics for the political involvement measure where 0 = 'not at all interested'/'never discuss' politics to 7 = 'very interested'/'very often discuss' politics.

from the frequency with which people talked about politics with family and friends and the level of interest a person claims to have in politics. The average level of involvement in Stockwell was higher than in the communitarian pit village. The highest involvement score was attained by 11% in Stockwell compared with 7% in Penrhiwceiber. In both areas it was those who were high on the locality index – the joiners and the socially active – who were also the politically involved rather than the communitarians (see table 9.3). Thus, in Stockwell, the high localists were more involved than the average resident (+0.16) whilst the high communitarians felt less politically involved (−0.10). This may reflect the general weakness of community sentiment. In Penrhiwceiber the contrast is less pronounced since the high communitarians there were slightly more than averagely involved (+0.12) but the localists were even more so (+0.23). In both areas those who were low on the locality index – less active in groups and with fewer friends – felt less involved. Overall, therefore, the evidence from these localities provides support for the interactionist thesis that political involvement reflects social interaction but no clear and consistent backing for the community-identification theory.

A sense of political efficacy – of confidence that one can affect political outcomes – is often held to be something important to the vitality of democratic institutions. It is sometimes interpreted as a precondition for participation, but one's level of political confidence is also a product of one's own experience and that of others with whom one identifies in encounters with authorities. There is an educative effect. Thus, a person

Table 9.4. *The effect of community and locality on political efficacy, controlling for other background characteristics*

	Score†			Mean*	SD*
	Low	Intermediate	High		
A Community					
Stockwell	+0.19	+0.01	−0.37	+0.11	1.09
Penrhiwceiber	−0.10	+0.06	−0.08	−0.33	0.99
B Locality				N*	Range*
Stockwell	−0.07	−0.03	+0.12	192	5.49
Penrhiwceiber	+0.02	−0.06	+0.14	253	5.08

† Standardised by local standard deviation (SD).
* Ns and unstandardised statistics for political efficacy measure (a 4-item factor scale).

active in social and political life might develop political confidence through experience of how the system operates or have confidence undermined by frustration at reversals or delays.

The standard test of efficacy is the extent to which people feel that persons like themselves can influence political authorities. However, efficacy can be enhanced by collective action and an alternative (or additional) measure would examine the degree to which it is considered that a *group* of people like the respondent could be effective. Accordingly, our efficacy scale incorporates both individual and group elements and combines them with a measure of a person's sense of understanding of how local politics works.

It appears that neither community nor locality has a great effect on the sense of political efficacy. Certain patterns are, however, discernible (see table 9.4). High communitarians turn out to be somewhat lower than average on political confidence. The high-scoring localists, who are active and well-integrated into the system, report a sense of efficacy which is above the norm for the areas without being remarkably strong.

Attitudes to community, and the likelihood of taking part in its political life, may also be related to positive or negative views of local politics and government. It is widely suspected that people have a cynical attitude towards politics but the extent of that attitude has remained a matter of debate. We have measured cynicism on a scale which incorporates measures of whether respondents believe that councillors, those active in community groups and protesters are out for themselves rather than concerned for the public good. These were combined with a measure of the respondents' readiness to trust local councillors to do what was right.

Table 9.5. *The effect of community and locality on political cynicism,*
controlling for other background characteristics

	Score†				
	Low	Intermediate	High	Mean*	SD*
A *Community*					
Stockwell	+0.53	−0.33	−0.11	+0.07	1.12
Penrhiwceiber	+0.89	+0.04	−0.17	−0.16	1.10
B *Locality*				N*	Range*
Stockwell	+0.12	−0.26	+0.28	156	6.17
Penrhiwceiber	+0.04	+0.02	−0.05	240	4.62

† Standardised by local standard deviation (SD).
* Ns and unstandardised statistics for political cynicism measure (a 3-item factor
scale).

The residents of Stockwell and Penrhiwceiber were inclined to take,
overall, a somewhat more cynical view of the political world than were
those in other areas. Even so, this meant that a majority of people dis-
agreed with cynical assessments of representatives, activists and protesters. The exception occurred in Penrhiwceiber where over half
expressed sceptical views of local councillors but where, by contrast, fully
68% were supportive of protesters.

Those high on the community index (see table 9.5) were less cynical than
the average in both Stockwell (deviation of −0.11) and Penrhiwceiber
(−0.17). A positive view of one's community thus appears to be connected
with a somewhat warmer appreciation of its political actors. Conversely,
the low communitarians and also the low localists were more cynical.
Detachment from the locality in terms of subjective identification and of
social integration would appear therefore to be associated with reservations about the motives of those active in local life. However, it is less
clear that the reverse is true and that a high degree of local social interaction reduces cynicism since, in Stockwell, the high scorers on the locality
index held more than averagely cynical views (+0.28). Whether hard
experience has taught them cynicism it is impossible to say.

The degree to which people were supportive of local political institutions was measured by a 'regime support' scale constructed from items
which probe normative values as well as assessments of local governmental performance. People were asked whether they believed that there
was a duty to vote in local elections and whether those elections provided
them with a favourable impression of how politics works. They were also
asked about their general view of local politics, whether it should undergo

Table 9.6. *The effect of community and locality on local regime support, controlling for other background characteristics*

	Score†				
	Low	Intermediate	High	Mean*	SD*
A Community					
Stockwell	−0.54	+0.21	+0.77	−0.49	1.12
Penrhiwceiber	−0.28	+0.03	+0.05	−0.16	1.02
B Locality				N*	Range*
Stockwell	−0.04	+0.11	−0.32	152	5.68
Penrhiwceiber	+0.14	+0.05	−0.06	218	4.94

† Standardised by local standard deviation (SD).
* Ns and unstandardised statistics for local regime support measure (a 6-item factor scale).

drastic change and were invited to rate the local council's performance on a scale of marks from zero to ten.

In both our areas the support for the local regime was below the average for all six localities in the study. Thus the plurality of those interviewed in both localities had a generally unfavourable view of how politics works, with only a fifth in Stockwell and a quarter in Penrhiwceiber being favourable. However, substantial numbers had no strong views in either direction. It should also be stressed that these were the two localities which could be said to be facing the most pressing social and economic problems amongst our six areas of study. Stockwell had the typical problems of the inner city and was ruled by a Labour Council which had been in deep conflict with the Conservative Government. This dispute concerned not only the provision of resources for local services but also whether the responsibility for local problems lay with the locality or with the centre. Penrhiwceiber, for its part, had extreme housing problems and faced the rapid decline of a mining industry that was its principal source of employment.

The patterns of support matched those for cynicism fairly closely. Thus, the high communitarians were more supportive than average, (see table 9.6) just as they were less cynical (see table 9.5). Low communitarians, on the other hand, were typically unsupportive and cynical to a marked degree. In Stockwell, the latter group's deviation from the mean was +0.53 in the direction of greater cynicism and −0.54 in the direction of lower support. The corresponding figures for Penrhiwceiber's low communitarians, who are admittedly few in number, are +0.89 on cynicism and −0.28 on support. The patterns for the localists in Stockwell are consistent, with high and low localists matching their cynicism by lower support. In our pit village the localists present a less clear picture but seem not untypical of the views of the area as a whole.

Looking at the set of values as a whole one gains an impression of the high communitarians as holding a generally consensual and supportive view of society and politics.[12] They perceive less class conflict, they are less cynical and more supportive of the system. But when it comes to feelings which might be thought especially related to the readiness to participate these are less strong. Their levels of political interest and discussion are modest to low and their sense of efficacy is on the weak side. The high localists tell a different story. Their support for the regime is below average and they think slightly more than the communitarians in terms of class conflict. In Stockwell they also display cynical views of politics. They are, however, more interested in politics and more inclined to discuss it. It remains, then to be seen how far the communitarian and localists holding these views actually take part in local politics.

5 LOCALITY, COMMUNITY AND POLITICAL PARTICIPATION

Having examined the ways in which a sense of community and the level of local social interaction are associated with social and political values we now turn to the crucial claims that community and interaction should be positively related to levels of political participation. In order to assess the independent effect of community and locality we have again controlled for a range of other potentially confounding factors such as class, wealth, education, age, gender, race and party allegiance.

Taken together all the factors we considered were highly significant in explaining overall participation[13] in our two areas. Equally, when the effects[14] of each factor were looked at separately, locality clearly had an important effect both in Stockwell and in Penrhiwceiber. Indeed, in this respect it rivals education which has repeatedly been shown in other studies to be one of the factors most closely related to participation (Milbrath and Goel 1977: 98–102; Barnes, Kaase *et al.* 1979: 370–9). Community, by contrast, had a very weak and inconsistent influence. It would appear, then, from the evidence of these localities that the communitarian hypothesis is not about to receive confirmation whilst social interaction theory will survive. However, a test more explicit than statistical significance is the extent to which the high scorers on each index are more politically active than the low scorers.

The people of Stockwell tend, by comparison with the nation as a whole, to be more politically active (see table 9.7). It is, perhaps, all the more striking, therefore, that those in the highest group of the locality index (scores of five or more) are much more likely to participate even than the

Table 9.7. *The effect of community and locality on overall political participation, controlling for other background characteristics*

	Score†			Mean*	SD*
	Low	Intermediate	High		
A Community					
Stockwell	+0.33	−0.04	−0.34	+0.30	1.44
Penrhiwceiber	+0.21	−0.07	+0.08	+0.08	0.91
B Locality				N*	Range*
Stockwell	−0.19	−0.17	+0.55	226	10.22
Penrhiwceiber	−0.08	−0.14	+0.48	291	5.89

† Standardised by local standard deviation (SD).
* Ns and unstandardised statistics for overall political participation measure (a second-order factor scale of 23 original items or 6 first-order factor scores).

average Stockwell resident. Indeed, they are amongst the most active quarter of the British population, judging by their average score (+0.55). Conversely, those in the low and intermediate categories on local integration are also below average on participation with deviations of −0.19 and −0.17 respectively. Penrhiwceiber displays a similar picture although it is less sharply drawn. The locally well-integrated are much more participatory (+0.48) and the weakest localists somewhat less participatory (−0.08) than the community average. However, unlike those in Stockwell, the people of Penrhiwceiber are generally much more like the nation as a whole in their overall levels of participation, even if they too tend to be on the high side.

It is apparent, therefore, that those who are active in the locality, by joining groups and having a wide circle of friends, also translate this social activity into public participation. Such a translation process, furthermore, seems to operate amongst both blacks and whites in Stockwell, although the threshold for converting local interaction into political participation is much higher amongst the non-white minority. However, whether black or white, those with a strong attachment to their area and who also see it very much in community terms are not led in a participatory direction in the way communitarian theory would suggest. Indeed, in Stockwell the reverse seems to be the case. Such high communitarians as exist tend to be low on participation (−0.34), whilst the less communitarian individuals participate more than average (+0.33). The pattern in Penrhiwceiber is less distinct but still gives little encouragement to communitarian theory. Thus, here, both those who are low and those who are high on the community index participate very slightly more than average, whereas those with middling scores are somewhat less active.[15]

Before attempting to assess the general significance of community and locality for participation it is also worth examining whether either measure is especially associated with any particular modes of participation. It is well-established that participation is a multi-dimensional activity[16] and it is at least plausible to suppose that those who are most committed to the community might be especially active in group life or that individuals who have a particularly wide circle of local friends and acquaintances, the localists, might be adept at contacting local leaders to press their demands.

The most striking pattern to emerge is that those who score high on the locality index participate more than the average in all five fundamental modes of participation in both Penrhiwceiber and Stockwell. On average they vote more regularly, are more active in groups, work more for parties, engage more often in protests and contact authorities more. Conversely, those low on the same scale are virtually the mirror image. They are less active than the average in every respect with the single exception of contacting in Penrhiwceiber. The strong 'localists' are particularly active in groups. In Stockwell, where group life is already above the national average, those high on the locality index have a score of $+0.71$ above the mean which certainly places them amongst the country's highest group activists. In Penrhiwceiber the figure of $+0.56$ above the mean is set against a background of much less vital group activity but reflects a similar pattern of involvement. Of course, it would be astonishing if this were not so, since an element in the locality scale is precisely the number of group affiliations. However, no tautology is involved since group *membership* is distinct from our measure of activity in support of informal and organised groups. The high localists are also very prominent in contacting in Stockwell $(+0.54)$ where, again, contacting is more frequent than in most places in the country at large. Both Stockwell and Penrhiwceiber also contain more residents than average who report being involved in protest activities, such as demonstrations and boycotts, and in both places those in high positions on the locality index have taken part in more such protests than the local average. This is especially true in Penrhiwceiber $(+0.25)$.

It is quite clear, therefore, that those who are joiners of groups, and who claim a wide social circle in the locality, are also more likely to participate politically. Hence the social-interaction hypothesis receives firm support. One may argue that people who are prompted by their interests to join groups also have the education, skills, time and other resources to participate. This consideration gives rise to one doubt about our locality index. It is possible that what is being identified is less the effect of 'place' than a propensity of certain types of individuals to interact socially. Such interaction occurs for the most part in the relatively restricted space of the locality but this may be merely contingent. Our localists might interact in much the same ways wherever they lived. However, this tendency of localists to participate at a higher rate is something over and above what might be expected from people's social class and education which, along with other factors, have been taken into account in the analysis. On the other hand, more extensive study of different areas might begin to probe whether local social interaction produces a consistently greater effect in some areas than others.

An examination of the five modes of participation does not, however, reveal any clear pattern which might retrieve the communitarian hypothesis even in part. Those who score highly on the community index are not consistently more active in one mode than another. Whilst, for example, they participate in groups above the local norm in Penrhiwceiber they are below the average in Stockwell. The strongest association is, indeed, between those scoring low on the index in Stockwell and the level of contacting. On the whole it is the least communitarian who are more active. Thus, if our measure is picking up a genuine sense of community – and its association with related values suggests that this is the case – then it appears to have relatively little impact on participation.

Moreover, the sense of community (and indeed also of localism) appears not to affect the kind of issues which are raised. Generally speaking, communitarians had the same sets of priorities as the rest of the local population. In that sense they could be said to identify well with their area. They showed little sign, however, of raising wider and less personal issues than their fellow citizens. Consistent with their greater activism it was those high on the locality index who raised most issues. In Stockwell each of these localists mentioned on average 2.75 issues compared with the average of two, and in total[17] provided 30% of all local issues. In Penrhiwceiber the pattern was similar though not quite so marked. The communitarians were close to the general population in the tendency to raise issues.

Attachment to the area in which one lives and the recognition of it as a community does not translate into local participation, at least in our case studies. It remains possible that other local areas would produce different findings but it is intriguing that these rather negative results should emerge from what would be regarded by many as a paradigm case of one type of community – the solidaristic mining village. Our findings are, indeed, borne out by those of earlier American studies which also reported that community attachment or identification contributed very little to creating local political involvement (Alford and Scoble 1968: 1,198–9; Putnam 1966: 643–6). It appears, therefore, that empirical confirmation of this persuasive theory is not readily forthcoming.

Determined advocates of the communitarian theory may not be totally dismayed by the findings. It could be contended that the communitarian sentiments which people at present report are not the genuine article. Only, so the argument might run, in a society which encourages communality – mutual support, the sharing of benefits and burdens – could people have a proper appreciation of their local world as a community. And only in the light of that recognition could they be led to contribute to their world by participation. The present condition of society is arguably very far from that state (Barber 1986). Moreover, if local government is to be related to the areas to which people feel most attached it must find a level of genuine self-government closer to the neighbourhood than any arrangement that currently exists. Community has always been both an image of the past and a dream for the future. For the present, however, community may give rise to feelings of 'loyalty" (to borrow the term of Hirschman, 1970) but not to any special readiness to use 'voice' to sustain that community by participating in its life.

NOTES

1　The measure of association used throughout this section was an asymmetric version of Somer's d (see Garson 1971: 161–2).
2　The scale ranges from 0 (not at all attached + strongly disagree that the locality is a community) to 6 (very attached + strongly agree).
3　Scores of 5 or 6.
4　The eta statistic for Stockwell (Garson 1971: 178–81) was significantly higher than the measure of linear association, whereas in Penrhiwceiber there was little difference.
5　This also helps to disprove the possible criticism that in combining formal and informal interaction scores we might be double-counting. It is not the case, in other words, that high levels of active group membership thereby entail or include knowing a lot of people on an informal basis. On the contrary, such formal attachments have seemingly very little to do with how many fellow residents one knows.
6　Scores of 0 or 1.
7　However, among the six localities it only ranks fourth on the locality index. Sevenoaks generates the highest average on this occasion – it was fourth on community sentiments – again strongly suggesting that high scores on local interaction tend to derive from different factors than for the community index.
8　Here we are using an eleven category scheme for measuring class in which the manual grades are category V (foremen and technicians), VI (skilled), and VIIA (semi and unskilled) respectively. For details, see A. Heath *et al.* (1985: 25, fn.6).
9　These comprise I (high grade professional and managerial) and II (low grade professional and managerial). For details, see A. Heath *et al.* (1985).
10　The specific technique utilised at this point was a form of multivariate analysis

of variance known as multiple classification analysis. This allows for the identification of the unique effect of any one factor (in our set of ten) controlling for all others. For further details see F. Andrews *et al.* (1969).

11 These comprise categories IIIA and IIIB of our class scheme.
12 Controlling for 'communality' (as measured in section 1) made only minor differences to the basic pattern of associations between community, locality and values.
13 The overall participation scale combines measures of voting, party activity, group activity, contacting and protesting (see further, chapter 3 above).
14 The 'main' effects only have been considered, setting aside any possible effects of interaction between factors.
15 Again few changes in the general pattern came to light when 'communality' was taken into account.
16 For the multi-dimensionality of participation see chapter 3 above.
17 The Stockwell high localists numbered 23.6% (see table 9.1).

10

In search of community spirit

PATRICK QUANTIN

In a work now 150 years old, Alexis de Tocqueville noted that 'in America, not only do communal institutions exist, but there is also a communal spirit which sustains and gives them life' (Tocqueville 1968: 81).[1] In pointing this out, the theorist of local democracy introduced a distinction which enables one to go beyond a purely administrative view of life of the commune and of its relationship with the State and society. The mere existence of communal institutions, sanctioned and protected by the State, is not sufficient to enable those who are administered to behave as citizens, or to take charge of running the affairs which directly affect all those who live in the commune, in a word 'to participate'.

In Tocqueville's view, to speak of a 'communal spirit' does not mean resorting to mysterious states of the soul, in the sense in which, for example, André Siegfried used to speak of the 'soul of nations'. As far as he was concerned, communal spirit results from the practical conditions in which the exercise of power is shared and even becomes routinised, so that each citizen may be called upon to perform a function or may possibly be forced to do so:

> With much care and skill power has been broken into fragments in the American township, so that the maximum possible number of people have some concern with public affairs. Apart from the voters, who from time to time are called upon to act as the government, there are many and various officials who all, within their sphere, represent the powerful body in whose name they act. Thus a vast number of people make a good thing for themselves out of the power of the community and are interested in administration for selfish reasons. (Tocqueville 1968: 82)

If we follow the theoretical model of local democracy proposed by Tocqueville, we have to recognise that this 'communal spirit' has nothing to do with a feeling of local patriotism expressing a collective unconscious, or some obscure desire to weld the community together. Quite the contrary; the citizens participate politically in the affairs of the commune only insofar as it is possible for them to exercise responsibility by themselves, and their share in sovereignty is not wholly delegated to others.

It is not surprising that the French commune is far from being ideally suited to the development of a flourishing communal spirit. First, because, for several centuries, the country has been weighed down with centralisation (see chapter 2); secondly because nothing has been done to disperse power within the commune, not even the celebrated reform of 1982, which strengthened the position of local elected representatives at the expense of the State, but did not concede an inch of power or effective control over the councillors to those who were administered. How then can one imagine a citizenry involved in actions aimed at influencing decisions taken by national government, when they seem to find so little attraction in participating in the affairs of the communes in which they live?

This, perhaps, arises from communal institutions being stronger in France than communal 'spirit'. In other words, the administrative framework has grown up independently of power-sharing along strictly democratic lines based on the primacy of the citizens. The French commune is indeed a centre for the exercise of power at the local level. But, in contrast to the etymological origins of the word, the commune is not seen as a political community. The fact that there are power struggles within the commune is evidence of a real pluralism which can be seen as the basis of democracy, but this process is fundamentally different from what might be called the 'natural' participation of all the citizens in local affairs, on which Tocqueville based his own conception of democracy.

These considerations perhaps go some way in explaining why the idea of a 'community' is so familiar in countries with an Anglo-Saxon tradition (the United States and Great Britain), whereas in France it is generally unknown both in theory and to the public at large. These circumstances in turn enable us to contrast two models or conceptions of local democracy. One is based on the primacy of the collective relationships which define a community. The commune in Britain – or perhaps what is its precise equivalent, the 'township' or even the 'parish' – seems to be looked upon as a community whose distinctive, but not fundamental, feature is territorial. But it is in principle no different sociologically from a non-spatial community, which brings together members who live in different places. Its basis is not localisation, which is merely a secondary characteristic.

The other model stems from an extrapolation from French practice. It does not presuppose the existence of preferential feelings of solidarity welding the inhabitants of the commune into a group defined sociologically as a 'community' and politically through the equality of the citizens. This other model takes account, above all, of the spatial proximity of individuals, and is built on the primacy of the idea of locality. Feelings of solidarity – if such feelings there be – are produced by the fact of the inhabitants being together on the same area of land. The locality is of major importance; the features which make up the community may perhaps derive from it, but are never the basis of the institution.

These two ideas of local democracy are not unconnected with the way in which one can set about analysing political participation. Of course, our task is not to set up a confrontation *a priori* between two empirical situations (the French and the British), but between two theoretical approaches: the one based on the primacy of the community, and the other studying first and foremost the effects produced by the localisation of political and social relationships. The sharp contrast between these two models which served initially as the basis for provisional hypotheses tended, in fact, to be weakened in the light of the findings from the empirical studies. The processes can indeed be looked at in different ways, depending on whether we wish to identify the effects of institutions on 'communal spirit' (the organisational approach) or attempt, following Tocqueville, to understand how 'communal spirit' can give life to local institutions (an attitudinal approach). But, in the last analysis, the object of the enquiry is the same, i.e. the relationship existing between an institutionalised framework, the use made of it by those involved, and the way in which they may possibly change it.

A thoroughgoing optimism lies at the core of the theory of local democracy. The claim is that it is enough to give free institutions to the people for them to learn, slowly but surely, how to use them. On this view, the history of the commune is part of a triumphant march of democracy from the village to the nation. The modern theory of the apprenticeship in democratic values through local political participation is an echo of Tocqueville's idea: 'the local institutions are to liberty what primary schools are to science; they put it within the people's reach; they teach people to appreciate its peaceful enjoyment, and accustom them to make use of it' (Tocqueville 1968: 74). It serves no purpose, at this stage of our enquiry, to indicate the inadequacy of this point of view for explaining the totality of the political relationships which are involved at the local level. But we might note that the division into 'activists' and 'spectators', the tendency of mobilisation to be intermittent, as well as the preponderant political weight of local oligarchies, suggest a need seriously to question possibly naive assumptions about political participation in the communes.

However, the hypothesis that there is a relationship between the integration of individuals into local society and their aptitude for undertaking actions, or involving themselves in political activities should not be excluded *a priori*. If there is perhaps no real question of arguing that community institutions are mainly based on such relationships, it is nonetheless interesting to ponder the specific internal mechanisms which predispose certain individuals, more than others, to participate, and to ponder the question, not from the point of view of their social characteristics (as was done in chapters 3 and 4), but with regard to the way they fit into the system of social relationships established in the locality.

These mechanisms may be only marginal, and provide no overall key to understanding. However, evidence about them may still provide important information about the different ways in which the local environment is experienced, and reflected in patterns of political participation. The fact of participating in the affairs of the commune reveals, in some respects, the characteristics of a kind of community which is reserved exclusively for those who do not perhaps take decisions, but who do at least have a degree of influence over them. As far as other citizens are concerned (those who never participate, or who do so only in exceptional circumstances), the commune may remain a much more distant entity, seen mainly as the manager of services of which they are merely passive consumers, or as the producers of a political 'show' which they observe as uninvolved spectators.

The problem then is to identify the relationships which may exist within the local community between participation and integration. But in what direction does this relationship hold? Do people participate to a greater extent because they are integrated? Or, conversely, are people integrated because they have participated? If the first hypothesis were confirmed, it would bear out Tocqueville's theory of local democracy. The commune would then be the school of democracy: the citizens participate all the more because the problems dealt with relate directly to themselves, and because they can discuss them with people they know. Examination of this first hypothesis involves, in effect, an extension of the analysis pursued in chapter 4 but incorporating additional variables.

The second hypothesis would, on the other hand, involve a more elitist interpretation, according to which participation would no longer be the effect of integration into the community, but would result from other factors which lead some individuals to participate more than others: their social status, their level of education, or the amount of leisure they have. This heightened propensity would have the effect of strengthening the solidarity of a participatory elite which, conscious of its influence in local affairs, would tend to become ever more active. At the same time, a gap would open up between it and the mass of those who felt excluded from, and less and less concerned by, public affairs. This hypothesis, which implies different behavioural patterns on the part of elites, involves some of the factors examined in chapter 7.

In French communes, everything seemingly combines to undermine the first hypothesis. Tocqueville's notion relies on the idea of sharing power – or powers – for which the organisation of the institution makes no provision. On the contrary, the commune offers the essential pre-requisites for the second view of participation, a view which finds expression in many contemporary theories of democracy: political participation is not the exercise of power, but an attempt to influence the decisions taken by those who legitimately hold power. In Tocqueville's view, citizens share power and the responsibility for exercising it. And they accept the duties deriving from it all the more readily in that their rights are significant ones. In the more restricted view of participation, on the other hand, citizens are essentially brought face to face with the consequences of decisions which they have not taken, and over which they may try to claim, through political action as it were, a right of veto or amendment. Here they act against 'bad' decisions, but do not demand the right to initiate and develop local public policies.

The analysis of the survey data collected at Mérignac (the town in the Bordeaux conurbation already described in chapter 4) serves to confirm the weakness of the Tocquevillian hypothesis when applied to France. However, this perhaps makes the diagnosis put forward by the author of *Democracy in America* even more valuable today, in that what distinguished the ideal model of local democracy from reality in France still holds true today. The interest which people show in local affairs and the fact that they feel they have a share in making decisions do not seem to fuel participation. Equally, the citizens who feel the greatest solidarity with their neighbours, or those who believe that they might expect to gain something from the distribution of local collective goods are not necessarily those most disposed to participate. A number do indeed give voice to their expectations, but only a few are ready to undertake any personal action. Thus, showing a concern for what is happening in the commune is not sufficient to ensure active political involvement in it. It is also necessary to possess the means to do so and, still more, a sense of efficacy. Only then can the local resident undergo a transformation into the 'fully-fledged' citizen.

It is not surprising, in these terms, to find that those who participate have a greater tendency to adhere to the locality than those whose participation is weak. Hence it is possible to argue that the locality takes on its full meaning only for the citizen who carries out actions intended to influence local public decisions. Conversely, the varied and subjective ways in which attachment to the commune are expressed have only limited value, and do not have any obvious relationship with the propensity to participate. For these reasons, the analysis which follows will be particularly concerned to identify various forms of integration in the locality and examine them in the context of patterns of local political action. In a few instances, however, it will be appropriate also to examine the converse relationship which sees integration as an influence in participation.

We shall look first, therefore, at how knowledge of the locality and its inhabitants varies according to each person's propensity to participate. Then, we shall see how the ways in which others are viewed differ according to the level of individual participation. Attachment to the commune, the subjective community variable *par excellence*, will provide an interesting test and interpretation for all that separates attachment to the locality from the determinants of participation. Finally, the significance of length of residence will be considered. Not least, this will provide an opportunity to discern the size of the gap between a large French commune of the end of the twentieth century and the ideal model worked out by Tocqueville at the start of the last century.

Indeed, as we find that the length of residence is one of the most significant indicators of attachment to the commune, we may wonder whether this is a consequence of weak political integration. For we may acknowledge, with the author of *Democracy in America*, that 'in general, men's affections are drawn only in directions where power exists... The New Englander is attached to his township, not so much because he was born there, as because he see the township as a free, strong corporation, of which he is part, and which it is worth the trouble of trying to direct' (Tocqueville 1968: 81).

I KNOWLEDGE OF PLACE AND OF RESIDENTS

Whilst political participation is a matter of individual initiative, it is nonetheless influenced by the milieu in which individuals develop and with which they interact. To this extent, a collective or contextual aspect is involved here. It is therefore of interest to establish whether the more fellow residents one knows, the more one is predisposed to participate. But, conversely, we can also ask whether those who participate tend to display a greater knowledge of their milieu. After looking briefly at the first aspect, we will concentrate on the second.

The analysis is based around responses to one survey question: 'Do you know many people around here?' A more elaborate investigation of social networks might have made for a more complex analysis. Nevertheless, even with this single indicator, we can identify a pattern: participation is not a matter of isolated individuals trying to defend their interests. Rather, it is a characteristic of individuals who know those around them. Equally, they have more precise ideas about the territorial area in which they live.

Knowing other people

Amongst those who said that they knew either everybody, or at least many other people (38%), one quarter 'often' contacted a local councillor.

Among the 56% who said that they knew only a few people, only about one person in ten had often done so. As for the 6% who knew 'nobody', none had contacted a councillor. But, putting it the other way around, as in table 10.1, among those who had never contacted a councillor, those who knew nobody were more than twice as numerous as those who knew many people. These proportions then change substantially for those who had done a lot of contacting.

Such figures are perhaps enough to establish the linkage between the local context and individual behaviour. Analysis of the other variables largely confirms these initial observations. Those who belong to associations are also those who know the greatest number of fellow residents. These activities, however, unlike contacts with local representatives, are usually collective in nature, so that this particular result is not at all surprising. Indeed, we may suppose that it is as much the fact of belonging to an association which leads an individual to know people as the reverse. But there is a similar tendency so far as those who sign petitions are concerned. Again, those who have been active in this way say that they know more people than those who have never signed.

However, more overtly politicised activities, such as 'attending a political meeting' or 'taking part in a protest demonstration' are less related to knowing others in the locality. This is probably because in a suburban community, such meetings and demonstrations generally take place outside the area and do not involve local questions.

The extent to which people know others in the locality is also related to other social characteristics. For example, in the Mérignac survey, knowing others increases with social status. Thus, for those who have no occupation, as many as 21.7% of them know nobody, a figure which is nearly four times the overall average (5.9%). Next come the employees and workers who also claim to know relatively few people. Industrial and commercial directors, senior managerial staff and those in the liberal professions, on the other hand, know the greatest number of residents.

Age also is connected with social interaction. Those aged under 25 and those over 65 know fewer of their fellow-citizens than the middle-aged. As many as 40% of this group say that they know 'everyone', or, at least, 'many' people. This compares with only about 25% for those under 25 and over 65. Similarly, women say they know fewer people than men; only 32% had high levels of interaction with others in the locality, compared with 43% for men. Finally, education is also relevant in that those with higher qualifications were distinctly more likely to report high levels. Thus, if we divide individuals into those with low, middle and high educational qualifications,[2] the proportions knowing a lot of other people are 33.3%, 37.8% and 50% respectively. Conversely, those who say that they know nobody decline (7.7%, 5.4% and 2.2%).

Table 10.1. *Participation and knowledge of other people in locality(%)*

Do you know many people around here?	Contacted a councillor			Been a member of an association concerned with a local matter			Signed a petition			Attended a political meeting			Taken part in a demonstration		
	Often	Rarely	Never	Often	Rarely	Never	Often	Rarely	Never	Often	Rarely	Never	Often	Rarely	Never
'Everyone' or 'many'	64.7	42.5	28.5	53.5	34.7	31.0	56.3	37.1	30.8	41.2	41.3	34.4	46.2	38.8	37.2
'Some' or 'very few'	35.3	56.2	61.5	43.3	57.3	63.0	43.8	56.3	61.5	55.9	52.9	58.3	53.8	56.5	55.5
'Nobody'	0.0	1.4	10.0	3.3	8.0	6.0	0.0	6.6	7.7	2.9	5.8	7.3	0.0	4.7	7.3
Total	100.0	100.0	100.0	100.0	100.0	100.0	100.0	100.0	100.0	100.0	100.0	100.0	100.0	100.0	100.0
N	34	73	130	60	75	100	32	151	52	34	104	96	13	85	137

With the exception of the first question, the total of responses is slightly less than 237 because of non-responses.

Overall, therefore, the relation between social status, age and gender and participation, reflects the degree to which each of these groups is integrated into the particular locality.

The boundaries of the commune

One of the difficulties faced in the study of a local community situated within a large urban conglomeration is the lack of clear geographical boundaries between the two. The fact that the commune is a centre of power and local political life does not usually escape even the least aware citizen. But it is much more difficult for him or her to say precisely within what territorial limits these activities are conducted. In asking respondents whether they knew the exact limits of the commune, the investigation is not claiming to measure such knowledge with great precision. Its aim is as much to evaluate the interest shown in the matter as 'real' knowledge. In any event, the results are interesting in that the picture they produce is almost identical to the patterns associated with knowledge of other people. Thus, knowledge of the boundaries of the commune is also correlated with political participation and displays the same relationships with social status, age and gender as were demonstrated for knowledge of fellow residents.

The same observations can also be made both for those with varying levels of interest in the affairs of the commune and for different degrees of understanding how local government works. In short, all these indicators, relating to knowledge of the locality, as well as of its inhabitants and institutions, are closely related to political participation.

2 THE CITIZENS' VIEW OF OTHER PEOPLE

We now turn to consider how citizens perceive other people in the commune, and to what extent these views are linked to their propensity to participate. For this purpose, the investigation draws on a range of questions relating to mutual help, equality, similarity of interests, and perceptions of the communal aspect of life in the commune. It also makes use of responses to a question as to satisfaction with the level of town hall services.

Each of these aspects of how the citizen sees others is related in differing ways to participation. But, in general, it is noticeable that the citizens who participate least tend to have the most optimistic view about the integration and solidarity of the local community. Communitarian thinking would appear, from this standpoint, merely to reflect a locally-generated mythology found amongst those least experienced in political participation and also least disposed towards it. The citizen who has gained some

Table 10.2. *Participation and perceptions of community interests (%)*

	Contacting*		
Shared interests**	Often	Rarely	Never
Agree	23.5	24.6	35.4
Disagree	73.5	71.2	46.2
Don't know	2.9	4.1	18.5
Total	100.0	100.0	100.0
N	34	73	130

  * 'Have you contacted a councillor?'
** 'People around here share the same problems and interests.'

local political experience, however slight, has more reservations about the idea of any collective and consensual mode of relations between individuals.

One example of the balance of opinion is provided by responses to the question: 'In your view, do the people here have the same problems and the same interests?' Those who participate can be seen to be less convinced of the existence of a community of interests than those who do not participate (the indicator of participation in this instance being contact with a town councillor). Moreover, the high rate of non-response in the latter group is significant in showing their relative ignorance of what the problems and interests of others might be.

Whether an individual has been in touch with a councillor often or only rarely makes no difference in this case. But those who have *never* participated in this way show a very distinctive response pattern indeed. A much greater number of them believe that others have the same problems, and fewer think in terms of a divergence of interests. They are also less inclined to give any definite answer to the question. The same general relationship can also be found for participation in local associations. Only 22% of those who are active members believe that people have the same problems and the same interests. Conversely, as many as 38% of those who have never belonged to an association, are of this opinion. Equally, more than 73% of active members think fellow residents do *not* share common interests as against less than half (44%) of non-members. It is true, however, that 18% of the latter were in the 'Don't know' response category.

It seems that the way in which the problems of others are seen is also related to the respondent's own social and economic circumstances. The more precarious that position – for example, those who in the broad

INSEE classification scheme are termed manual workers (*ouvriers*) and employees (*employés*) – the more pronounced is the view that, in effect, 'everybody is in the same boat'. For example, 44% of manual workers think that 'people around here have the same problems and interests', as against 25% of senior managers and members of the liberal professions and only 10% of the 'intermediate professions'. Conversely, 26% of manual workers do *not* hold this general view compared with 33.3% of senior managers and 42.5% of the 'intermediate professions'.

When we turn to educational differences, these results are largely repeated. Thus, the greater the individual's educational achievement (and hence, no doubt, the more secure his or her social position), the less are people in the commune seen as having similar problems and interests. Nearly one-third (32.5%) of those who have a low level of education hold such a view, as against only 13% of those with a higher level.

These differences of attitude become clearer if we move on to consider, beyond the question of shared problems in general, what concrete problems respondents in fact have uppermost in their minds. Amongst these, unemployment is seemingly the great issue of the moment for Mérignac citizens – 60% of responses refer to it. The others comprise a variety of problems ranging from refuse collection to law and order and racism. If we then look at those who think that the inhabitants of the commune all have the same problems, they, more often than the rest of the population, also think that unemployment is the main problem.

This particular finding, though perhaps counter-intuitive, is in fact extremely interesting since, at the local level, it is not the case of an awareness of major shared problems leading those people who are conscious of their community of interests to undertake actions to resolve those problems. On the contrary, those who mention the most salient problem (namely, unemployment) and who also share with others interests which need to be defended are those who actually show *less* propensity for political participation. Conversely, those who participate by contacting local councillors, or are active in a local association, or who sign petitions, are much less inclined to regard their problems as collective ones, and see themselves rather as people with different interests from others.

This analysis runs counter to some of the classic patterns of collective action. But perhaps we are faced here with one of the distinctive characteristics of political participation at the local level. The problems raised are part of a much wider range than one might encounter in a national-level investigation, in which only the great political issues would be raised. However, by opening up our observation to the whole range of questions which come within the competence of a local council, or even those which affect one district, we inevitably end up with a whole mixture of types of issue which would complicate any analysis. Yet the existence of a relatively

Table 10.3. *Participation and satisfaction with the council (%)*

Satisfied with council**	Contacting*		
	Often	Rarely	Never
Very true	23.5	16.4	20.0
Fairly true	50.0	56.2	42.3
On the whole untrue	14.7	17.8	16.2
Completely untrue	11.8	1.4	3.8
Don't know	0.0	8.2	17.7
Total	100.0	100.0	100.0
N	34	73	130

* 'Have you contacted a councillor?'
** 'The town hall handles the town's affairs well.'

strong correlation between, on the one hand, being on the margin of society and raising general problems such as unemployment and, on the other, between integration and a form of participation which is more concerned with local questions, forms a clear pattern.

In these terms, it is then easier to understand why the level of individual political participation is not apparently related to expressions of discontent with the way in which the town hall deals with the affairs of the commune. Indeed, over the question whether the town hall handles affairs well, there appear to be few differences in the level of satisfaction expressed by those who contact the council a lot and those who never do so. Nor are there any when we look at our other indicators of participation.

When we examine the effect of partisan preference, we find that it plays only a small part. Whether respondents are on the same side as the mayor (i.e. on the left) or opposed to him (the right), is only weakly related to levels of satisfaction. In other words, a person's attitude towards the running of the town's affairs appears to be a depoliticised variable not only in the partisan sense of the term, but also in a wider sense that includes levels of political participation. Should we conclude from this that the citizens of Mérignac behave in a strictly pragmatic way in relation to the local institutions of government? Do they look upon them merely as an agency for providing services? This seems to be the most appropriate conclusion to be drawn from the results of the investigation.

Nonetheless, the interpretation of these results is a very delicate matter since there is a large measure of self-censorship amongst those who voted for parties of the right (UDF or RPR) who seem to take refuge either in 'Don't know' responses, or else refuse categorically to answer. This apparent evasiveness can be further detected when we compare our survey results on party preferences with the most recent electoral results in the area. However, these possible complications do not arise in relation to views about how pleasant life in the commune is. Here, it is clear that citizens who are more participatory are also more ready to take a positive attitude towards local life.

However, the optimists change sides when they are asked whether the population of the commune forms 'a real community', a term left to respondents to define for themselves. In this instance, greater local integration through collective activity is associated with a non-communitarian perspective. It is not that those who participate fail to find the commune a pleasant place, and even less that they wish to leave it, but nevertheless their experiences seem to lead them to have a less than idyllic view of the relationships which exist between local people. Within the group who say that they have 'often' contacted a councillor, 73.5% feel that the commune is not 'a real community'; in the intermediary group who have 'rarely' made such contacts, only 52% take this view, and this figure falls to 48.5% among those who have never engaged in contacting. Conversely, of course, the largest percentage of individuals who believe that a community exists is found among those who do *not* have contact with elected representatives (about 35%), whilst only 23.5% of non-contactors share this view. The number of those who did not answer the question also rises (from 2.9% to 18.5%) when we move from those who participate strongly to those who are the least participatory.

Views about community are also closely correlated with levels of education. The lower the level of educational qualification, the greater the chance of encountering the view that the commune forms a community. Thus, 42% of those of a 'lower' educational level see the commune as a 'real community', whereas this is the case with only 27% in the group with a middle level of qualifications, and drops to 20% for those with higher education.

In the final analysis, the views people have of others and of their own milieu are related in various ways depending on the particular questions asked. However, it seems clear that the idea of a 'community life' finds many more supporters among those who are not much involved in collective action within the locality. Indeed, it is the most active citizens who tend to express reservations about an integrated and solidaristic vision of life in the commune. This general disparity persists when we look at the patterns of individual attachments amongst different categories of citizens.

3 DISTANCE FROM OTHERS

Whereas individuals' views of other people referred to their general perceptions of fellow residents and to their notion of community, the idea of distance here refers to the linkages with groups which are not based on the commune itself. This may involve, for example, a sense of attachment to people in the same kind of job, or those with shared political opinions, or even the same leisure pursuits.

Feeling close to other people in the same job or occupation is one factor which might arguably predispose the individual towards political participation. A degree of 'solidarity' with fellow workers or professionals might prompt action in defence of these sectional interests which, from another point of view, have been alleged to constitute potential new kinds of non-spatial community (Plant 1978; Wellman and Leighton 1979). This would confirm the view that professional occupation is an important factor in social integration. In the event, however, this is not generally confirmed by the results, which show no significant correlation between such attachments and participation. On the other hand, this sense of attachment does vary across socio-professional categories. Thus, owners of industrial and commercial firms express the greatest level of solidarity with their particular socio-professional group (72.7%), followed by senior managers and the liberal professions (62.5%) and the intermediate professions (also 62.5%). The least occupational solidarity is shown by employees (48.7%).

The way in which solidarity with people of the same social background (*milieu social*) is perceived does offer a modest contrast across types of participants. Those individuals in the habit of contacting councillors tend to feel closer to those of similar background than others – 62% as against only 47% amongst those who have 'never', or 'rarely', contacted a councillor. This particular attachment is also linked to the mention of unemployment as the main problem. Among those who say that this is the main problem, 57% feel close to those people who belong to the same background as themselves. The figure is only 39% among those who do not see unemployment as the major problem.

This suggests that a relationship exists between the perception of problems affecting individuals and their families, and the expression of solidarity with the social group to which they belong. Involvement in some form of political participation cannot, however, be the result of this kind of predisposing factor because it does not point to any precise objective, merely to a particular sensitivity to social problems. Those individuals who refer to more limited problems, such as questions which may be dealt with directly by the mayor, are not seemingly so clearly motivated by this sort of solidarity. They are, rather, motivated more by the need to find a

Table 10.4. *Neighbourhood attachment and age (%)*

	Age			
Attachment*	18–24	25–44	45–64	65+
Yes	31.0	38.9	56.3	84.6
No	69.0	61.1	43.7	15.4
Don't know	0.0	0.0	0.0	0.0
Total	100.0	100.0	100.0	100.0
N	29	108	87	13

* 'Do you feel a sense of attachment to your neighbourhood?'

solution to the particular problem which affects them without being concerned whether the problem is one of more general importance to others.

Perceptions of distance from others, especially in terms of work and of background are, therefore, not factors strongly associated with political participation. Furthermore, by broadening our analysis to other kinds of proximity which individuals might feel, the results show that there is no difference between, for example, those who claim to be close to others who have the same political opinions and those who claim to have no such feelings of solidarity. The same is also true of attitudes towards people who have the same leisure activities.

In general, therefore, such outlooks may well be significant in cultural terms but they seem to have relatively little to do with political participation. The consequence is to reinforce, once more, the importance of feelings of solidarity *within* the framework of the local community. Whilst such measures do not do full justice to the multi-dimensional character of solidarity, nevertheless it is clear that in this highly urbanised context, being integrated into a specific urban complex has an important influence on the perceptions which individuals have of the world in which they live. Equally, attachment to a place and to its inhabitants throws light on the predispositions of people to participate.

Perhaps the most remarkable aspect of attachment to neighbourhood (*voisinage*) is the way in which it is related to age. The older the inhabitant, the more he or she feels attached to this area. Now, we know from other sources that people aged over 65 are, together with those under 25, those who participate least in politics. It is all the more striking, therefore, that despite the tendency for older (and more attached) people to participate

Table 10.5. *Neighbourhood attachment and participation (%)*

	Contacting*		
Attachment**	Often	Rarely	Never
Yes	76.5	39.7	43.1
No	23.5	60.3	56.9
Don't know	0.0	0.0	0.0
Total	100.0	100.0	100.0
N	34	73	130

* 'Have you contacted a councillor?'
** 'Do you feel a sense of attachment to your neighbourhood?'

less, there should still remain a strong relationship between attachment and participation.

This finding is supported by the answers to a further question concerning the respondent's attachment to his or her area of town (*quartier*). Like the neighbourhood item, this question was seemingly well understood in that nobody failed to give a definite answer. The word '*quartier*', unlike the idea of 'community' or 'social background', seems to belong to the system of ideas shared by all the social groups in Mérignac. It has few emotional overtones, and it is unlikely to give rise to significant misunderstandings, even if the extent of the area referred to may differ somewhat in the minds of different people. From the responses, it is apparent that those residents who have often contacted a councillor tend to have the deepest attachments to their *quartier*. As many as 79% of them felt such a bond compared with only about 56% of non-contactors. If we look at the relationship the other way round, the linkage is still apparent. Among those who say that they are attached to their *quartier* (60% of the total), 19% have often contacted a councillor, whereas only 7% of the remainder had taken this action.

These few observations show quite clearly that the local community is a significant frame of reference for political participation. Whether this takes the form of actions to obtain demands or simply of prudent loyalism, it puts into the same active category those citizens who wish to continue living in this framework. By contrast, the rest (those who feel little or no attachment) seek no personal involvement in the life of the commune. But could it be that this sense of attachment to the commune is merely something which reflects one's becoming accustomed to a place after living there over a long period of time, as might be inferred from the fact that attachment increases with age? Or is a sense of attachment a feeling which has nothing to do with how long the individual has lived in the commune?

Logically, the theory of local democracy would seem to imply that socialisation within a particular locality offers a training in specific norms and values which should then lead the individual to make better use of local institutions – and to participate more. But here we are far from the vision of the founders of this theory, Tocqueville and J. S. Mill, and closer to an approach to 'community spirit' based on ideas of political culture. Our data, however, do not support such a conclusion unambiguously as we have found that participatory activity has relatively little to do with where the citizen spent his or her adolescence. The fact that he or she came to social awareness in this commune rather than in another, in the same department or elsewhere in France, has no great influence on any of our measures of political activism.

Furthermore, a town of 50,000 inhabitants which has recently undergone considerable expansion is perhaps an insufficiently integrated entity for the fact of being a 'native' to be a stimulus to greater participation. A study of a rural milieu or of a small town with a static population might give different results. Here, the 'age' variable is of primary importance in determining the extent to which a person is settled in the locality, and any interpretation of the link between length of residence and participation has more to do with questions of generation than with questions of socialisation in the locality or elsewhere. Among the under-25s, more than half have lived in the commune for less than 5 years, while more than three-quarters of the over-65s have lived there for more than 20 years.

Even though the present case-study has enabled us to undertake only a relatively limited investigation into the processes of participation within the framework of one newly urbanised locality, it allows us, nonetheless, to formulate some provisional conclusions related to the problems studied in this book.

First, participation at the local level is linked to the ability of individuals to integrate themselves into the local social fabric. Participation is therefore broadly an effect of sociability, which leads those who most readily maintain relationships with the other inhabitants of the commune also to take their place in the networks of the local political system. However, a propensity to participate in local politics does not engender a 'community mystique' on the part of those who are most involved. The experience of participation tends, rather, to lead to images of the local collectivity as heterogeneous in nature, and even conflictual in its modes of operation. Belief in the existence of a communal identity is, rather, the sign of a certain naivety which can be attributed to a lack of knowledge of the milieu. This naivety can also be found among those who do not involve themselves in participatory actions.

The background characteristic most closely associated with participation is neither age, nor gender, nor profession, but education. Political participation is, indeed, a more or less direct effect of the access to knowledge allowed by the educational system – and hence of the specific processes of socialisation through school – just as much as of the particular social status with which those having different qualifications are generally associated.

The local collectivity does not appear from this study to be a centre for mobilising people to deal with the major political and social problems. We find that the more individuals are sensitive to what is seen as the major problem nationally (i.e. unemployment), the less they tend to be involved in local activities. This may be, of course, because this problem is not regarded as amenable to local treatment. Moreover, satisfaction with the conduct of affairs by the town hall is also not related to individual activity, although there is a modest association with political party leanings at the national level. The degree of solidarity which the individual perceives between himself, or herself, and others appears to be influenced more by an ability to enter into close social relationships than by the expression of professional identity or, if one prefers, class consciousness. The expression of solidarity of any kind, other than that resting on roots within the local community, is not the basis for a propensity to participate in local politics. Attachment to the locality is, however, a reasonably good indicator of how individuals see themselves in relation to local institutions. Attitudes may vary from 'loyalty' which expresses a somewhat passive view and only modest levels of participation, to 'voice', which implies greater levels of participation. In each case, however, these attitudes are not the same as indifference or voluntary 'exit' by those who might wish to live elsewhere, or who might expect to gain nothing from participation.

In the last resort, the findings serve to emphasise the delocalised nature of political participation. To belong to a locality may provide the actors with a framework for action or for commitments but only rarely is this the source or basis for participation. If the French political system is a participatory democracy, one cannot expect to discover its bases at the local level. From the point of view of Tocquevillian theory this may be regrettable but, as is well known, no man is a prophet in his own country.

NOTES

1 We employ throughout the Lawrence translation (Tocqueville 1968). However, in this instance, 'communal spirit' has been preferred to Lawrence's 'municipal

spirit' as the rendering of the original *esprit communal*, since this perhaps serves to bring out the problematic relationship between the commune and communal feelings which is one of the themes of the chapter. Reeve's original translation used 'public spirit'.

2 The levels of educational attainment are as follows: lower – up to the third level (i.e. qualifying for upper secondary school); middle – up to the baccalaureat or equivalent diploma; higher – above baccalaureat.

Conclusion

The idea that local democracy is properly rooted in something called 'community' has a long history in western thought. It has had its protagonists in French political thinking, although its most notable exponents, Rousseau and Tocqueville, are in certain, if differing, respects outside some of the mainstreams of French political argument. However it is, as one of its critics has said, 'primarily an Anglo-Saxon theory (in the Gaullist sense)' (Bulpitt 1972:282). The prime components of the theory (also termed by Bulpitt 'territorial democracy') are, first, the view that communities are not the artificial constructs of central authorities, but natural units which arise out of the habitual patterns of social life. Secondly, such units should, ideally, be small allowing people to develop mutual knowledge and understanding. This will, thirdly, encourage a concern for the area and its people which will result in higher levels of participation, especially where the community has a genuine degree of autonomous governmental control over its affairs.

It is of course fundamentally a normative theory but it is in a form to which empirical evidence about the attitudes and practices of people in local life is pertinent. To the degree that localities are seen by their inhabitants to be communities one should be able to discover higher levels of participation.

Ranged against this communitarian theory is a more sober hypothesis that participation will be a reflection of social interactions which have nothing to do with a sense of community, but could be as much concerned with the pursuits of sectional interests within the framework of a locality which may, in any event, be entirely arbitrarily defined.

Chapter 10 gave ample reason for expecting that the communitarian hypothesis would have little meaning in France. The fundamental premise that there might be an association between administrative units such as the commune and natural 'community' units is lacking. In Britain there was at least reason to think that a relationship might be found and community was seen in chapter 6 to have been a potent symbol in the Carmarthen study, yet in these two test cases the theory met a severe rebuff. There may indeed be found persons with a syndrome of positive community sentiments, but they were not those who participated most, nor did they tend to raise a distinctive set of issue priorities that might possibly embody communitarian assumptions. Nor in either country was there any evidence of solidarities based upon non-spatial 'communities', such as occupation, providing an alternative stimulus.

Instead, it is the theory of local interaction which appears to possess more substance. In the French and the British case studies, it is those who have a wider circle of social acquaintanceships in the locality or who are joiners of groups, who are more likely to be involved in political activities. The direction of the causal relationship involved is problematical. Does participation enhance integration with fellow residents or is integration the basis for participation? The answer no doubt is that both interpretations capture a part of the complex ways in which the individual and his or her local milieu interact. Moreover, both sets of studies discovered that such individuals tend to have a somewhat less sanguine view of relationships and political institutions in their locality. The French study found such people less inclined to think of their area as characterised by shared interests. Similarly, in the British cases the 'localists' were somewhat more ready to perceive their local political life as conflictual and were less confident about the local system. The evidence begins to suggest that conflict and tension are the spur to action whereas community sentiments induce benign neglect. Indeed, there is some reason to think that involvement in local politics actually destroys the ideal of a harmonious society.

However, even this conclusion needs to be treated with some caution. It does not follow from such patterns of local interaction that they are entirely prompted by local considerations. People may be 'joiners' in whatever locality they happen to live. Individuals may simply be predisposed towards both social interaction and participation.

This is not necessarily to conclude that the local polity has no impact on participation. At the very least it could be said that the direction given to action will be determined by the particular local issue agenda. Yet even in this respect due caution must be exercised. The issues which prompt participation or collective movements of mobilisation may be entirely local, or merely localised versions of wider concerns or may be national. We saw in chapter 4 that in the French town people gave priority to national problems lying outside the competence of the local authorities. The very organisation of local administration, moreover, promotes the interpenetration of national and local concerns. In Britain, for all the dependence of local government on the centre, there are signs that people still think in terms of a distinct local arena. The evidence of the British study suggests a greater tendency of people to give prominence to local issues. Even when, as in the national survey which was the counterpart of the present local case studies, people were asked to discuss the major issues facing them without any restriction as to scope they tended to mention local problems, especially concerning environment and planning, before national ones (Moyser, Parry and Day 1986). These were matters for which the local authorities can be held responsible and towards whom action can be directed. Yet, at the same time, when it comes to electoral party politics at the local level, in both countries it is very often the decentralised expression of national struggles rather than the reflection of purely local issues and, in consequence, voting is notoriously affected by nation-wide factors.

Modern life is clearly in an important sense 'delocalised'. Yet the very mundane fact that most people live and work within a circumscribed area ensures that local politics and administration have to play a significant role in their existence. Virtually every service has to be localised. Nevertheless, it would seem that this fact does not tend to generate a sense of 'community' which translates into participation, even amongst those for whom the notion of community carries some meaning. In France the idea of a local community has only a weak resonance because local issues tend to be interwoven with the great national debates. In Britain, too, community remains more of an aspiration. It constituted part of the language of politics in Carmarthen. At the least it is an element in symbolic politics but one which, as a result of the very frequency of such terms as 'community worker', 'community centre', 'community activist' or 'community workshops', is in danger of becoming devalued.

It may be wondered, however, whether even this restricted symbolic sense of community can survive in the face of growing inroads into the autonomy of local government in Britain. In its quest for financial control and for educational standardisation, the Conservative Government has aspirations to reduce the degree of control of local authorities over a number of services which have traditionally been the jealously guarded preserve of local government. The power over economic and environmental developments in the cities is one instance. Education is another, where discussion of the imposition of a national curriculum has frequently evoked the example of France. Both are areas over which citizens have hitherto taken local action and where local distinctiveness has to some degree survived. New procedures, some more centralised, but all involving a reduced local political presence are bound to affect the patterns of participation, and may further reduce the importance of communitarian sentiments. Although France has moved somewhat in the opposite direction of decentralisation there could not be any question there of a resuscitation of 'community'. In Britain critics of the current centralising tendency may well find that the only alternative ideological defence is a revival of notions of community and participation despite the evidence that they appear to have little to link them. Such participatory communities would possibly be at levels rather smaller than the present local government authorities which are so much under attack. In reality any solution will involve a mix of central direction and local responsibility for which until recent years France and Britain have provided alternative models.

11

Participation and the local polity in France and Britain

ALBERT MABILEAU, GEORGE MOYSER, GERAINT PARRY
and PATRICK QUANTIN

The underlying theme of this study is the notion of local democracy. This notion rests on a fundamental ideal of political liberty. Tocqueville not only grasped the significance of this ideal, but also many of its contradictions, which manifested themselves in the course of the political developments of the nineteenth century. The idea of local democracy was, to a considerable extent, undermined by the processes of centralisation and modernisation, as well as by the rationalisation of political authority typical of the modern period. And yet this ideal rose again from the ashes at the end of the 1960s, and in Western countries, especially France and Britain, produced a set of attitudes which was widely shared. 'Participatory democracy' was very much the vogue, and if the expression, with its abstract tone, is more familiar to the French than to the British, it nonetheless became one of the major preoccupations of the great commissions on government reform which were set up in both countries (in Britain the Redcliffe–Maud Commission in 1969, and the Layfield Committee in 1976; in France the Peyrefitte Commission in 1975 and the Guichard Commission in 1976) aimed, amongst their objectives, at adapting the system of local government to new democratic circumstances. In Britain, it had been thought that the effect of the new system introduced in 1974 would be to increase citizen participation at the local level, to improve the quality of the elected representatives, and to build up new communities which would in many instances bring together the town and the countryside. In France, democratisation was also firmly stated to be one of the guiding principles of the decentralisation reform, which was finally brought into force in 1982 and which guaranteed some autonomy at the local political level (Guichard 1976; Mabileau 1983).

The rediscovery of local democracy is the result of the conjunction of two phenomena. The first is a crisis of representative democracy – or more

239

precisely, parliamentary democracy – which has possibly been more pronounced in France than in Britain because of the traditional absence of
local self-government in France. The second factor was the background of
growing economic and social crisis in which local communities or collectivities (the commune being the basic cell of French democracy) have had
to face up to demands and pressures from a variety of different social
forces. Participatory democracy thus appeared as a new form of democracy which might provide a basis at the local political level for the regulation of the political system as a whole. In order to achieve this, however,
participatory democracy requires a number of social and political preconditions. First, it supposes the recognition of genuine local autonomy. In
this respect there was something of a convergence between the two local
political systems, as France decentralised in the direction of greater autonomy whilst in Britain local independence was being diminished by centralising pressures. Participatory democracy requires, therefore, the
existence, or else the creation, of 'local communities' which would allow
the local sub-system to organise its own activities internally rather than be
shaped by the play of external influences. Finally, such democracy supposes some kind of 'sense of community' which is akin to the phenomenon
of political cooperation identified by Almond and Verba, which makes
local participation a crucial indicator of a civic culture.

The findings of the various studies into the actual extent of democratic
participation reported in the preceding chapters often run counter to what
one might have anticipated, even though some allowance may have to be
made for the possible effects of differences in methodologies and for the
influence of any special factors at work in the areas chosen for the case
studies. Although only a low level of local democratic activity is to be
found in either country, it appears higher in France. Political participation
at the local level is the pursuit of only a minority of citizens and, if we
discount electoral participation (in which the French, unlike the British,
are relatively active), we have to conclude that both countries are basically
non-participatory cultures, if we go by the behaviour of three-quarters of
the population. At the other extreme we can speak of people who are
virtually professionals in political participation, such as elected representatives and leaders of voluntary associations, who are, indeed, sometimes the same individuals. Stable representative democratic institutions
allow the elected representatives a degree of autonomy from pressures
from individual citizens. At the same time this very independence of action
of the representatives gives a special weight to what one might call processes of 'downward participation' in the relationships between local
councillors and citizens, in that often it is the local leaders who approach
groups in order to activate demands from the population as a whole. The
main picture presented by the local representative process is one in which
elected representatives are essentially mediators between the electors and

local government, charged with responsibility for finding solutions to local problems. Only to a much lesser extent do they reflect or mirror in a passive manner the population at large.

Our findings thus point towards the existence of a version of local democracy a good deal less strong than that advanced not only by some recent theorists of democracy, but also in much of the political ideology and rhetoric of the last few decades. Yet it would be wrong to conclude that citizen attitudes towards local politics are necessarily unchanging. We are looking at local democracy at a particular point in time and we cannot determine, in an explicit manner, the degree to which local individual and group behaviour might change with respect to either the nature or the intensity of participation. The same is possibly true of the citizens' demand to participate, the encouragement of which was widely regarded – in France at least – as one crucial objective of the reform of local administration. It is also difficult to detect that there are signs of an emergence of a new form of representation in which both representatives and electors are brought closer together, with both playing a more active political role. It is also not possible to provide evidence for the further decline of local communities, the real existence of which – even if all could agree on the meaning of the sociological phenomenon of community – has not in any event been established for periods in the past. However, the absence of an explicitly historical perspective does not prevent us either from drawing up a balance sheet of participation (the results of which have already been set out in the conclusions to each section of the book) or from considering its overall significance. We propose to consider here various perspectives on participation and its analysis by looking at it in relation to the local community, community leaders, and the processes of political mobilisation. We also, in this final chapter, will try to consider the institutional context in which participation is able to flourish and how this relates to national politics. Finally, we will ask about the possibility for a viable and genuinely local political system.

7 WHO PARTICIPATES?

Measuring participation by means of a questionnaire (as in chapters 3 and 4) administered to a representative sample of the population of a town provides a distinctive angle on the political processes at work at the local level. The picture presented is, in some respects, reductionist, since it gives as much weight to the attitudes and behaviour of those who never participate as to the small number of those whom Verba and Nie (1972) call 'complete activists'. Just as an election counts votes without assessing the real influence exerted by each elector, so a survey takes account of everyone's opinions, and can dilute the activities of a few in an ocean of inaction.

In the eyes of those who look for the triumph of local democracy, such results are somewhat disconcerting. It might be argued that in order to study participation it would have been more appropriate to have looked more intensively at actual political processes of decision-making. One might, that is to say, have concentrated on those situations in which a particular section of the population attempted to influence local policy-making. However, our aim was different. It was not a matter of showing how certain 'active minorities' managed to make their views count or succeeded in defending their interests. That would have required alternative methodologies. Our intention was primarily to investigate the activities and attitudes of the population as a whole, within the political structures of their immediate locality. For these purposes survey methods are particularly appropriate.

Looked at on the level of the 'atomised' individual, the measurement of participation is based on actions which can be categorised into those which the citizens habitually perform, those which they have only performed on exceptional occasions and those which they have never undertaken. There is a danger that this type of approach might take no account of context, that is to say of the fact that signing a petition or taking part in a demonstration are not simply individual, but collective, actions which the individual joins in after being encouraged, or even pressured, to do so by those around him. However, both in the questionnaire itself and in the mode of analysis the present study has sought to counter this danger by looking at individual behaviour in relation to forms of collective action and to the context of issues and, thereby, to place it in its local setting. The aim of the surveys was not, therefore, to draw up a profile of the 'ideal participant' but, rather, to show how the tendency to undertake actions which can be regarded as 'political participation' or to be involved in organisations is related to various predispositions and social characteristics. With this common framework, the research carried out in the two towns, whose socio-economic characteristics provided some basis for comparison (Sevenoaks in the London greenbelt and Mérignac near Bordeaux), has produced results which appear to reveal something about participation in the two countries.

After making due allowances for the differences in social structures and also in the way that certain factors, such as social class, are measured, some similarities in patterns emerge. The possession of high educational qualifications is, in both countries, related to the propensity to participate. So is membership of formal groups or associations as well as of parties. On the other hand, in neither town do we find clear and consistent support for what is often taken to be a standard relationship between high social status or class and participation. Moreover, the different partisan complexion of the councils – Conservative in Sevenoaks and Left coalition in Mérignac –

made no difference to the relative rates of participation by people in working-class occupations.

Another factor which might be expected to influence who participates and who does not is the way in which an individual relates to the 'community'. The potential relationship was examined in the work of Verba and Nie, on whose study we are building, though adopting different approaches. The community dimension has two aspects. There is the question of the extent to which individuals feel that they form part of a community. There is also the question of whether a feeling of solidarity with others living in the same area results in some actual form of political behaviour. Chapters 9 and 10 sought to look at this community dimension in the hope of clarifying some of the ambiguities which surround it. The results suggest, however, that in those cases the notion of community had little to offer in explaining local political participation. Feelings of solidarity did not appear to produce local action. Participants were more likely to be those moved by particular or sectional interests than those who have an all-embracing, consensualist image of local political life. Only in the rural Welsh market town, discussed in chapter 6, did the ideology of community appear to possess some genuine resonance in response to outside threats.

2 THE STRUCTURE OF LOCAL SOCIETY AND LOCAL PARTICIPATION

The aim of these studies has been to shed light on the characteristics of local political participation whilst also endeavouring to show how such participation occurs within the general context of local institutions and structures. Accordingly, we have focused our attention on actions undertaken (or contemplated) by citizens who are seeking to influence policies which affect local interests. Clearly, such action will be influenced by the social structures of the localities concerned which we have not set out in detail but have treated more as a backdrop. In some cases 'political participation' can be merely an extension of what might be termed 'social participation' and for this reason the relationship between the social and political aspects of participation has to be borne in mind. A whole variety of activities can affect the local scene and shape the setting for political action without their being directed specifically at the local political authorities themselves. Are all such activities to be regarded as 'political' on the grounds that they have an indirect bearing on local governmental decisions? In some instances the principal mode of participation in local affairs may be through the activities of institutions which are not formally connected to the local political system itself but which nevertheless play a crucial role in the life of the locality. Trade unions and churches provide two illustrations.

In the Welsh mining village of Penrhiwceiber social relationships are decisively shaped by an economic structure which is dominated by the presence of a single source of employment. At the time of the study the most fundamental feature of local life was the conflict between the National Union of Mineworkers and the National Coal Board which had led to the national strike. Involvement in the strike could, in principle, be interpreted as being as much a social or economic act as an act of political participation. In the event, 14% of residents of Penrhiwceiber said that they had either on this occasion or in the past five years taken part in a strike which they would call 'political' – a figure much higher than the average for the country. However, this should not be construed to mean that other union activity in more 'normal' times in the area would be regarded by them in a political light

Although churches and other religious bodies did not appear in any of our case studies as significant bases for participation, we do not need to delve back very far into the French past in particular to discover situations in which the activities of the parish had far greater importance than those centred around the town hall. In instances such as these people can come to influence local politics through their involvement in what are strictly speaking 'non-political' institutions, such as trade unions or organisations run by the clergy. Such organisations may even act as the chief local spokesman to the extent that, in the French case, one might have concluded that individual 'political' participation scarcely existed.

However, the situation changed far earlier in Britain than in France, with the growth of party organisation at local level, a change which could be interpreted as replacing 'social participation' by 'political participation'. This is manifested in the decline of the local notables or spokesmen and their replacement by a more specifically political market-place. In Britain this was more rapidly achieved as a result of the long-standing existence of stable and highly-structured political parties, operating at local level and providing a more favourable environment for the development of 'political' participation, understood in a strictly partisan sense of the term. Even if issues and actions are not necessarily always defined as 'political' solely by reference to their partisan or non-partisan character, the parties are in a position, at least, to take up issues and thereby to 'politicise' them.

In France, by comparison, the weakness in the past of the parties at the local level, their less crucial role in the running of national institutions and the fact that the party system itself has actually changed from generation to generation means that extra-political factors continue to play a considerable part in local affairs. As a result local 'notables' still retain an important position. Their ability to put themselves forward as the spokesmen for their localities is a consequence of their social standing and not of their status as party activists. The exercise of local political office is thus seen as an extension of their social position.

The actual room for independent action by local political leaders in either country is not necessarily very great. To a considerable extent the role of the politician is expected to be to solve, case by case, the particular problems of individual voters. In France, clientelism, which is the reflection in the political structure of the social role of the elected representatives, establishes and maintains a system in which decisions about collective goods are separated off from the handling of particular, individual interests. And in both countries one could see the system as one in which the ordinary citizens unload onto the elected representatives the task of defining and defending the 'general interest' of the locality, in exchange for assistance with solutions to their particular personal problems.

One illustration of this distinction between collective goods and individual demands is provided by the Mérignac study. Not a single person interviewed made mention of the lack of a large-scale cultural centre in the commune. Yet at the same time the council was putting a major financial investment into building a theatre. Was this perhaps a case of anticipating demand – a classic instance, perhaps, of agenda manipulation? Certainly, our evidence implies that the theatre could not be interpreted as a response to a collective need actually felt by the population as a whole. Rather, it was an example of a public good being promoted by a very small number of groups (in this instance cultural associations) and then taken over by organisations linked to the parties and involved in the political battle for control of the town hall. The decision to initiate this particular project was in fact taken by the controlling group which helped to make an electoral issue out of it and thereby forestall criticisms from the opposition, which would otherwise have used the supposed 'lack' of a theatre as part of its campaign.

The situation in the British case of Sevenoaks was rather different. There people did tend to take action on problems which were, at one and the same time, particular and collective. Thus, the two major issues (the construction of the swimming pool and the closure of the hospital) concerned the provision of public goods, although private interests were also partly at stake. One should therefore be cautious about inferring the existence of universal patterns of issues, even if it is generally true that more collective goods tend to be raised by groups and be seen as a special council responsibility.

The Mérignac study provided a further example of the differences in the ways collective and individual issues are viewed, in the case of problems of employment. Whilst the council took the view that it was a fundamental part of policy to protect existing industry and, if possible, attract new ones, the population as a whole seemed to look to the national government for a solution to unemployment problems. This is not to say that the ordinary citizens are mistaken in their view. It is simply to point out that the solution to an issue, which more than half of those interviewed regarded as the most important of all, was not thought to be achievable through policies designed to defend purely local interests. Likewise in Britain it was found that unemployment was viewed more as a national rather than a local issue by the citizenry, but was given a higher local priority by the councillors themselves.

In ways like this the council leaders, and also sometimes the opposition, can come routinely to define the local issue agenda. There is no mechanistic process which ensures that the more people are socially integrated through active involvement in local group life the more they will participate politically and through that bring influence to bear on local issues. Only in part does the population in general determine the local issue agenda. By comparison, this is more a reflection of party competition – even if in France this often merely amounts in reality to a system which sustains the dominance of the notables.

3 LOCAL LEADERS: AN ELITE OR MERELY INTERMEDIARIES?

In France even more than in Britain, local decision-making power is highly concentrated. Compared with France the situation in Britain does allow for a certain limited dispersal of power which can permit a number of local elite groups to exercise a degree of influence. These might include councillors (or, rather, those in the inner circle of the ruling party), the senior local government officials and certain strategically placed groups amongst business, professions and the unions. However, in France, power is so much concentrated in the hands of the mayor and his very immediate circle, that one cannot readily identify other elites exercising genuine power. There it is better to think of the local elite more as the pool of people from whom can emerge potential holders of power.

In both countries one can find in local politics individuals who do not so much exercise power as act as intermediaries between the citizens and those in decision-making positions. The generality of councillors can be looked at in these terms in both Britain and France. The careers of French councillors before gaining office provide some evidence of this intermediating role, first entering politics as advocates or representatives of these interests, often of a sporting or cultural nature. The situation in Britain appears to vary. Service in the party is essential and, in the case of the Labour Party, trade union work is often the stepping stone. Elsewhere, as in France, group activities may lead to invitations to stand for the council. What is clear is that councillors are well-integrated into local group life which enables them to perform a linkage function, which is not necessarily to say that councillors are part of anything as structured as a local power elite. Elected representatives, and even many French mayors, are seldom in a position to impose their will on decisions or shape local policy according to their own preferences. Instead they are more often intermediaries and brokers.

Individual citizens often formulate their demands in the expectation that the elected representatives or other reputed influentials will intervene to provide assistance with their individual problems. Such interventions usually amount to mediation rather than to decision-making. Most often what is required is that the file should be forwarded to the right person in authority who is in a position to deal with the matter. The elected representatives and local administrators are often past masters at this game of passing difficult decisions on to others. It might be argued that, even where such demands for solutions to individual problems also involve policy decisions with potentially more general repercussions, they do not constitute 'political participation' in a strict sense of the term. Getting matters settled incrementally, case by case, requests for some special dispensation and demands for interpretations of rules are, however, in day-to-day terms, the most fundamental ways in which citizens influence the local political systems. The flow of 'micro-decisions' through the system is one of the essential means whereby it can adapt to local needs, through its capacity to respond to individual demands. In order for this process to work properly, it is vital that the local authority has at its disposal a communications network efficient enough to process demands. This function is performed by the councillors and by some of leaders of local groups and associations. From this point of view, they behave much more as intermediaries than as an elite. Their role as channels of communication is more important than their involvement in the decision-making process.

This is, of course, only one aspect of council activities. Councils also have to make general policy decisions, which often bring groups into conflict with one another. But here too the same network of group contacts can be valuable in providing channels through which the council can defend and justify its decisions to the various sectors of the electorate who are affected. The ideal kind of support for the council would be one which rested on a local consensus. A prime role for 'local elites' is therefore in maintaining a communications network which keeps the processes of political participation running smoothly. If such arrangements break down it is possible that protest movements may mobilise around issues.

4 POLITICAL MOBILISATION AND LOCAL PROTEST

The concept of political mobilisation was first used to explain the processes of rapid change at societal level and was often linked to the idea of modernisation in development theories. Here, however, it is being employed in a different, but related, sense to look at a particular kind of process which may shape the way in which people become involved in local decision-making. Mobilisation thus refers to protest movements which result in collective action usually directed around a single issue. Those involved in such movements are not necessarily well-integrated into the local system through involvement in conventional forms of political participation. As the case studies in this book show, mobilisation may even to some degree compensate for the low incidence of local conventional political participation by providing an alternative mode of action which will draw people into the political debate who are normally excluded – or who exclude themselves – from the regular operation of the local political system. An *ad hoc* single issue grouping is more flexible than, for example, a conventional party organisation which is weighed down by a multiplicity of different objectives. Such a movement, set up around one specific issue, is likely to generate more enthusiasm or to channel anger over policies it opposes more effectively and it can go in for spectacular demonstrations in support of its position. On the other hand it has normally only a limited life-span and rarely becomes properly institutionalised. The outlook for such protest movements is often poor. The political system is usually able to survive the storm, either because its own forces have taken control of the movement, or else because the movement itself has run out of steam and finally been extinguished. The case studies carried out in a Welsh community provide one example of the pattern such protests may take. The issue of the defence of the Welsh language is one which, in a sense, admits of no final solution. It arises in different ways at different times, in almost a cyclical manner, as the distribution of the Welsh-speaking population changes. Thus new protests are mobilised with each different phase of the issue, involving sometimes new leaders and new protest techniques.

The French cases related to issues each of which was, taken by itself, a one-off affair (although similar issues recur regularly in both countries). As such, they display different patterns of events. Mobilisation against the building of a nuclear power-station and against the opening of a ring-road generated issues which, however, were of short duration. But whilst one can fairly readily explain the course of the development of such movements it is less easy to explain why they are sparked off by some problems rather than others, nor why over some issues they are more successful than others. Neither the risks of nuclear accidents nor the urban traffic problems were removed with the 'demobilisation' which followed the original outburst of protest. In the former case, the policy was put into effect; in the second, it was rescinded. It so happened that, in this instance, a nationally conceived plan (for French self-sufficiency in energy) succeeded, and a policy devised by the local authorities (for improving traffic flows) failed. There have been other cases, however, in which the reverse has occurred. The intensity and duration of protest movements appear to have nothing to do with the importance of the issue itself. Issues do not exist in themselves. They need to be created by groups and it is up to these groups to speak for the matter and push it forward onto the agenda.

Conventional political participation, involving small groups of activists in more established groups, usually has a better chance of sustaining issues on the local political agenda than protest movements, which may be able to mobilise considerable public support at a particular moment, but which employ their resources in areas which the local political system can often find difficult to handle. The authorities then have to choose between trying to take over, or incorporate, the movement or allowing the risk of letting it develop without intervening. In that case the protest group might be tempted to try to deal directly with the political system at national level.

Whilst there are differences between the ways in which such protest movements operate and the established routines of conventional participation it would be wrong to suppose that the two phenomena are not related. The French case studies suggest that when a protest movement mobilises in a particular locality, but also recruits members from outside (as was the case with the anti-nuclear movement) the local political system faces difficulties in being accepted as a full party to the dispute. Accordingly the capacity of the system to resolve problems and achieve a level of local integration through the ordinary channels of conventional political participation is shown to be limited. Where the mobilisation movement is entirely confined to the particular local authority area the situation is different, and more complex. The new issue becomes part of the agenda of the mayor and council, and it is often the case that activists involved in the conventional process turn up as leaders of the protest movement. Just as political activists often move into non-political associations so some are equally apt to infiltrate mobilisation movements. But this is by no means always the case. The Welsh examples show that the party political activists are sometimes held at arm's length in order to prevent the movement becoming split on party lines. However, where the established political leaders succeed in taking over the protest, its unconventional character is negated and the ordinary rules of the local political system begin to be applied to the problem.

Although there may occasionally be an overlap in personnel amongst the activists, the actual processes of mobilisation and conventional political participation differ in certain respects. The question arises how far they are antithetical rather than complementary. It is doubtful whether, at the local level, such episodic political mobilisation leads to a revival in levels of conventional participation. The French evidence suggested that the established groups in the conventional process were more likely to employ their resources so as to become the 'gravediggers' rather than the saviours of the protest movements. There may be some validity in the idea that mobilised protest movements are an indication of levels of 'potential participation'. To the extent that there is a reserve army of citizens who do not participate but who would be ready to do so in certain circumstances, it is possible that they would be more likely to be mobilised around single issues, which have not been handled by the ordinary system, than become regular, conventional participants. Local political mobilisation may be a 'safety valve' allowing conflicts to be kept at the boundaries of the system without exerting excessive pressure on it. This possibility of resorting to protest activity over single issues may be one of the reasons for the low levels of political participation in regular, established processes. Whilst the ordinary operations of local democracy are able to sort out routine conflicts, there may be other major disputes which it cannot resolve so readily and which may lead to protest, on the one hand, or may, on the other hand, fall outside the capacity of local government to handle. The extent to which this is so depends on the ability of local institutions to absorb conflicts.

5 LOCAL INSTITUTIONS AND POLITICAL PARTICIPATION

The institutional context of political participation was discussed comparatively in chapter 2 where it was argued that any assessment of the effect this context might have on levels of involvement would have to await an examination of citizen behaviour, pressure groups and elected representatives. Clearly on an instrumental view of participation the degree to which local institutions either promote or impede effective action is an important factor. Yet comparisons between the institutional structures of the two countries suggest a number of indicators which point in contrary directions.

If we look at electoral participation – and we have already pointed out that this is a basic, but episodic form of political involvement – the situation in the two countries appears paradoxical: a strongly centralised system of government coupled with high levels of turnout in the municipal and cantonal elections in France; a tradition of local government alongside low levels of interest in local elections in Britain. Can we therefore find any relationship between other forms of participation and the ways in which local institutions are structured in the two countries? It will be recalled that the various case studies (which obviously cannot claim to provide a comprehensive treatment) suggest that the structure of participation in the two countries, in the sense of the distribution of the various types of participants, is almost identical. The overall level was, however, higher in France. This suggests some possible, though tentative, lines of interpretation of the relationship between institutions and participation.

Certain institutional factors appear to facilitate participation. The problems over which people are most ready to take action are those which arise in their immediate surroundings. They are able to direct their concern about such problems to authorities who are close at hand and whose decisions are immediately known and felt. It also tends to be such problems which generate attempts to mobilise protest. In France the proximity of the authorities is an important factor helping the administration to keep in touch with those whom it administers. There is, as was pointed out in chapter 2, a considerable difference between the two countries in the size of local authority areas, especially after the 1974 reform in Britain. This might appear to facilitate participation in France. However, one should be cautious in drawing such a conclusion. It is difficult to establish any clear relationship between the size of local authorities and the sense people have of their proximity to centres of decision-making, and the effect that this in turn has on levels of participation. Although participation is low in the most rural of the areas studied in the British research, where the local authority's head offices are indeed remote, it is difficult to establish any further clear correlation between participation and size and remoteness. Such a relationship, even if it were to appear to exist, could not in any event be readily isolated from many other factors affecting participation which point in a variety of directions.

One such factor is the cognitive one of the extent to which the population is actually aware of the exact responsibilities of the local authorities. Here, the institutional environment would seem in principle to favour local participation in Britain, where the division of responsibilities is relatively more straightforward and comprehensible. In France the situation is more complex because, in addition to the responsibilities of the elected local representatives, there are those which fall to the local representatives of the State. This may be why decentralisation does not seem to have had an appreciable impact on local participation. The division of statutory responsibilities between the various tiers of government has an indirect influence both on the levels and the subject matter of citizen participation, in that these are very much shaped by the local political agenda, which is itself affected by the functions of the several authorities. This might explain the overriding interest which the British display in locally-provided public services, whereas in France it is social problems within the purview of the local authorities which are given particular emphasis (such as the problems of the young, the elderly and difficulties over social security). At the same time in both countries there are certain major problems, notably unemployment, which are regarded as national responsibilities and, hence, not the occasion for local citizen action.

The varying degrees to which local political power is wielded on a more personal basis or is, alternatively, exercised through parties may also have its effects, though once again the experiences of the two countries differ. The personalisation of local power is a feature which marks France off quite sharply from Britain. It is arguable that such personalisation can encourage participation insofar as it helps to identify the target for citizen and group action and to pinpoint responsibility for decisions. This pattern would appear to be counterbalanced in Britain by the much greater penetration of the political parties, at least in the electoral arena. It has been seen that there is a positive relationship between participation and party membership or commitment, although the actual numbers of party activists are small. By providing a special avenue of access through the party to centres of local decision-making such politicisation of local government in Britain could have some effect in stimulating participation.

The degree of access to decision-making is clearly a significant general factor. When access is closed it can, in extreme cases, lead to the mobilisation of protest groups. Although the joint presence in France of local authorities and of local representatives of the state makes for a more complex system, it has some advantages in offering the citizens a dual channel of action and in multiplying access points, even if the sub-prefect and the services of the prefecture are sometimes situated at a relative distance. Access can also be measured in terms of the capacity of the local institutions in relaying citizen demands. In this respect there is little to distinguish between the two countries. The integration of local councillors in their society and their relationships with groups is well developed in both France and Britain. In the case of Britain, although the councillors are involved in groups including especially civic associations, these retain an autonomy from political control which may make for a more independent process of communication compared with France where, in those areas with strong party control, the parties penetrate group life.

In each country there are, therefore, factors which appear to promote participatory opportunities and others which seem to put obstacles in the way, the balance of argument shifting from one side to the other. As a consequence any estimate of the overall comparative participatory potential of local institutions in Britain and France still remains extremely difficult and open to debate. At the same time the political relevance of local participation in both countries is being affected by the various pressures which indirectly influence the exercise of power at the local level. In particular, the conditions of economic crisis in both countries have increased the impact of the general economic environment on local policy-making. Whilst planning problems in Britain and social problems in France may actually generate citizen participation, it is hardly surprising that it is issues of unemployment and of the local economy which, in both countries, exercise the active attention of the local authorities themselves. Thus the national economic and political environment is increasingly another important force shaping local political actions.

6 LOCAL PARTICIPATION AND NATIONAL POLITICS

Until recently most studies of the processes of political participation and mobilisation have been conducted mainly at national level. National studies have the disadvantage that they are less closely concerned with the actual context in which a great deal of participation occurs. They consequently tend to highlight broader patterns of participation. The present studies are, however, in two particular respects 'localised'. In the first place, they deal with the participation and mobilisation of citizens in response to local problems. Secondly, the focus of the investigation is on the local community or authority, and there is no attempt to extrapolate from the cases to the national level, in contrast to the method adopted by many American political scientists and sociologists in the 1960s. Does this approach permit us to identify a form of political participation which can be distinguished from the behaviour of citizens in respect of national issues?

The answer is by no means obvious, because it is increasingly apparent that there is a growing convergence between local and national politics in contemporary society. The interconnections between these two levels of politics almost certainly still remain stronger in France than in Britain, by reason of the closer relations between centre and periphery which, as was pointed out in chapter 2, are a long-standing feature of the political system. This is not to say that the local political arena is regarded as more politicised by the French than by the British. There are many indicators to the contrary, although this remains a matter of some uncertainty. In France, the case studies suggest that citizens attach more importance to national problems than to those which fall within the purview of the local authorities, whilst in Britain people appear to show a greater concern for local issues. In this instance, however, due caution must be exercised because of some differences in the frame of reference within which responses about issue concerns were elicted. On the other hand, evidence from the related national survey in Britain indicates that, even where a frame more strictly comparable with that used in Mérignac is employed, English respondents still think disproportionately in terms of needs or problems that affect themselves, their family or the neighbourhood. Indeed a rating of their most important issue in such terms showed a very significant disjuncture between the perception of their high impact in the immediate locality and their much lesser prominence at the regional or national level. In short, when it comes to issues that Britons see as being of personal concern, they think largely within a very localised or parochial context (see Moyser, Parry and Day 1986). In these terms, therefore, albeit indirect ones, perhaps there is substance to the conclusion drawn here, notwithstanding technicalities of wording. There has been, in any event, a degree of nationalisation of participation in both countries brought on by the fact that national and local politics have become increasingly interwoven, especially as the local authorities take on new roles in implementing national government policies.

Even so, the distinction between the two levels of politics, and consequently the two levels of participation, has not entirely lost its significance. These studies have shown that it is strictly local types of problems and issues which generate more citizen and group participation than the national problems, about which the citizen often senses that no locally-based action is feasible. It has also been seen that, where citizens do raise issues, they are concerned in very large part with individual, particularised benefits whilst the elected representatives are left with taking initiatives over the provision of more collective goods.

There are, therefore, differences between local and national patterns of political behaviour, but it is not clear whether they are sufficient to be able to distinguish a purely local form of participation which is independent of national influences. Participation in local elections may, for example, be thought of at first sight, as clearly local. However, leaving aside the question of the importance of this mode of political action as a measure of participation in general, local elections are becoming increasingly affected by national politics, inasmuch as the behaviour of voters is largely determined by the attitudes they take to national political divisions and to the performance of central government. Apart from voting, the most distinctively local form of conventional political participation is constituted by the activities of voluntary groups with strictly local objectives, or of 'localised' groups (such as the local branches of wider organisations, including trade unions) which directly or indirectly seek to influence local authorities. One might also think to find genuine local political activity in the examples of protest movements which have been mobilised in particular areas and which might be indicative of a political society in which new forms of unconventional or aggressive participation are emerging. However, here too, as we have seen in the several case studies, these movements are more often 'localised' than strictly local. Where they are purely local they remain on a correspondingly modest scale. Finally, the shape of local political agendas is also not an entirely reliable indicator of the local character of politics. We saw that the agenda depended as much on the initiative of the elected representatives as on the demands emanating directly from local groups and citizens. Consequently the agenda could show the imprint of national preoccupations of which the councillors tended to be very conscious. When looked at in isolation, there is, therefore, no single feature which is sufficient in itself to mark off a distinctively local style of political participation. Taken together, however, these various factors could be said to constitute a pattern of activity which, as these studies have sought to demonstrate, is neither merely peripheral nor entirely dependent for its meaning on national level politics.

One last way of seeking to identify a distinctively local type of participation, and one which raises new questions, would be by delimiting the sphere of 'legitimate politics', the extent of which would not be the same at the local as at the national level. Here we are again dealing with the boundaries between the 'social' and the 'political' touched upon earlier. These are not necessarily viewed in entirely the same way in the two countries. If one were to confine 'political participation' to those spheres which are recognised as properly and legitimately 'political', the effect, certainly in France, would be to reduce the arena of local political participation, in that in France there persists a distinctively apolitical ideology and language amongst the elected representatives which are not paralleled to the same extent in Britain. What counts as the legitimate sphere of politics depends on the extent to which local politics is institutionalised. There is a gulf between 'total politics', which characterises the national politics of contemporary societies, and the limited domain of what is regarded as legitimate politics at the local level in France. The varied conceptions of 'the political' which result make it impossible to define local political participation by reference to a commonly agreed notion of what is properly politics. This problem, however, raises the question as to whether there is such a thing as a local political system.

7 IS THERE A LOCAL POLITICAL SYSTEM?

The idea of a local political system has been examined in contemporary political science literature mainly within the context either of the study of institutional structures or that of centre–periphery relations: the 'local politico-administrative system' and 'restrained Jacobinism' in the case of France (Crozier and Thoenig 1975; Gremion 1976), or the interdependent asymmetry of Britain (Rhodes 1984: 282). From these various studies it is clear that the degree of structural differentiation and of functional specialisation has not gone as far at the local level as it typically has at the national level in Western democracies. On the other hand, there is a recognisable over-institutionalisation of local politics, which the 1974 reform of local government in Britain sought to curtail by reducing the number of authorities but which the French reforms of 1982 actually appeared to increase. Within this changing local institutional structure, can the study of the processes of political participation offer any different insight into the ways in which a distinctively local political system might be identified and defined?

We have already seen that it is difficult to identify the local political system by reference to a commonly agreed understanding of the legitimate sphere of politics. This concern for the legitimacy of local 'politics' appears, in any event, a peculiarly French one. To the extent that activities at local level have become politicised, which in France is a relatively recent occurrence, it can be regarded as a better indicator of the way in which the wider, national political system has spilled over into local politics than evidence for the existence of a specifically local set of political relationships. The idea of an autonomous sphere of local political activity has been by contrast a presupposition, in theory at least, of British politics, where it has tended to be regarded as a specific defining characteristic of the local community. But this traditional presupposition no longer holds, as local authorities become ever more dependent on central government. This can be regarded as marking the decline, even the erosion, of a distinctive, independent local political system. In France, the presupposition has been quite the opposite, and local processes have, as a whole, been seen as largely determined by the relationship between the centre and the periphery. The familiar terminology of 'local government' in Britain and 'local administration' in France is a reminder of this contrast. However, citizen attitudes and behaviour, which in this respect appear, on the basis of our case studies, to be very similar in the two countries, do not suggest that there is such a marked sense of local autonomy such as to give rise to distinctive patterns of local activity and, hence, to a highly differentiated local political system.

The activity of the elected representatives also betrays, in many ways, the influence of the national system. However, a more genuinely distinctive function played by the local political system is to be found in the role of the elected representatives and of the groups in the processes of communication. Their role consisted very much in acting as intermediaries in response to citizen demands, even though in doing so they often did as much to generate demands from local residents as to satisfy them. The study of local participation thus suggests that a purely local political system can exist only intermittently to the limited extent nowadays that it is able to deal with situations which arise exclusively at the local level and which can also be successfully resolved at the same level.

In the final resort there is no such thing as a completely local political system. This is true whether we analyse it in terms of institutional structures or of centre-periphery relations. And it is also confirmed by the study of local political participation. The behaviour of local political actors, both citizens and leaders, displays an inescapably dual character. In Britain and in France there has been a steady nationalisation of local politics and yet, as these studies have sought to show, locality and, consequently, local decision-making have remained important to the lives of most people. This mixed nature of local politics in the two countries is reflected in the patterns of issues raised, the modes of citizen participation and in the roles played by the political leaderships. Like other aspects of local politics, participation cannot be understood entirely apart from the national context in which it operates. But it would not be correct to conclude from this that it is wholly circumscribed by nationally determined patterns and arrangements. In both France and Britain, for all the national pressures towards uniformity, political activity still retains some of its distinctive local flavour. Indeed it is one of the tasks facing all modern democracies to ensure the survival of what is both particular and valuable in local political life in the face not merely, nowadays, of national interests but of growing international interdependence. Local political participation can help to shape, and will certainly in turn be shaped by, the way in which France and Britain cope with this task within their respective political traditions.

Bibliography

Alexander, A. 1982. *Local Government in Britain since Reorganisation*. London, Allen and Unwin.

Alford, R., and R. Friedland. 1985. *Powers of Theory*. Cambridge, Cambridge University Press.

Alford, R., and M. Scoble. 1968. Sources of Local Political Involvement. *American Political Science Review*, 62:1,192–206.

Almond, G., and S. Verba. 1963. *The Civic Culture: Political Attitudes and Democracy in Five Nations*. Princeton, Princeton University Press.

Andrews, F., J. Morgan, and J. Sonquist 1969. *Multiple Classification Analysis*. Ann Arbor, Institute for Social Research.

Ashford, D. 1976. The Limits of Consensus: The Reorganisation of British Local Government and the French Contrast. *Western Societies Programme, Occasional Paper No. 6*. Ithaca, Cornell University.

1982. *British Dogmatism and French Pragmatism. Central–Local Policy-Making in the Welfare State*. London, Allen and Unwin.

Autrement. 1976. Special number: 'Contre-pouvoirs dans la ville: enjeux politiques des luttes urbaines'. Vol. 6.

Bachrach, P., and M. S. Baratz 1962. The Two Faces of Power. *American Political Science Review*, 56:947–52.

Barber, B. 1984. *Strong Democracy: Participatory Politics for a New Age*. Berkeley, University of California Press.

Barker A. and Keating M. 1977. Public Spirits: Amenity Societies and Others. In *British Political Sociology Yearbook, Vol. 3: Participation in Politics*, ed. C. Crouch, London, Croom Helm.

Barnes, S., M. Kaase, *et al.* 1979. *Political Action: Mass Participation in Five Western Democracies*. Beverly Hills, Sage.

Bealey, F., and J. Sewel. 1981. *The Politics of Independence: A Study of a Scottish Town*. Aberdeen, Aberdeen University Press.

Becquart-Leclercq, J. 1983. Cumul des mandats et culture politique. In *Les pouvoirs locaux à l'épreuve de la décentralisation*, ed. A. Mabileau. Paris, Pedone, 207–34.

Belorgey, G. 1984. *La France decentralisée*. Paris, Berger-Levrault.

Benzecri, J. P. *et al.* 1973. *L'analyse des données*, 2 volumes. Paris, Dunod.

Boaden, N. *et al.* 1982. *Public Participation in Local Services*. London, Longman.

Boyd, L. H. Jnr. 1971. Multiple Level Analysis with Complete and Incomplete Data. Ph.D. dissertation, Ann Arbor, Michigan, University of Michigan.

Brudal, L. F. 1982. The Case Study as Scientific Evidence: A Critical Evaluation. *Nordisk Psykologi*, 34: 337–50.

Bulpitt, J. 1972. Participation and Local Democracy: Territorial Democracy. In *Participation in Politics*, ed. G. Parry. Manchester, Manchester University Press, 281–302.

1983. *Territory and Power in the United Kingdom*. Manchester, Manchester University Press.

Byrne, T. 1985. *Local Government in Britain. Everyone's Guide to How it All Works*, 3rd edn. Harmondsworth, Penguin Books.

Cadène, P. 1982. Collectivités rurales et résistances à l'intégration: la construction de l'autoroute de Toulouse. *Revue de Géographie des Pyrénées et du Sud-Ouest*, 53: 105–28.

Carmarthen District Council. 1985. *Planning and the Welsh Language*. Carmarthen.

Chamboredon, J. C., and M. Lemaire. 1970. Proximité spatiale et distance sociale: les grands ensembles et leur peuplement. *Revue Française de Sociologie*, II: 3–33.

Chazel, F. 1975. La mobilisation politique: problèmes et dimensions. *Revue Française de Sociologie*, 25: 502–16.

Chombart de Lauwe, P. H. 1965. *Des hommes et des villes*. Paris, Payot.

Cibois, P. 1983. *L'analyse factorielle*. Paris, Presses Universitaires de France.

Cobb, R., and C. Elder. 1972. *Participation in American Politics: The Dynamics of Agenda-Building*. Boston, Allyn and Bacon.

Converse, P., and G. Dupeux. 1966. Politicization of the Electorate in France and the United States. In *Elections and the Political Order*, ed. A. Campbell, P. Converse. W. Miller and D. Stokes. London, John Wiley, 269–91.

Cook, C. 1976. *A Short History of the Liberal Party, 1900–1976*. London, Macmillan.

Crenson, M. 1971. *The Un-Politics of Air-Pollution: A Study of Non-Decision-making in the Cities*. Baltimore, Johns Hopkins University Press.

Crozier, M., and J. C. Thoenig. 1975. La régulation des systèmes organisés complexes. Le système de decision politico–administratif en France. *Revue Française de Sociologie*, 16: 3–32.

Cynon Valley Borough Council. 1984. *House Condition Survey*. Aberdare.

Czudnowski, M. 1976. *Comparing Political Behavior*, vol. 28, Sage Library of Social Research. Beverly Hills, Sage.

Davies, M. 1985. *Politics of Pressure: The Art of Lobbying*. London, British Broadcasting Corporation Publications.

Dogan, M., and D. Pelassy. 1982. *Sociologie politique comparative. Problèmes et perspectives*. Paris, Economica.

Dunleavy, P. 1980. *Urban Political Analysis*. London, Macmillan.

Duverger, M. 1964. *Political Parties*. London, Methuen.

Easton, D. 1985. *A Systems Analysis of Political Life*. New York, John Wiley.

Eldersveld, S. J. 1964. *Political Parties: A Behavioral Analysis*. Chicago, Rand McNally.

England, J. 1986. The Characteristics and Attitudes of Councillors. In *The Local Government Councillor*, Research Vol. 2, of *The Conduct of Local Authority Business*. Cmnd. 9799: 9–123. London, HMSO.

Erikson, R., J. H. Goldthorpe and L. Portocarero. 1979. Intergenerational Class Mobility in Three Western European Societies: England, France and Sweden. *British Journal of Sociology*, 30: 415–41.

Frankenberg, R. 1969. *Communities in Britain*. Harmondsworth, Penguin Books.

Frey, F. W. 1970. *Cross-Cultural Survey Research in Political Science. In The Methodology of Comparative Research*, ed. R. Holt and J. Turner. New York, The Free Press, ch. 6.

Gallie, W. B. 1955–56. Essentially Contested Concepts. *Proceedings of the Aristotelian Society*, 55: 167–98.

Garraud, P. 1979. Politique électro-nucléaire et mobilisation: la tentative de constitution d'un enjeu. *Revue Française de Science Politique*, 29: 448–74.

1980. Politique électro-nucléaire et strategies de l'information. In *L'information locale*, ed. A. Mabileau and A. Tudesq. Paris, Pedone, 129–45.

Garson, G. D. 1971. *Handbook of Political Science Methods*. Boston, Holbrook Press.

Gaventa, J. 1980. *Power and Powerlessness: Quiescence and Rebellion in an Appalachian Valley*. Oxford, Oxford University Press.

Gaxie, D., ed., 1985. *Explication du vote: un bilan des études électorales en France*. Paris, Presses de la FNSP.

Goldsmith, M., and K. Newton. 1983. Central–Local Government Relations: The Irresistible Rise of Centralised Power. *West European Politics*, 6:216–33.

Goodin, R., and J. Dryzek 1980. Rational Participation: The Politics of Relative Power. *British Journal of Political Science*, 10: 273–92.

Grant, W. 1977. *Independent Local Politics in England and Wales*. Farnborough, Saxon House.

Greenacre, M. 1984. *Theory and Applications of Correspondence Analysis*. London, Academic Press.

Gremion, P. 1976. *Le pouvoir périphérique*. Paris, Editions du Seuil.

Guichard, O. 1976. *Vivre ensemble*. Paris, Documentation Française.

Gyford, J. 1976. *Local Politics in Britain*. London, Croom Helm.

Gyford, J., and M. James. 1983. *National Parties and Local Politics*. London, Allen and Unwin.

Hampton, W. 1970. *Democracy and Community*. London, Oxford University Press.

Hatzfeld, H. 1986. Municipalités socialistes et associations. Roubaix: le conflit de l'Alma-Gare. *Revue Française de Science Politique*, 36: 374–92.

Hayward, J. 1983. *Governing France: The One and Indivisible Republic*. London, Weidenfeld and Nicolson.

Heath, A., R. Jowell, and J. Curtice. 1985. *How Britain Votes*. Oxford, Pergamon Press.

Himmelweit, H. T. *et al.* 1981. *How Voters Decide*. London, Academic Press.

Hirschman, A. 1970. *Exit, Voice and Loyalty*. Cambridge, Mass., Harvard University Press.

Hymes, D. 1970. Linguistic Aspects of Comparative Political Research. In *The Methodology of Comparative Research*, ed. R. Holt and J. Turner. New York, The Free Press, ch. 7.

Inglehart, R. 1977. *The Silent Revolution*. Princeton, Princeton University Press.

Jennings, R. 1982. The Changing Representational Roles of Local Councillors in England. *Local Government Studies*, 8: 67–86.

Jollivet, M. 1974. *Sociétés paysannes ou luttes de classes au villages? Problèmes théoriques et méthodologiques de l'étude locale en sociologie rurale*. Paris, A. Colin.

Jones, B. D. 1981. Party and Bureaucracy: The Influence of Intermediary Groups on Urban Service Delivery. *American Political Science Review*, 75: 688–700.

1983. *Governing Urban America: A Policy Focus*. Boston, Little, Brown.

Kaase, M. 1976. Party Identification and Voting Behaviour in the West German

Elections of 1969. *Party Identification and Beyond: Representation of Voting and Party Competition*, ed. I. Budge, I. Crewe and D. Fairlie. London, John Wiley, ch. 5.

Kadushin, C. 1968. Power, Influence and Social Circles: A New Methodology for Studying Opinion Makers, *American Sociology Review*, 33: 685–99.

Kornhauser, W. 1959. *The Politics of Mass Society*. Glencoe, Illinois, Free Press.

Kukawka, P. 1980. *Manufrance. Radiographie d'une lutte*. Paris, Editions Sociales.

Lacoste, Y., ed. 1986. *Géopolitiques de la France*. Paris, Fayard.

Lagroye, J. 1985. La legitimation. In *Traité de Science politique*, ed. M. Gravitz and J. Leca. Paris, Presses Universitaires de France, I: 395–467.

Lagroye, J., and V. Wright, eds. 1979. *Local Government in Britain and France. Problems and Prospects*. London, Allen and Unwin. (English edition.)

  1982. *Les Structures locales en Grande-Bretagne et en France*. Paris, Documentation Française. (French edition.)

Ledrut, R. 1973a. *Sociologie urbaine*, 2nd edn. Paris, Presses Universitaires de France.

  1973b. *Les images de la ville*. Paris, Antropos.

Lijphart, A. 1971. Comparative Politics and the Comparative Method. *American Political Science Review*, 65: 682–93.

  1975. The Comparable-Cases Strategy in Comparative Research. *Comparative Political Studies*, 8: 158–77.

Lukes, S. 1974. *Power: A Radical View*. London, Macmillan.

Mabileau, A., ed. 1972. *Les facteurs locaux de la vie politique nationale*. Paris, Pedone.

  1983. *Les pouvoirs locaux à l'épreuve de la décentralisation*. Paris, Pedone.

Machin, H., and V. Wright. 1980. Centre-periphery in France. In *New Approaches to the Study of Central-Local Government Relationships*, ed. G. W. Jones, Aldershot, Gower.

McCulloch, C. 1984. The Problem of Fellowship in Communitarian Theory: William Morris and Peter Kropotkin. *Political Studies*, 32: 437–50.

McCulloch, C., and G. Parry. 1986. Pluralism, Community and Human Nature. In *Unity, Plurality and Politics: Essays in Honour of F. M. Barnard*, ed. J. M. Porter and R. Vernon. London, Croom Helm, 162–87.

MacIntyre, A. C. 1971. Is a Science of Comparative Politics Possible? In A. C. MacIntyre, *Against the Self-Images of the Age: Essays on Ideology and Philosophy*. London, Duckworth.

MacIver, R. 1924. *Community: A Sociological Study*. London, Macmillan.

Martlew, C. 1988. *Local Democracy in Practice: The Role and Working Environment of Councillors in Scotland*. Aldershot, Avebury Press.

Memmi, D. 1985. L'engagement politique. In *Traité de Science politique*, ed M. Gravitz and J. Leca. Paris, Presses Universitaires de France, I: 310–66.

Milbrath, L. W., and M. L. Goel. 1977. *Political Participation: How and Why Do People Get Involved in Politics?*, 2nd edn. Chicago, Rand McNally.

Miller, W. L. *et al.* 1982. *Democratic and Violent Protests? Attitudes Towards Direct Action in Scotland and Wales*. Studies in Public Policy, 107. Strathclyde, University of Strathclyde.

Molnar, G. 1967. Deviant Case Analysis in Social Science. *Politics*, 2: 1–11.

Moran, M. 1985. *Politics and Society in Britain: An Introduction*. London, Macmillan.

Moyser, G., G. Parry and N. Day. 1986. Political Participation in Britain: National and Local Patterns. Paper presented to Annual Meeting of the American Political Science Association, Washington D.C.

Muller, E. 1979. *Aggressive Political Participation*. Princeton, Princeton University Press.

Naylor, E. L. 1986. Milk Quotas in France. *Journal of Rural Studies*, 2:153–61.

Nettl, P. 1967. *Political Mobilization*. New York, Basic Books.

Newton, K. 1976. *Second City Politics*. Oxford, Clarendon Press.

Newton, K., and T. Karran. 1985. *The Politics of Local Expenditure*. London, Macmillan.

Nie, N. H., G. B. Powell and K. Prewitt. 1969. Social Structure and Political Participation. *American Political Science Review*, 63: 361–78 and 808–32.

Nisbet, R. 1967. *The Sociological Tradition*. London, Heinemann.

Nordlinger, E. 1981. *On the Autonomy of the Democratic State*. Cambridge, Mass., Harvard University Press.

Oberschall, A. 1973. *Social Conflict and Social Movements*. Englewood Cliffs, N.J., Prentice-Hall.

Office of Population Census and Surveys. 1984. *A Classification of Occupations*. London, HMSO.

Olson, M. 1971. *The Logic of Collective Action*. Cambridge, Mass., Harvard University Press.

Orbell, J., and T. Uno. 1972. A Theory of Neighborhood Problem Solving: Political Action versus Residential Mobility. *American Political Science Review*, 66: 471–89.

Page, E. 1983. La marginalisation des élites politiques locales en Grande-Bretagne. In *Les pouvoirs locaux à l'épreuve de la décentralisation*, ed. A. Mabileau, Paris, Pedone, 189–205.

Parry, G. 1972. The Idea of Political Participation. In *Participation in Politics*, ed. G. Parry. Manchester, Manchester University Press, 3–38.

  1974. Participation and Political Styles. In *WJMM: Political Questions*, ed. B. Chapman and A. Potter. Manchester, Manchester University Press, 190–204.

Parry, G., and P. Morriss 1974. When is a Decision not a Decision? In *British Sociology Yearbook*, vol. 1: *Elites in Western Democracy*, ed. I. Crewe, London, Croom Helm, 317–36.

Parry, G., and G. Moyser. 1984. Participants and Controllers. In *Comparative Government and Politics: Essays in Honour of S. E. Finer*, ed. D. Kavanagh and G. Peele. London, Macmillan, 169–84.

  1988. What is 'Politics'? A Comparative Study of Local Leaders and Citizens. In *Democracy, State and Justice: Critical Perspectives and New Interpretations, Essays in Honour of Elias Berg*, ed. D. Sainsbury. Stockholm, Almqvist and Wiskell International, 33–54.

Parry, G., G. Moyser and M. Wagstaffe. 1987. The Crowd and the Community: Context, Content and Aftermath. In *The Crowd in Contemporary Britain*, ed. G. Gaskell and R. Benewick. London, Sage, 212–54.

Pateman, C. 1970. *Participation and Democratic Theory*. Cambridge, Cambridge University Press.

Plant, R. 1978. Community: Concept, Conception and Ideology. *Politics and Society*, 8: 79–107.

Putnam, R. 1966. Political Attitudes and the Local Community. *American Political Science Review*, 60: 640–54.

Rhodes, R. 1984. Continuity and Change in British Central–Local Relations: 'The Conservative Threat', 1979–83. *British Journal of Political Science*, 14: 261–83.

1986. *The National World of Local Government.* London, Allen and Unwin.

Rich, R. 1979. The Roles of Neighborhood Organizations in Urban Service Delivery. *NASPAA Urban Affairs Papers,* 1: 2–20.

Richards, P. 1980. *The Reformed Local Government System,* 4th ed. London, Allen and Unwin.

Ritaine, E. 1979. L'espace local. In *Encyclopédie de collectivités locales.* Tome introductif. Paris, Dalloz.

Rondin, P. 1985. *Le sacre des notables. La France en décentralisation.* Paris, Fayard.

Rossi, P. 1972. Community Social Indicators. In *The Human Measuring of Social Change,* ed. A. Campbell and P. E. Converse. New York, Sage, 87–126.

Rusk, J. 1976. Political Participation in America: A Review Essay. *American Political Science Review,* 70: 583–91.

Saunders, P. 1979. *Urban Politics: A Sociological Interpretation.* London, Hutchinson.

    et al. 1978. Rural Community and Rural Community Power. In *International Perspectives in Rural Sociology,* ed. H. Newby. Chichester, John Wiley, 55–86.

Schumpeter, J. A. 1954. *Capitalism, Socialism and Democracy,* 4th ed. London, Allen and Unwin.

Segal, D. R., and S. H. Wildstrom. 1970. *Community Effects on Political Attitudes: Partisanship and Efficacy.* Reprint Series No. 39, Michigan, Ann Arbor, Center for Research on Social Organization, University of Michigan.

Thoenig, J. C., 1985. Le grand horloger et les effets de système. De la décentralisation en France. *Revue Politique et management public,* 3:135–58.

Thomassen, J. 1976. Party Identification as a Cross-National Concept: Its Meaning in the Netherlands. In *Party Identification and Beyond: Representations of Voting and Party Competition,* ed. I. Budge, I. Crewe and D. Fairlie. London, John Wiley, ch. 4.

Tocqueville, A. de 1968. *Democracy in America,* ed. J. Mayer and M. Lerner, trans. G. Lawrence. London, Fontana Library, Collins.

Tönnies, F. 1963. *Community and Association,* trans. C. P. Loomis. New York, Harper and Row.

Verba, S., and N. Nie. 1972. *Participation in America: Political Democracy and Social Equality.* New York, Harper and Row.

Verba, S., N. Nie, and J.-O. Kim. 1978. *Participation and Political Equality: A Seven-Nation Comparison.* Cambridge, Cambridge University Press.

Walker, S. G. 1973. Case Studies and Cumulation: The Study of Divided Nations. *Journal of International Affairs,* 27: 261–7.

Weber, M. 1947. *The Theory of Social and Economic Organisation,* ed. T. Parsons. New York, Free Press.

Wellman, B., and B. Leighton. 1979. Networks, Neighbourhoods and Communities: Approaches to the Study of the Community Question. *Urban Affairs Quarterly,* 14: 363–90.

Winch, P. 1958. *The Idea of Social Science.* New York, Humanities Press.

Worms, J. P. 1966. Le préfet et ses notables. *Sociologie du Travail,* 3: 249–75.

Wright, V. 1986. Le parti conservateur et les collectivités locales en Grande-Bretagne en 1984–85: L'accentuation de la crise. *Revue Française d'Administration Publique,* no.38.

Young, M., and P. Wilmott. 1957. *Family and Kinship in East London.* London, Routledge and Kegan Paul.

Index

Note: Most references are to local politics except where otherwise specified.

For EU product safety concerns, contact us at Calle de José Abascal, 56–1°,
28003 Madrid, Spain or eugpsr@cambridge.org.

www.ingramcontent.com/pod-product-compliance
Ingram Content Group UK Ltd.
Pitfield, Milton Keynes, MK11 3LW, UK
UKHW010034140625
459647UK00012BA/1384